_____ Comics as

PHILOSOPHY

Comics as
PHILOSOPHY

Edited by
JEFF McLAUGHLIN

University Press of Mississippi / *Jackson*

www.upress.state.ms.us

The University Press of Mississippi is a member of the
Association of American University Presses.

Copyright © 2005 by University Press of Mississippi
All rights reserved
Manufactured in the United States of America

First edition 2005

Library of Congress Cataloging-in-Publication Data

Comics as philosophy / edited by Jeff McLaughlin.— 1st ed.
      p. cm.
   Includes bibliographical references (p.   ) and index.
   ISBN 1-57806-794-4 (cloth : alk. paper) 1. Comic books, strips, etc.—Moral
and ethical aspects. 2. Comic books, strips, etc.—History and criticism.
I. McLaughlin, Jeff.
    PN6712.C58   2005
    741.5′09—dc22   2005004453

British Library Cataloging-in-Publication Data available

To my late brother Gord,
for letting me read his *Fantastic Four*.
To my dad,
for giving me my allowance to spend on
comic books.
And
To my wife Deanna,
Just because I love her.

Contents

Acknowledgments

Obviously putting together an anthology involves more than one person. Thus I must thank a variety of people who were instrumental in getting this book into your hands. First, I must single out Gene Kanneberg Jr., for without his kindness and knowledge this book would not have been born. Even though Gene and I were strangers at the time we met at the 2002 International Popular Culture Conference in Toronto, he introduced me to a number of important people who have played central roles in this project. In fact, Gene literally took me by the hand and walked me over to the publisher at University Press of Mississippi.

Director Seetha Srinivasan and Assistant Editor Walter Biggins at the University Press of Mississippi have been extremely supportive towards this project. At times when I felt I was being a real pain nagging the contributors to get their work in on time (or at least only a few months late), Seetha's first words to me would come back to haunt me. "You'll find out that writing a book is often easier than editing one." This may be true but to do so would have meant that I would not have been able to learn from the papers assembled here. "Assembled" is probably the wrong term since these essays required very, very little editorial reshaping. A poke here and a nudge there was all that was required. Accordingly, I'm honoured to be have been able to collect the ideas of R. C. Harvey, Amy Nyberg, Stanford W. Carpenter, Laura and Paul Canis, Pierre Skilling, Jeremy Barris, Iain Thomson, Kevin LaPlante, Aldo J. Regalado, and Terry Kading.

Anne Stascavage helped me with the nuts and bolts of the manuscript. As my editor at UPM she was infinitely resourceful and patient with all my "green" questions.

A debt of gratitude is owed to Thomas Inge for it was he who suggested the title *Comics as Philosophy* to me as we sat on a hotel shuttle bus heading to the airport after the Toronto Popular Culture conference.

Thanks must also be given to Annette Dominik who provided the French-English translation of Pierre Skilling's essay on Tintin.

I'd also like to express my deepest appreciation to all of the reviewers who helped with the evaluation process including Dr. Bruce Baugh, Dr. John Belshaw, Dr. Christine Daigle, Dr. Annette Dominik, Dr. Michael Gorman, Dan O'Reilly, Dr. Kate Sutherland, and Dr. Robin Tapley. Their insightful comments gave me confidence in the selections that I had made and their suggestions helped make these fine essays even better.

Doug Sulipa started with a small comic shop in the attic of an old house in Winnipeg, Manitoba where I first met him some thirty years ago and now he has one of the largest collections in North America. As a senior advisor to the Overstreet Comic Book Price Guide, he was instrumental in providing me with some suggestions and back issues that helped move my investigations along.

Sadly, when it came time to go to do my doctorate work, I had to give up my monthly purchases because it was a matter of either eating or reading. Nevertheless, the mere fact that you hold this anthology in your hand shows you that comic books have continued to play a role in my life. In fact, I remember one of my first philosophy essays used the Death of Jean Grey of the X-Men as a discussion point. Hence, I must express my gratitude to all those artists who gave me hours and hours of enjoyment over the years. To attempt to name them would be a disservice to the one or two that I would mistakenly overlook.

Lastly I have to thank you dear reader. Whether you're a student, a professional, or a comic book enthusiast, reading this collection shows that your interest in philosophy is as genuine as your interest in comic books. May you always find pleasure in both.

—JEFF McLAUGHLIN
June 2004

Introduction

When we read comics, we make a series of aesthetic and philosophical choices. Although these choices are usually made subconsciously, they're nevertheless real decisions that we face every time we open the comics section of the newspaper or crack open a new comic book.

From the very outset, then, the form of comics—its language and how we understand it—is rife with philosophical quandaries. Once we start analyzing the contents of comics, we can face its theoretical concerns through its various storylines, narrative arcs, drawing styles, and commentary. *Comics as Philosophy* is a collection of essays that explores the ways in which comics, both in form and content, can articulate and complicate philosophical concerns, and vice versa. The essays here, written by scholars from diverse critical perspectives, also discuss related issues such as audience reaction and censorship, showing how comics have been a key battleground in cultural debates in the courtroom, the op-ed page, and the academy.

This collection shows how a cartoonist's careful construction of a world in comics form can give insight into the world in which we live. The contributors to *Comics as Philosophy* reveal how the issues and questions that philosophers deal with can be found not just in some remote branch of academia but in unassuming and easily accessible places. In doing so, they achieve the most noble goal of informing and educating individuals who may or may not be sitting in a university classroom. As the eleven authors present you with a variety of philosophical perspectives and draw from what they consider to be philosophically significant comic books and comic book genres, readers will see how these fields may be used to provide intellectually stimulating insight about the other.

The essays that make up this collection address two fundamental questions and provide a sense of the breadth and depth of the branches of philosophical inquiry. The first question asks: "What is the Good?" Thus the topics touched upon in this collection include: What constitutes a good life? What is a good thing to do? What is a good form of government? What is a good society? The second enduring question is "What is the Truth?": What is the truth about reality? What is the truth about the human condition? What is the truth about the nature of art?

The first essay, "What If?: DC's Crisis and Leibnizian Possible Worlds," argues that the multiple universes that were home to the superheroes of DC Comics—including Superman, the Flash, Batman, and Wonder Woman—depict the well-known metaphysical concept of possible worlds. The necessity of multiple universes was used by DC artists and writers to explain the interrelationship of DC's Golden, Silver and Bronze-aged characters, but the essay analyzes how this construct ultimately became an overwhelming continuity problem for the publisher. After nearly fifty years of production, DC was forced to confront the fact that cataclysmic events that occurred in *Superman* comics, for example, weren't even mentioned in *The Flash*, despite the fact that both heroes ostensibly lived in the same world and were produced by the same publisher. DC's writers and artists realized that these disparate narratives needed to be unified because the internal conflicts of its comics were too startling to ignore. This crisis was eventually resolved in an expansive storyline, documented in several DC comics ventures, that destroyed several alternate worlds and ultimately collapsed others into a single universe.

A few hundred years previous to DC's 1986 predicament, German philosopher Gottfried Leibniz wondered whether the world that we live in with all its grief and pain is the best one that God could have created. In determining that the answer had to be "Yes," Leibniz also raised the question about the possible existence of other worlds. Can we imagine a more perfect world than this one? Might there be another philosopher in another universe wondering the same thing? This scenario is similar to the Flash reading a *Flash* comic book or Superman wondering whether his world would be considered the "Bizarro world" to Bizarro Superman, but it's not a fiction.

The possibility of other worlds is a metaphysical concept that helps one to understand that there can be different ways of looking at the world, not only to question whether this is a single world, or the even best one, but also whether our perceptions correspond correctly to the way the world actually is. DC's *Crisis on Infinite Earths* indirectly addresses this question.

The next essay, Robert C. Harvey's "Describing and Discarding 'Comics' as an Impotent Act of Philosophical Rigor," addresses aesthetics. Providing the reader with background information regarding where (and how) comic books fit into the aesthetic world, Harvey comments on the historical development of comic books. More significantly, he examines what it is for a comic book to be called a "comic book" and not something else. In alluding to Mark Twain, Harvey expresses this requirement powerfully, noting that "the right word lights the way. It illuminates the dimmer recesses of the brain where, otherwise, ideas and thoughts lurk unnamed and therefore only faintly perceived and vaguely understood. The task of philosophy is to bring such furtive notions into sharp focus and thereby to discern their meaning and discover their import."

Having an acceptable aesthetic definition of comics is necessary since discussions and evaluations of the form are most fruitful when there is an agreed-upon understanding of what the form is. If there is disagreement about the dynamics of comics, the same words will be used but with different meaning and intent depending upon the speaker. Part of the exploration of aesthetics involves determining what we mean by "art" and what role art has to play in our lives.

So if we can discern what a comic book is, or at least argue about what sorts of things it isn't, we can then turn to examine what role it has in culture and what meaning it imports to its readers. In the next essay, " 'No Harm in Horror': Ethical Dimensions of the Postwar Comic Book Controversy," Amy Kiste Nyberg examines a well-documented moment in which this disagreement about the aesthetics and ethics of comics came to a head.

Several comics publishers produce comics intended only for adults, and even the two major all-ages companies—Marvel and DC Comics—have flirted with lines intended for "mature readers." In fact, one of DC's most enduring and critically acclaimed series of the 1980s and 1990s—Neil Gaiman's *Sandman*—was published by Vertigo, the company's "mature readers" subsidiary. At the same time, Marvel has consciously tried to broaden its appeal towards children, recently creating a subsidiary catering specifically to younger readers.

As Nyberg points out, this dichotomy is nothing new. She explores the cultural climate in which EC Comics' controversial horror and crime comics were produced in the 1950s. These popular books were seen by concerned parents and activists as contributors to juvenile delinquency. Accordingly, the content of the books, and the legal battle that erupted around them, exemplifies a variety of ethical concerns.

Nyberg looks closely at the Senate Subcommittee hearings on juvenile delinquency, revealing how they place the individual rights of comics publishers, including freedom of expression, against society's interest in protecting its youth. She asks crucial questions: how can a distinction be made between a work being harmful and merely offensive? When should the government intervene in the production and distribution of art? Is censorship ever acceptable and, if so, when?

Stanford Carpenter's "Truth Be Told: Authorship and the Creation of the Black Captain America" presents a case study, complete with interviews, that details how comic books are developed from conception to finished product.

The team-based approach to creating a mainstream comic book has built-in restrictions regarding what can and cannot be done. Indeed, as his essay shows, the final product cannot be evaluated independent of its creation process. With comic books, artists must confront compromises and creative control issues, copyright and corporate ownership conflicts, and even marketing strategies. Carpenter's interviews with the creators allow firsthand insight into the relationship between art and the artist, and between business obligations and artistic freedom.

Another topic that arises through Carpenter's work is central to epistemology or the theory of knowledge. Underlying Carpenter's paper is the theme of "Truth Be Told" itself which also happens to be the title of the comic book series that is dissected. The truth revealed here is that Steve Rogers was not the first Captain America. Thus what faithful readers of the comic believed for several decades turned out to be untrue, and Carpenter examines both the creation of this storyline and its audience's need to revisit the sixty-year mythology of *Captain America*. While this fictional bombshell isn't like discovering that the sun doesn't revolve around the Earth, it nevertheless reminds readers that what is taken for granted may not actually be true, and what was once unimaginable may in fact be real.

While Carpenter explores the notion of how knowledge of the external world is acquired, Jeremy Barris's "Plato, Spider-Man, and the Meaning of Life" looks inward. The Socratic motto "Know Thyself" remains a central tenet of philosophy, and Barris parallels Plato's dialogues with *The Amazing Spider-Man* to explore the issue further.

When Stan Lee and Steve Ditko launched *The Amazing Spider-Man* in 1962, the American comics community had rarely been exposed to an angst-ridden or neurotic protagonist. While Spider-Man enjoys the ability to climb walls and sling himself around Manhattan on his own spider webs, his continual popularity springs primarily from his mundane, human problems. Unlike most superheroes, but very much like most people, he struggles to pay the rent, hold down a job, keep a steady girlfriend, and satisfy the demands of his family and friends. Even when fighting supervillains, Spider-Man is constantly revealing his internal conflicts through thought balloons and quips to others. He is a superhero beset with the most familiar of adult anxieties: "Who am I, and what is my purpose in this world?"

Barris looks at how Spider-Man and Plato both approach the question "What is the meaning of life?" and finds startling similarities. The essay focuses on four interconnected themes stressed both in *The Amazing Spider-Man* and Plato's *Dialogues*: sex; the shadowy dimensions of our lives and the need to get beyond those limitations; self-trivializing humor that connects with more serious ironies; and the central, but inadequate, role sensory images play in our awareness. Barris argues that Plato and Spider-Man are heroes in parallel because they recognize their limitations and as a result can move beyond them.

Continuing with the use of mainstream superheroes, Aldo Regalado's "Modernity, Race, and the American Superhero" argues that superheroes serve the function of reaffirming the primacy of humanity for individuals who have felt threatened or constrained by the world in which they live. While these heroes may personify various ideals, some comics have not been able to transcend the times and prejudices in which they exist. Accordingly, by tracing the historical interactions between superhero comics and changing notions of race in America, Regalado analyzes the possibilities and limits of the superhero's potential to affirm the dignity of the human condition. The essay looks at the multitude of economic, political, and cultural changes that have come about by the evolution of the urban and industrial landscapes during the twentieth century. An essay of social philosophy, Regalado's work offers new insights into the meaning of American superheroes as well as the social dynamics of popular culture and race.

This spirit of superhero deconstruction moves forward in Iain Thomson's "Deconstructing the Hero." Existentialist philosopher Martin Heidegger argues that society gains self-understanding through its choice of a hero. The hero defines the people, giving focus to their sense of what really matters, telling them *which* battles are most worth fighting—and *how* they might go about fighting them.

But what does it mean when an age seeks not only to destroy its own heroes and to expose their all-too-human failings but goes even further to deconstruct the very idea of the hero? To address this question, Thomson provides us with a remarkable analysis of Alan Moore and Dave Gibbons's *Watchmen*. Published in twelve monthly issues in the late-1980s, *Watchmen* is widely recognized as one of those seminal comic books with which the art form "grew up." It helped accomplish this by deconstructing the idea of the hero from within and shattering this idealized reflection of humanity. *Watchmen*'s heroes are angst-ridden, ineffectual, plagued by personal demons, and unsentimental.

Existentialists who reflect upon the qualities of humanity offer anything but idealized visions. They question whether life has any meaning and examine what role human despair and suffering play in defining our fleeting presence on the planet. The shocking events of World War II acted as a precursor to those philosophers such as Jean-Paul Sartre who viewed the world as an inherently irrational place. And given that it is irrational, our attempts to make rational decisions seem futile. The resulting sense of angst is often associated with the developing awareness of teenagers as they struggle to make sense of out it all.

In the mid-1990s, Daniel Clowes tackled existential angst in his graphic novel *Ghost World*. Its hero Enid Coleslaw (an anagram of Daniel Clowes) is a sullen teenage girl in emotional limbo. She hasn't quite graduated from high school—she needs to take a summer art course to fulfill her requirements—and her few friendships are slowly breaking apart. Stuck in a world full of fast-food commercialization that she detests, but unable to find a culture that is intellectually and emotionally sustaining, Enid is dazed by her attempts to find something honest and real.

Laura and Paul Canis's "Jean-Paul Sartre Meets Enid Coleslaw: Existential Themes in *Ghost World*" explores the ways in which Sartre's existential struggle is reflected in Clowes's teenage protagonist. Enid confronts fundamental human questions with brutal honesty, refusing to accept ready-made answers on the authority of anyone other than herself. She is on an existential journey, coping with the Sartrean predicaments of anxiety in the face of an absurd world. She experiences abandonment and despair and struggles for authenticity amidst her own feelings of alienation. Rather than belittling teenage angst, Canis and Canis discuss how Clowes uses it instead to confront serious philosophical concerns.

The next essay moves away from considerations on the human condition to an elucidation on how humans interact with the environment. Kevin de Laplante's "Making the Abstract Concrete" uses Paul Chadwick's long-running comic *Concrete* to explore the complex dimensions of environmental philosophy. Concrete, a former political speechwriter who has been turned into a 1,200-pound rock-like creature, is more meditative than his physical form would lead one to believe. Throughout the series, but particularly in Chadwick's graphic novel *Think Like a Mountain*, Concrete gets involved in debates about humanity's moral obligation to the world it inhabits, in a manner that engages both intellect and emotion.

In the context of political philosophy, the question "What is the good?" involves determining the best form of government. Through *The Adventures of Tintin*, the artist Hergé introduced millions of children to politics and awakened in them an interest in history and current events. While Tintin never openly advocates one form of government over another, his actions consistently combat dictatorships, be they in Latin America or in Eastern Europe.

Instead, Tintin appears to be on the side of humane monarchs, shown in the comic as the only statesmen who can defend the common good. Pierre Skilling's essay, "The Good Government According to Tintin: Long Live Old Europe?" explores the models of power seizure and government which the Belgian hero rejects (i.e., dictatorship, sometimes with characteristics of totalitarianism), as well as the legitimate form of government according to Hergé's comics (i.e., monarchy). Skilling asks whether Tintin's political choices are still relevant in our time as, for Hergé, the denunciation of dictatorship appears to be more a plea for a moderate government than for democracy itself. Teasing out the allusions and metaphors in *The Adventures of Tintin*, Skilling connects them to actual political events and debates.

Philosophical debate about governmental rule is one area of human inquiry that has met with violent opposition and resolution. Violence, especially violence towards the innocent as a means to a political end, remains a festering wound upon the body politic.

Philosopher George Santayana stated "Those who cannot remember the past are condemned to repeat it." Shockingly, however, it is also the case that those who do remember repeat it willingly. We remember the holocaust of World War II but people continue to commit genocide and other atrocities. The attack on the World Trade Center reaffirmed this fact. With that in mind, the last selection gives one of the clearest and most powerful examples of how themes in comics can "cross-over" with our own world as it comments upon how even "escapist" comic books cannot escape worldly events. Indeed, even the lives of superheroes have been affected by the terrorist attack on New York City on September 11, 2001.

In "Drawn Into 9/11, But Where Have All the Superheroes Gone?" Terry Kading argues that the world established in the superhero genre has often mirrored our own scientific and technological advancements and the related concerns of the modern world. In superhero comics, it is not unusual to find the same urban topography and related social problems, but with the noticeable addition of powerful beings doing battle in the skies above. The nature of the conflict in the superhero genre tends to be on a far grander scale, involving more complex forms of "good versus evil" and with higher potential costs. It is with the events of September 11, 2001, that Kading examines several parallels between our contemporary sense of high insecurity and that of the worldview and individual experience within the superhero genre, suggesting that more than ever before we have been drawn into the superhero narrative. Kading notes that this merging of reality and superhero narratives has left the world with super-villains, but no superheroes. Thus, without the benefits of any superheroes to restore a sense of safety, we are forced to engage in activities that further heighten our insecurity and diminish (if not reverse) our aspirations and the prospects for positive global developments.

With or without superheroes, comics can explore with philosophical and moral concerns. By means of several critical lenses, *Comics as Philosophy* allows for re-examination and deeper engagement with an art form too long dismissed as trivial. Like the comics they discuss, the essays are springboards for thought and the continuing debate about what it means to be human.

_____ Comics as
PHILOSOPHY

What If? DC's Crisis and Leibnizian Possible Worlds

—JEFF McLAUGHLIN

DC comics' *Crisis on Infinite Earths* was a landmark series that signaled the start of many crossovers to follow and along with Marvel's *Secret Wars*, signaled the end of the Bronze Age of comics. In the 1985 twelve issue set writer Marv Wolfman and artist George Pérez collapsed DC's ever-expanding number of universes into one. While clearly significant from the perspective of comic-dom in that it simplified DC's overly complex superhero realm and conveniently wiped out a few trillion lives in the blink of an eye, the underlying metaphysics of the multi-universe concept has a rich 300-year philosophical tradition. DC's *Crisis* can be shown to be a perfect example of what we call "possible worlds" talk. Furthermore, if one looks past the red capes and tight spandex, the premises behind this comic book are not all that far-fetched.

First, here is a very brief sketch of why the crisis (with a small "c") came about for DC Comics. According to Jonathan Woodward:

> In the late '40s, superhero popularity declined, and through the mid-'50s only Superman and a precious few others heroes remained in publication. In 1956 a new Flash (Barry Allen) was introduced inaugurating the Silver Age of comics. Barry Allen was in part inspired to become [the Flash] by the comics he had read as a child; comics about Jay Garrick, [the first Flash]. [Allen's Flash] later joined the Justice League of America alongside Superman, who was of course,

still around. [The problem was that] Superman, who had fought beside [the first] Flash [Jay Garrick]; was now fighting beside [the second] Flash [Barry Allen]. But to [Allen], [Garrick] was a fictional character.

Later, [to try and make some sense out of this] the Silver Age Earth of Barry Allen [the second Flash] was dubbed "Earth-1" and the world of Jay Garrick, [the first Flash] "Earth-2." (Woodward, para 2–4)

Interestingly, and equally confusing perhaps is that the "earlier" Earth is referred to as the second Earth while the later Earth of the Silver Age era becomes the first Earth. As the decades passed and as new storylines got created, numerous more Earths appear thus leading to the ultimate supposition by both the DC creators and their characters that there are an "infinite number of Earths" which exist within an infinite number of universes. In the *Crisis* series, Wolfman claims that some 3,000 universes were killed off. While not quite the infinite number of universes that were claimed to exist, it is still a remarkable catastrophe.

Now for those who are not familiar with the series' storyline, here's an overview of the crisis storyline depicted by Wolfman and Pérez. Krona from the planet OA seeks to learn the origin of the universe. He creates a machine to peer into the past but a "cosmic bolt" (and aren't they always cosmic?) surges forth and . . . "the universe shuddered and the evil anti-matter universe was formed. But more than that—the single universe was replicated. What was one became many. At that moment was born both the anti-matter universe and the multi-verse. The Earth . . . and all the planets were duplicated. Only one was without its doppelganger: Oa." (Wolfman, Pérez, 183). In these universes the powerful entities known as the Monitor and Anti-Monitor were also born. Feeling guilty at what one of their own had done, the immortal Oan's created the Green Lantern Corps as atonement for Krona's evil meddling into things best left untouched.

Eons later, a brilliant scientist (and aren't they always brilliant?) also sought to find the origin of the universe and created an anti-matter chamber to "penetrate the barrier between universes." Unfortunately, matter and anti-matter cannot exist together and so came the death of this universe. The void that this created was filled by the anti-universe and freed the Anti-Monitor. As his power grew, more and more positive universes fell. Now let us skip ahead a few million years. . . .

Aware of the spreading threat, the Monitor sends a messenger to round up the superheroes from different Earths (and other assorted planets). The messenger is herself possessed by the Anti-Monitor and kills the Monitor. But the Monitor foresaw this tragedy and welcomed it as his death would release his positive energy to temporarily protect Earth-1 and Earth-2 from being consumed. Three more Earths, 4, X, and S, are also temporarily protected but continue to threaten each other's existence. In a battle against the Anti-Monitor, Supergirl is killed but her actions stop the five Earths from continuing to occupy more of each other's space. Our superheroes then travel to the dawn of time and kill the Anti-Monitor and the multi-verse is reborn as one universe only.

Of course, since we are dealing with the comic book universe, there is always the danger that the "dead" character really didn't die or is reincarnated as someone else.[1] Marv Wolfman writes:

> For those hundreds of people who have been asking how I intended to bring back Barry Allen [Flash II] from death in *Crisis on Infinite Earths* the answer will now be revealed once and for all! If you remember, Flash was moving backward through time, from the future to the (1985) present. Occasionally he would pop up for an instant before the time stream closed up on him once again. My idea was to pluck him out of one second of time. From this moment on Barry would know that the time stream could close in on him for the last time at any instant. For the first time in his life, Barry understood that every moment mattered to him. He therefore had to do as much good as he could, knowing that any moment might be his last. Because it was felt by some (not me) that Barry wasn't as dynamic a character as many others, I thought this character alteration would make him more interesting to the readers at large. I could bring him back from the dead and add a dynamic tension to the character that others felt he lacked. I proposed this solution from Day one, but for good or bad—your decision—it wasn't taken. Was I right? Well, I think it would have given Barry the "oomph" some thought he lacked. On the other hand, Wally West as the new Flash has been an incredibly popular character for fifteen years now.

In the end, one Earth survives, an amalgam of the remaining others. Lost in the new DC Universe are the Earths that we loved to read about including Earths 2, 3, 4, 5, 6, K, S, and X. Lost also are such significant superheroes such as Supergirl, Flash II, Aquagirl, Robin I, and many more.[2]

Given the sacrifices made, the lives lost and the tragedies that befell all, we have to ask whether this new DC world is the best of all the possible ones that could have been created. The simple answer has to be "no" just because this particular (fictional) world had human creators. The "new" world that is created within the *Crisis* setting proper isn't perfect of course. Nevertheless, I'm not about to critique Wolfman's decisions as his creation is quite philosophically instructive. To explain, we have to go back three hundred years.

Gottfried Liebniz (1646–1716), who is probably the greatest German philosopher prior to Immanuel Kant (1724–1804), argued that this world, that is, the one where you are currently reading this essay, is the best of all possible worlds simply because it is the only world that is *actualized*. There are other worlds and in some of them I didn't write this article and in others, you did; and still in others you and I may not even exist in the twinkle of our parents' eyes. However, we're talking about *this* one, right here and right now. If you think about it, it makes sense (at least from a personally subjective point of view) to believe that if there were many worlds then this world has to be the best one. Even if we just narrowed our candidates down to just two worlds to this one that I exist in, and an imaginary one where I'm rich and famous, this one (where I'm not rich and not famous) has to be considered better from my point of view since this world *exists*. The imaginary one would be less than perfect *for me* for even though my life is better in it, that life is merely a possible one. I don't exist in that world because there is no world to exist in.

Still, the fact that I believe this world to be the best of all worlds simply because I'm included in it, doesn't mean that truly it is. I'm just one person among billions and I may be slightly bias in thinking that the best world has to have me in it. A person who's life seems to be horrific, for instance, that proverbial blind, mute, friendless, starving orphan who just had his only pair of (albeit it ill-fitting) dentures stolen might disagree. Besides, wishing it so, doesn't make it so. Other individuals may find other worlds better for them even though they might be worse for me. Perhaps surprisingly, Leibniz argued that this world is the best of all possible worlds for *everyone*. So how did Leibniz derive this particular view?

In his *Theodicy*, Leibniz argued that God's existence is required to stop the infinite causal chain of explanation. That is, when we try to explain how A happened, we refer to cause B. When we ask how B came to be, we have to refer to a previous causal event C and so on. To avoid an infinite regress of causes, there has to be a first cause, and that cause is God.[3]

But there must also be sufficient reason for contingent truths, or truths of fact, that is for the succession of things extended throughout the created universe, where their resolution into individual reasons would know no bounds on account of nature's vastness and the infinite divisibility of bodies. There is an infinity of shapes and movements both present and past that enters into the efficient cause of my present writing, and there is an infinity of minute inclinations and dispositions of my soul that enters into its final cause. (Leibniz, *Theodicy* sec. 36, 37, 44, 45, 52, 121, 122, 337, 340, 344 qtd. in *Monadology* sec. 36)

And as all this detail just contains other preceding and more detailed contingencies, each of which requires a similar analysis to arrive at its reason, one is no further forward. The ultimate and sufficient reason must lie outside the succession of things or the series of detailed contingencies, however infinite it may be. (Leibniz, *Monadology* sec. 37)

Thus it is that the ultimate reason for things must lie in a Necessary Substance, one in which the complex detail of all changes is contained merely eminently, as their source. This is what we call God. (*Theodicy* sec. 7 qtd. in *Monadology* sec. 38)

God must be the first cause since there *must* be a first cause. And because the first cause must have intelligence in order to choose between the alternatives, God must exist. "This existing world being contingent and an infinity of other worlds being equally possible, and holding, so to say, equal claim to existence with it, the cause of the world must have had regard or reference to all these possible worlds in order to fix upon one of them." (*Theodicy* sec. 7). But just being able to choose a world (which Leibniz defines as "the whole succession and the whole agglomeration of all existent things" see *Theodicy* sec. 8), doesn't mean that an all-powerful being would necessarily choose the best one. Leibniz also needed to argue that God was absolutely perfect and that in being perfect, he would choose the perfect world.

We may also infer that this Supreme Substance—which is unique, universal and necessary, having nothing beyond it that is independent of it, and existing as a simple consequence of being possible . . . (Leibniz 40) . . . From which it follows that God is absolutely perfect (*Theodicy* Preface, sec. 22 qtd. in *Monadology* sec. 41)

Clearly this assumes that in order for something to be perfect, it is necessary that that entity must also exist. The reasoning parallels my preference for a world that I'm in rather than the one I'm not. In other words, if God did not exist; we could imagine a greater being, namely one that *did* exist.

> We may also infer that this Supreme Substance . . . must be incapable of being limited, and must contain as much reality as is possible. (*Monadology* sec. 40)

Not only then is God the first cause, but since He is all powerful and perfect, from God springs forth all the other perfections of the world. Furthermore, given that he is perfect, he cannot be the cause of the flaws that we know to exist.

> It also follows that the perfections that created things have are due to God's influence; their imperfections, though, are due to their own natures, incapable as they are of being without limits. It is in this that they are distinguished from God. This original imperfection that belongs to created things is manifest in the natural inertia of bodies. (*Monadology* sec. 42)

God is all-powerful and all good and because He has these characteristics, the world that He chooses to create as part of His divine plan must be the best one possible. *Our world is that world.*

Leibniz's possible worlds argument is neat and tidy. If there is a God, then He must necessarily exist. The conjunction of His perfect and all-powerful nature with His being the first cause ultimately leads to the existence of our world which is the best of the infinitude of possible worlds. . . . Now we might object that Leibniz is merely *defining* God into existence, or that there is no reason to not postulate that there are many gods fulfilling this role, but these criticisms don't give us a true appreciation of the philosophical beauty concerning why *this* world is the one that God produces. Leibniz writes:

> Now, as there is an infinity of possible universes in the ideas of God and because only one of them can be actual, there has to be a sufficient reason for God's choice which determines Him in favour of one rather than another. (*Theodicy* sec. 8, 10, 44, 173, 196–99, 225, 414–16 qtd. in *Monadology* sec. 53)
>
> And this reason can only be found in the fitness or in the degrees of perfection that these worlds contain, each one having as much right to claim existence as there is perfection in it. . . . (*Theodicy* sec. 74, 167, 350, 201, 130, 352, 345–47, 350, 352, 354 qtd. in *Monadology* sec. 54)
>
> What brings about the existence of the best is that God's wisdom has Him recognize it. His goodness has Him choose it, and His power has Him create it. (*Theodicy* sec. 8, 78, 80, 84, 119, 204, 206, 208. Abridgement, Objs. 1 and 8 qtd. in *Monadology* sec. 55)

Compared to the other possible worlds, this is the best and we have to trust God's judgment on this matter. This doesn't mean that our world is wholly perfect since moral imperfections are a necessary part of it due to the non-divine nature of human beings. Although we may be readily able to point to physical flaws in the world, Leibniz argues that given *our* inherent limitations, we are neither able to know what changes would be required to improve the world, nor able to know what the consequences of our changes would ultimately result in. This sort of thinking is evident when we speak of "the cure being worse than the disease" such as when we try to interfere with the natural world and wind up creating more difficulties than if we left it alone. One could also point out that in order to know what is good, we must have something to contrast it with, thus, we need to also know evil. Moreover, flaws or "evil" can be instrumental in contributing to the "greater perfection in him who suffers it" (*Theodicy* 24).

But why do we need evil to see what is good? If God is all powerful (and all good I might add) then why *must* we suffer? Furthermore, if we must suffer, would not just one example of evil be sufficient for us to have something to compare goodness with? Do we need to be continually reminded by the deaths of innocents? One might suggest that God could have made us perfect beings as well, with the powers required to improve our lot in life. In fact, Rene Descartes wondered about this very point. If God is perfect, why did he not create us as perfect beings as well? Descartes was attempting to respond to the skeptics who argued that we couldn't know anything about our world (not to mention any possible ones). While he admitted that he could be deceived, for example, that he was actually dreaming when he thought he was awake, the foundation for his rationalist theory of knowledge was based on the perfection of God. God does not deceive us for that would imply God's imperfection. In an argument that echoes Leibniz's views regarding the imperfections of human beings, Descartes states that error (which includes perceptions about imperfection) is initiated within us and that it comes from our understanding and freedom of choice. As finite beings we just are incapable of knowing God's purposes and plans; or in more simplistic terms: God works in ways that are mysterious to us, but not to Him. Descartes tells us that isolated instances of error or defect must be viewed within the context of the goodness of the whole.

> It further occurs to me that we must not consider only one creature apart from the others, if we wish to determine the perfection of the works of Deity, but generally all his creatures together; for the same object that might perhaps, with some show of reason, be deemed highly imperfect if it were alone in the world, may for all that be the most perfect possible, considered as forming part of the whole universe. (*Med. IV*. Para. 7)

Although we can debate the validity of the assorted arguments put forward by Leibniz and Descartes (as philosophers have done for centuries), one of most intriguing things that Leibniz did was to posit the existence of possible universes. This "multi-verse," to use the terminology adopted in the DC *Crisis* series is populated with an infinite number of possible Earths, each with its own degree of perfection. When philosophers talk about the existence of these Earths, we mean they are *real*, we can talk about them meaningfully, but they are not *actual*. In other words, we can describe what they might be like but we can't climb into a space ship and travel to these Earths because their existence is only that of possibility. They do not exist in *actuality*.[4] For Leibniz, these worlds do not exist because they are not fully perfect.

These infinite worlds aren't just something out of the imaginations of comic book writers or long-dead philosophers. The "Infinite Earths" crisis need not just be seen as a creative way to extricate DC Comics from an artistic mess that had been building up since the 1930s. Ordinary people talk about the infinite number of worlds all the time when they speak of things that are contrary-to-facts. They just don't know that they are doing this and that these worlds are real.

The term we use to capture possible worlds talk is "counterfactuals." Counterfactuals occur when we describe how the world would be if it weren't the way it actually is. In other words, we are offering a counter to the fact of the matter. Here are a few simple examples.

- If the mug had slipped off the table, it would have broken.
- If I had left for the airport a few minutes earlier, I would not have missed my flight.
- If Hitler had died at age ten, Nazism would not have arisen in Germany.
- If Elvis were alive today, he'd be really, really fat.

Counterfactuals are just "What If?" types of questions where we present a different version of the world and try to determine what it would look like.

Individuals may do this when they regret the performance of an action or lament the occurrence of a particular action. Marvel Comics examines counterfactuals with the aptly named *What If* series. "What if Gwen Stacey didn't die?" "What if Captain America had been revived today?" "What if Dr. Strange did not become Master of the Mystic Arts?" And so forth.

Counterfactuals are controversial since it is not possible to determine the accuracy of most of the scenarios. One can't just pop over to another world to see if the consequences would have changed if the circumstances were different. On one world, I did leave the house early but still missed the plane because I had a flat tire. On another I left late but the plane was delayed so I was able to catch it. On still yet another I didn't even manage get out of bed. Since there are an infinite number of possible worlds, there are an infinite number of possibilities. Some will look very similar to the actual one, others will be radically different. In those possible worlds my hair will be a different colour while in others, I'm completely bald, or female, or Austrian . . . Indeed, sometimes I wish I could fly like Superman and in perhaps in one possible world I do.

When tragedy befalls us, it is natural to think of how things could have been if things were different. Perhaps it is just a part of human nature to second guess what could have been the case by comparing this world with the infinite number of possible ones but the events that happen in our world are simple actualities. For better or worse, the world is how it is and it is not another way. This isn't cause for existential dread as it is simply a truism. "What happens, happens" really isn't very profound.

Our actual world is *this* one while the major concern that motivated the DC *Crisis* series was that there were too many fictional worlds colliding. While Wolfman and Pérez allowed a new world order to unfold in the DC universe such that five Earths competed to become the "actual" one,[5] our actualized world is the one where we are reading about the adventures of individuals whose lives exist only between the pages of a comic books.

Possible worlds allow us to understand each other when we are talking about superheroes. These superheroes *are* real but not actual because they are living lives in real possible worlds but not actual possible worlds. Accordingly, we can honestly claim that Superman and Lois Lane finally tied the knot and that Supergirl really died at the hands of the Anti-Monitor back in '86. Of course, we have to be careful how we talk and remind ourselves that although Supergirl *really* did die, she didn't *actually* die at the hands of the Anti-Monitor because she doesn't actually exist.

Are you puzzled? Don't be. We can and need to be able to make these kinds of statements about the real nature of fictional characters for if we tried to suggest otherwise, we would create even more awkward and potentially contradictory claims. If I asked: "Did Supergirl die?" You might respond by saying: "Yes, she was killed in a battle"; and this is completely acceptable. However, if we didn't make the distinction between reality and actuality, you would state: "No, Supergirl didn't die because she's a fictional character. Fictional characters don't exist. One has to have existed before one can go out of existence. So Supergirl didn't die because she never lived." This is a fair enough explanation, but it doesn't capture what really happened. If *actual* existence were a requirement for talking about anything in a meaningful way, then many of our ordinary and commonly accepted discussions would become nonsensical. Consider:

"The Green Lantern's powers are not nullified by yellow objects. Why? Because there is no such person as the Green Lantern."

Yet Yellow does hinder GL!

"Bruce Wayne was never motivated to become the Batman due to the murder of his parents. Why? Because his parents *weren't* murdered. They weren't murdered and they weren't parents because they weren't in a dark alley and they didn't have a son named Bruce. Why? Because Bruce doesn't exist and, as a matter of fact, neither do his parents."

But I read the books, and this is what happened!

The point of these examples is that we can and do ascribe attributes to mythological beasts, fictional characters, and comic book superheroes that don't exist in actuality. They exist in the important sense that we can meaningfully refer to them and make statements about them that are true or false. It is false that a unicorn has two horns—not because they don't exist in actuality—but because they only have one horn. It is false that Sherlock Holmes is the world's "second best detective" because he is the world's *greatest* detective. And so we do continue talk about these individuals, often with love and passion and excitement at all their trials and tribulations.

This is not a just game of semantics. You and I know that there is no Santa Claus, but ask any adult "Who delivers presents to good boys and girls on December 25th and laughs with a hearty 'Ho Ho Ho!'?" and you'll be told "Jolly St. Nick!" or "Santa!" Being able to understand that we are *describing a person who doesn't actually exist* is essential to how our natural language works. Logicians refer to this practice as "Hypothetical Import" for what we mean when we are talking about Santa is this: "*If* Santa existed, he'd bring toys to all the good boys and girls." "*If* Bruce Wayne actually existed, *then* he would be the Batman." "*If* Kara Zor-el actually existed, she'd be Kal-El's cousin and would be known as 'Supergirl.'"

What attracts people to comic books and to fiction in general is that they give us a peek at just a few possible worlds. Our imaginations are not limited to documenting what goes on around us. *DC's Crisis on Infinite Earths* illustrates how we can not only see these other worlds, but it also presents us with an instance of how we can come to understand the metaphysical discourse surrounding our own. Reading fictional accounts of the adventures of superheroes is often considered escapist entertainment. But fictional worlds can provide the means by which reflect back upon our own lives and thus they can offer insight about our own world. When our favourite comic book characters are faced with crises we can in some small way identify with them because we get caught up in their real lives; lives that we can't actually live; lives that *they* don't actually live.

Really.

NOTES

1. In fact, I wish to ignore everything including the revisions and the reinventions that came after this series—they aren't relevant for my purposes here.
2. Again, citing Jonathan Woodward. Other deaths Woodward notes include the Crime Syndicate, Luthor III, Lois Lane-Luthor, The Losers, Nighthawk, Kid Psycho, Princess Fern, Lord Volk, The Justice Alliance, Luthor I, Icicle, Mirror Master, The Lieutenant Marvels, Dove, Green Arrow I, Prince Ra-Man, Clayface II, The Ten-Eyed Man, Kole, Huntress. Jonathan Woodward, *The Annotated Crisis on Infinite Earths*, http://www.io.com/~woodward/chroma/crisis.html (visited 02/12/02).
3. An infinite regression is not only troubling to theists, but it is also a puzzling concept for those who rather offer a scientific explanation of the universe. Here, there is no beginning, no starting point. And if there is no starting point, how did the whole thing *get going* in the first place?
4. This is an overgeneralization since there are different theories posited by philosophers about what the "existence" of possible worlds means. The point here however is that these worlds exist—in a sense—and thus one can excuse the reader if the distinctions between "actual worlds," "real worlds," and "possible worlds" are fuzzy.
5. Obviously, it is "actual" only from the perspective of the characters portrayed in the series.

Describing and Discarding "Comics" as an Impotent Act of Philosophical Rigor

—ROBERT C. HARVEY

We have it on pretty good authority (Biblical, in fact—Genesis II:19) that it was Adam who gave every living thing its name. This stunning feat of denomination took place, Bishop Butler tells us, on October 4, 4004 B.C. On that day, God paraded "every beast of the field and every fowl of the air," indeed "every living creature," before Adam "to see what he would call them; and whatsoever he called them, that was the name thereof."

Some wag of note, perhaps the ever-quotable Mark Twain, imagined God's bemusement as He witnessed Adam's performance.

"Lion," saith Adam, as the shaggy King of Beasts slouched by him, cat-like.

"How do you know it's a lion?" God asked (bemused, as I said).

"It *looks* like a lion," said Adam, scoffing somewhat.

Dunno what Adam would have done about comics. Comics don't look like comics at all. They can be found, usually, in a nimbus of light at the far end of a darkened room, where they stand, entirely alone, often gripping a microphone in one sweaty hand, delivering themselves of bad puns, all manner of verbal incongruities, and assorted manifestations of syntactic surprise, which they accompany, sometimes, with distorted facial expressions.

For this, they are rewarded with the laughter of a multitude that has assembled before them for the purpose of laughing.

But as every schoolboy knows, comics do not stand alone at microphones in the dark. Indeed, we cannot even read them in the dark. We need light, the more, the better. And we enjoy comics best in solitary, by ourselves, not in crowds; although large numbers of people read comics, they generally do it by themselves, in silence.

Even in the light, bewilderment ensues. Newspaper comics are sometimes funny and sometimes quite serious. The reasons for this anomaly are evident in the history of the medium. Newspapers had published cartoons before 1894, but it was in the fall of that year that the *New York World* started publishing a Sunday supplement that became embroiled in a circulation war, which, taking place in the nation's largest city where the media set a pace for the rest of the country, had ramifications beyond the city limits. In devising the Sunday supplement in color for the *World*, Morrill Goddard imitated weekly humor magazines like *Life, Judge,* and *Puck.* Offering comical drawings and amusing short essays and droll verse, these magazines were dubbed "comic weeklies" in common parlance—or, even, "comics." So when the *World* launched its imitation "comic weekly" as a supplement to its Sunday edition, it was lumped together in the popular mind as another of the "comics." And then, once the *World* had shown the way, papers in other cities began publishing humorous Sunday supplements full of funny drawings in color and risible essays and verse. In a relatively short time, obeying the dictates of demand, newspapers eliminated the essays and verse and concentrated on comical artwork, which was increasingly presented in the form of "strips" of pictures portraying hilarities in narrative sequence. It was but a short step to the use of *comics* to designate the artform (comic strips) as distinct from the vehicle in which they appeared (the Sunday supplement itself). Once that bridge was crossed, meaning deteriorated pretty rapidly. Storytelling (or "continuity") strips arrived soon after, and even when the stories they told were serious, they were called "comics" because they looked like the artform called *comics* and they appeared in newspapers with all the others of that ilk. Finally, when comic strips began to be reprinted in magazine form in the 1930s, the now-generic term was applied to those magazines, too—comic books became *comics.*

Whether the evolution of the term followed these lines precisely or only generally (the *Oxford English Dictionary* is not explicit in its etymology), it is certain that a confusing coinage was soon in wide circulation. And the perplexity was compounded by the form of the word itself. What do we make of the assertion "comics are art"?

Or is it "comics *is* art"?

Or are comics stand-up comedians?

The confusion inherent in the word *comics* has been apparent to those writing in the field for years. The word has a plural form but is singular in application. And in its singular form, *comic*, it can be an adjective for something humorous or another name for a comedian. In short, *comics* lacks the precision it ought to have for ordinary communication let alone serious philosophical deliberations. Comics might very well be freighted with ontological messages, but, as a purely philosophical matter, they (or it?) ought to have a name that can be readily understood. We ought to have the right word for the artform before we plumb its metaphysical depths.

The difference between the right word and the nearly right word, Mark Twain remarked, is the difference between lightning and the lightning bug. The right word lights the way. It illuminates the dimmer recesses of the brain where, otherwise, ideas and thoughts lurk unnamed and therefore only faintly perceived and vaguely understood. The task of philosophy is to bring such furtive notions into sharp focus and thereby to discern their meaning and discover their import.

We may discuss comics as philosophy without taking the time to devise more precise language. After all, as Humpty Dumpty, the most frequently quoted authority on these matters, is reputed to have said: "When I use a word, it means just what I choose it to mean—neither more nor less."

"The question," he continued a scant breath or so later, "is which is to be master—that's all."

But Humpty Dumpty, remember, had a great fall, and all the king's men couldn't put him together again. Probably because they couldn't understand the written instructions he'd supplied against such an eventuality.

Clearly, we can make words mean whatever we want them to mean, willy nilly. Comics can be anything we choose to say they are, assuming two or three of us can agree on each fresh nuance of meaning. Still, calling a motor scooter a Sherman tank doesn't guarantee that the scooter will be able to run through a brick wall. In short, before we determine the word or words to use in discussing comics, we ought to be reasonably sure that we can recognize representatives of the artform when we see them. And so we approach the abyss of definition into which nearly every serious discussion of comics has descended, sooner or later. I'd like to avoid the pitfall by declining to define comics. What I'll offer is a description, not, exactly, a definition. But by way of paving the way to that intention, let me touch upon other forays in this direction.

As others have said before me, definitions of *comics* these days tend to be essays rather than simple definitions. Partly, that's because it's difficult to define comics in ways that include everything we think of when we think of "comics."

In *Understanding Comics*, Scott McCloud famously defines comics as "juxtaposed pictorial and other images in deliberate sequence, intended to convey information and/or to produce an aesthetic response in the viewer."[1]

Pascal Lefevre and Charles Dierick, editors of a collection of essays entitled *Forging a New Medium*, while acknowledging that everyone defines a comic strip differently, offer a "prototypical definition." The advantage to this device, they say, is that each term in the definition identifies a group of artifacts or works, but a work that does not satisfy all of the terms of the definition is not necessarily excluded. Their definition of comics, then, is "the juxtaposition of fixed (mostly drawn) pictures on a support as a communicative act."[2] The "support," a puzzling term at first blush, denotes, usually, "a piece of paper" although a T-shirt would suffice. "Pictures" means "images" which might include text, or verbal content. So if you wear a T-shirt with several verbose speech balloons imprinted on it, it's comics.

Thierry Groensteen, in the same collection, defines a comic strip as "a visual narrative, a story conveyed by sequences of graphic, fixed images, together on a single support," adding that "the concept of sequence *in praesentia* (in what Henri Van Lier called a 'multicadre' or multi-frame) constitutes the principal basis of the language of the comic strip. No other criterion appears absolutely essential to me."[3]

David Kunzle, one of the pioneering scholars in the field, adds, in the first volume of his massive *History of the Comic Strip*, the requirements that there be a "preponderance of image over text" and that the medium be a mass medium.[4]

Omnibus as these definitions seem to be, they have led us to embrace a history of comics that includes many works that are clearly not comics.

In our search for holy writ, we may have overlooked the most conspicuous shortcoming of these definitions. While all of these "juxtaposed pictorial and other images in deliberate sequence" concoctions include verbiage (those "other images" can be written words), all of the lexicographers imply or maintain that comics do not have to contain words to be comics. But words are clearly an integral part of what we think of when we think of comics. Words as well as pictures. These definitions are simply too broad to be useful as anything except as springboard to discussion. Guided by these definitions, we wind up at the Bayeaux Tapestry and Mexican codices. Both are comics. So is written Chinese. So are the Stations of the Cross as depicted in the stained glass windows of medieval cathedrals.

These definitions include what we call comics just as *quadruped* includes horses. But dogs are not exactly horses even though dogs also have four legs. A more accurate definition of each contains other distinguishing characteristics that make it possible for us to tell a dog from a horse. Clearly, when we think about "comics," an image of the Bayeaux Tapestry is not the first that leaps up before the mind's eye, and our definition should acknowledge this commonplace mental predisposition.

The traditional definition of *comics* is that conjured up by Coulton Waugh in his book *Comics* (1947). And he says *comics* consist of three elements: (1) sequence of pictures that tell a story or joke, (2) words incorporated into the picture usually in the form of speech balloons, and (3) continuing characters.[5] last item snatches at sophistry. It's there under false pretenses. Its function is purely rhetorical—to eliminate anything that came along before the Yellow Kid, the most conspicuous of the combatants in New York's newspaper circulation battles of the 1890s. The Yellow Kid was seen as the first comic strip character mostly because he was a highly visible and successful commercial enterprise—the commercial aspect establishing the value to newspapers of comic strips. But "continuing characters" clearly have nothing much to do with the intrinsic form of a comic strip, and I usually leave that part out. But the rest of Waugh's definition is a pretty good basis for starting. By way of making a start, however, we must return to an era earlier than that of the Yellow Kid and a form more primitive, more basic. And so I do, for a moment only:

There are stories, narratives. There are verbal narratives (epic poems, novels), and there are pictorial narratives (Egyptian tomb paintings, the Bayeaux Tapestry). In my view, comics are a sub-set of pictorial narrative; therefore, all comics are pictorial narratives, but not all pictorial narratives are comics. Horses are quadrupeds, and dogs are quadrupeds, but horses are not dogs, and dogs are not horses. There are different kinds of quadrupeds, and there are different kinds of pictorial narratives. Egyptian tomb paintings are a species of pictorial narrative, but they aren't comics. It seems to me that the essential characteristic of *comics*—the thing that distinguishes it from other kinds of pictorial narratives—is the incorporation of verbal content. I even go so far as to say that in the best examples of the art form, words and pictures blend to achieve a meaning that neither conveys alone without the other.

To McCloud and Groensteen and the rest, "sequence" is at the heart of the functioning of comics; to me, "blending" verbal and visual content is. McCloud's definition relies too heavily upon the pictorial character of comics and not enough upon the verbal ingredient. Comics uniquely blend the two. No other form of static visual narrative does this. McCloud includes verbal content (which he allows is a kind of imagery), but it's the succession of images that is at the operative core of his definition. I hasten to note, however, that regardless of emphasis, neither sequence nor blending inherently excludes the other.

Rodolphe Topffer, often dubbed the "father of comics" these days, seems to lean in my direction. Commenting upon his verbal-visual creations, he wrote: "The drawings, without their text, would have only a vague meaning; the text, without the drawings, would have no meaning at all. The combination makes up a kind of novel, all the more unique in that it is no more like a novel than it is like anything else."[6]

Topffer's comics would include even the humble single-panel gag cartoon in which, usually, the humor of the picture is secured, or revealed, by the caption below—and vice versa. The gag cartoon falls outside McCloud's definition because it is not a sequence of pictures. In fact, gag cartoons fall outside most definitions of comics. But not outside my description. In my view, comics consist of pictorial narratives or expositions in which words (often lettered into the picture area within speech balloons) usually contribute to the meaning of the pictures and vice versa. A pictorial narrative uses a sequence of juxtaposed pictures (i.e., a "strip" of pictures); pictorial exposition may do the same—or may not (as in single-panel cartoons—political cartoons as well as gag cartoons). My description is not a leak-proof formulation. It conveniently excludes some non-comics artifacts that McCloud's includes (a rebus, for instance); but it probably permits the inclusion of other non-comics. Comics, after all, are sometimes four-legged and sometimes two-legged and sometimes fly and sometimes don't.

But leak-proof or not, this proffer of a description sets some boundaries within which we can find most of the artistic endeavors we call *comics*. Even pantomime, or "wordless," comic strips—which, guided by this definition, we can see are pictorial narratives that dispense with the "usual" practice of using words as well as pictures. But that doesn't make the usual practice any the less usual. Pantomime cartoon strips are exceptional rather than usual. Usually, the interdependence of words and pictures is vital (if not essential) to comics—"vital" meaning "characteristic of life" rather than "indispensable."

The presence of verbiage in the same view or field of vision as the pictures gives immediacy to the combination, breathing the illusion of life into the medium. In a letter to me, Richard Kyle (who coined the term "graphic novel" in 1964) elaborated on the need he felt then, in 1964, for a new terminology for comic books instead of the terms already in circulation (albeit not very visibly by then—"illustories," concocted by Charles Biro, and "picto-fiction," the EC Comics invention): "Biro and the others apparently did not think about the fundamental nature of comics or understand some of the characteristics of our language. Comics are not 'illustories'—'illustrated stories.' In comics, ideation, pictures, sound (including speech and sound effects), and indicators (such as motion lines and impact bursts) are all portrayed graphically in a single unified whole. Graphics do not 'illustrate' the story; they *are* the story. . . . In the graphic story, all the universe and all the senses are portrayed graphically" [i.e., in the static visual mode].

Kyle's point, and mine (although he makes it better than I have), is that in comics everything is portrayed and conveyed in the same manner, visually. And the concurrent presence in the visual mode of speech as well as action, locale, etc., makes comics what they are, a unique kind of pictorial narrative. In fact, this concurrence, if not interdependence, may actually define the medium.

The importance to me of the verbal content in determining whether a pictorial narrative (or exposition) is *comics* may be best illustrated by a discussion of comic strips. Comic strips include an ingredient that gag cartoons do not. The technical hallmarks of comic strip art—the things that distinguish it—consist chiefly of narrative breakdown and speech balloons. Narrative breakdown is an aspect of sequencing images and is therefore peculiar to the comic strip branch of the cartooning family tree and to pictorial narrative in general. The narrative is broken down into separate key moments that can be depicted visually in ways that clearly convey the essential elements of the story. But in speech balloons, we have something that is unique to the comics medium. Speech balloons breathe into comics their peculiar life. In all other graphic representations—in all other pictorial narratives—characters are doomed to wordless posturing and pantomime. In comics, they speak. And they speak in the same mode as they appear—the visual not the audio mode of representation. This is unique.

If speech balloons give comics their life, then breaking the narrative into successive images gives that life duration, an existence beyond a moment. Narrative breakdown is to comics what time is to life. In fact, "timing"—pace as well as duration—is the second of the vital ingredients of comics. "Vital" but not, here, "unique." The sequential arrangement of panels cannot help but create time in some general way, but skillful manipulation of the sequencing can control time and use it to dramatic advantage.

My description seems to exclude Harold Foster's *Prince Valiant* and Burne Hogarth's *Tarzan* and Warren Tufts's *Lance*. Exactly. These are not comics. They consist of pictures with text underneath telling a story. They are illustrated narratives, and they were published in the Sunday comics section of newspapers. But the place of publication doesn't make them comics. Nor is William Donahey's *Teenie Weenies* a specimen of comics: the feature was published in the Sunday funnies, but it consisted of a single picture illustrating a text short story. Not comics despite its venue.

Comics are a species of illustrated narrative. So is a rebus. So is *Prince Valiant*. So are many of today's children's books. "Illustrated narrative" includes all of these as subsets. But the subsets are not interchangeable: each has distinguishing characteristics that set it apart from the others.

The notion of comics as a visual-verbal blend does more than merely describe the artform. It also suggests a critical criterion: in the best examples of the medium, the words give a meaning to the pictures that the pictures otherwise lack, and vice versa. The blend creates a new meaning that is not present in either of the two vital ingredients alone without the other. I must emphatically add, however, that visual-verbal blending is only one of numerous criteria by which the cartooning artistry of comics should be judged—only one, albeit the first one.

The visual-verbal blend principle is the first principle of a critical theory of comic strips for two reasons. It is first in importance: it derives directly from the very nature of the art. But it is first also because it is the first step in the process of evaluation, a process that involves making a successive series of "allowances" by which the visual-verbal blend principle is modified to accommodate the various categories and genres of comic strips. Many comic strips (those that tell continuing stories, particularly) cannot consistently meet the visual-verbal blend criterion. And yet many of them are excellent strips. But their excellence derives from other aspects of the art.

Dondi and *Peanuts* are both about children, but *Dondi* is a storytelling strip about an orphan boy, and it seeks in its soap opera tales and realistic rendering an illusion of real life. *Dondi* can be faulted when it falls short of achieving that illusion; *Peanuts*, which, ostensibly, aims simply to make us laugh, cannot. We can look for visual-verbal blend in both strips, but if *Dondi* fails to achieve it as consistently as *Peanuts*, there may be good reasons for that failure—reasons peculiar to the continuity genre.

Because storytelling strips tell stories that continue from day-to-day, they are freighted with an expository burden that gag strips, those that tell a different joke every day, never have to shoulder. Continuity strips tend to be much more verbal than gag strips, and the more exposition needed, the more verbal and less visual the strip becomes. A diligent cartoonist, however, attempts to restore the visual-verbal balance by resorting to variety in his compositions. Changing perspective, camera-distance, texture, and the like gives emphasis to the visual component and thereby revives the impression of visual-verbal blending. To the extent that a cartoonist tries to maintain the visual character of his strip in the face of the expository imperative for more verbiage, so is his work better than that of a cartoonist who gives us a panel-by-panel parade of talking faces, all the same distance from the camera. Other criteria that apply more to storytelling strips than gag strips include such things as characterization, realistic illustration, authentic-sounding dialogue and so on.

In a book of mine, *The Art of the Funnies*, I outline many more of the "allowances" that must be made in applying a visual-verbal criterion of evaluation and discuss other criteria, too. And in the last analysis, visual-verbal blending is scarcely all there is to the art of the comic strip. The notion, however, stresses both the visual and the verbal nature of the medium, and any examination of the art form must consider both if we are to achieve the kind of analytical perception that is not only appreciative but articulate, not only evaluative but appropriate. Too often, despite McCloud's insistence upon the visual sequential nature of the medium, critical consideration concentrates on the essentially literary aspect of the work, the narrative and its implications. To look first for a visual-verbal blend, then, is to perform a sort of mental sleight-of-hand, a trick of perception by which we focus our attention on the visual character of the medium as well as the verbal means by which we otherwise suppose the narrative and thematic thrust is conveyed. Only by fully embracing the visual as well as the verbal can we see that together they *are* the artform. But there's more to understanding the comics than simply appreciating and evaluating visual-verbal artistry.

The kind of analysis I've suggested makes no attempt to explain or examine what makes a certain strip so peculiarly appealing to its readers. The success of a strip may arise from such things as the exotic and mysterious personality of Milton Caniff's Dragon Lady in *Terry and the Pirates*, the indomitable innocence (or is it ignorance?) of Elzie Segar's *Popeye*, the brittle anachronistic wit of Johnny Hart's *B.C.* and company, the commanding illusion of reality of the pictures in Alex Raymond's *Flash Gordon*, or the masterful blend of vaudeville, allegory, satire, and caricature in Walt Kelly's *Pogo*. A thorough-going analysis of any representatives of the medium must consider these aspects of a cartoonist's work as well as basic visual-verbal blending.

But let's not call the medium "comics." For the sweet sake of intellectual precision, let us call it something else. Let me submit an alternative. Let us derive a usage from the history of the medium. And let us start with the root of the word that is used for those who practice the art, *cartoonist*.

A *cartoonist* is one who draws *cartoons*. But *cartoon* is a relatively old word; *cartoonist* is wholly modern. *Cartoon* comes from the Italian *cartone*, meaning "card." Italian tapestry designers and fresco painters and the like drew their designs on sheets of cardboard at full scale before transferring those designs to the cloth or walls they were intended for. These designs were called by the name of the material upon which they were drawn—*cartones,* or *cartoons.* Later, the word *cartoon* was applied to any preliminary study for a final work.

But none of the artists who used cartoons in those days were called *cartoonists.* The word *cartoonist* is associated only with the medium known in modern times as *cartoon.*

The modern usage of *cartoon* began in London in the 1840s. It was first employed in the modern sense in reference to *Punch,* the London humor magazine. The Houses of Parliament had been all but destroyed in a fire in 1834. The building that took the place of the gutted relic was called the New Palace of Westminster and was built over the next decade. By the mid-1840s, it had been determined that the New Palace would contain various murals on patriotic themes, and a competitive exhibition was held to display the cartoons (in the ancient sense) submitted as candidates for these decorations. *Punch,* then only a couple years old, entered the competition on its own, publishing in its pages satirical drawings about government and calling them "Mr. Punch's cartoons." The first of these appeared in the weekly magazine dated July 15, 1843, and was greeted, we might as well imagine, with howls of joyous appreciation.

At first, *Punch* continued to call its humorous drawings "pencilings." Eventually, it applied the term *cartoon* to any full-page satirical drawing. But to the man in the street, any funny drawing in the magazine after the summer of 1843 might be termed one of "Punch's cartoons," and by this route, the word came into use for any comic drawing.[7] By the time Americans launched their imitations of *Punch* in the mid-to-late 1800s, *cartoon* was well on its way to being established in the modern sense. And so was *cartoonist.*

As we've seen, the modern American newspaper cartoon started in the extravagant Sunday magazine supplements that New York newspapers launched to attract buyers for their newspapers in the 1890s, frank imitations of the weekly humor magazines, *Life, Judge, Puck,* and a host of others—all of which traced their lineage back to *Punch* (and hence to its French inspiration, the Parisian journal, *Charivari*).

The persons who drew the humorous pictures in the supplements were sometimes called *comic artists* (because the pictures they drew were funny), but the term *cartoonist* was in use, too (and had been since at least the 1860s, if we are to judge from the *OED*). Thus, *cartoonist* is a word that has always referred specifically to the medium we now call *comics*; and *cartoonist* is the only word reserved exclusively for those who ply their skill in this medium. *Cartoonist* refers to nothing else. A *comic artist*, on the other hand, could refer to a comedian (who is sometimes termed "a performing artist") or to an illustrator who draws humorous paintings (which are not necessarily cartoons).

Finally—to complete this historical review—comic books began when M. C. Gaines and a few like-minded entrepreneurs of the 1930s started reprinting newspaper cartoon strips in magazine format. With the success of the first of these ventures, the demand for material for such magazines grew so insistent that new stories had to be generated to fill the pages, and this original material drawn especially for the magazines continued to use the form of the cartoon strip to tell short stories. The magazines, then, might well be termed *cartoon story magazines* rather than *comic books* (particularly since many of them were not at all humorous and none of them were books). But an even more apt term is possible anon.

By means of this etymological safari, we come at last to the terms I offer for the medium—terms exclusive to the medium and therefore incapable of the kind of semantic corruption that blurs meaning and distinction. I begin, then, with *cartoonist*, the most exclusive of those terms.

A cartoonist may produce single-panel cartoons, animated cartoons, newspaper cartoon strips, or cartoon short stories (or cartoon story magazines)—or (better) paginated cartoon strips. The word that embraces all these media is *cartoon*. It is the generic alternative to *comics*. And by adding the appropriate modifier, we can make *cartoon* accurately and precisely describe any of the genre in the medium.

I have no illusions that this campaign of mine will win any converts. And even if it does, I doubt that even legions of the converted would impinge much on the common parlance in which the term *comics* has come to apply to the medium. Language is like that. Its terms and usages are established by general practice, not by prescription. And English, perhaps more than any other language, is particularly open and receptive to this kind of evolution. Indeed, linguistically speaking, "English" is not a language at all: it is, rather, a sort of accumulation of usages and vocabularies, most derived from other languages. And this accumulation leaves us with *comics*, a term washed up on the beaches of the medium after weekly humor magazines had sunk into obscurity. We're doubtless stuck with its wobbly imprecision even if we can think of better, more exact, terminology. But the firefly, for all its low voltage, remains a joy to behold and a challenge to try to trap in a bottle.

NOTES

1. Scott McCloud, *Understanding Comics* (Northampton, Mass.: Tundra, 1993), p. 9.
2. Pascal Lefevre and Charles Dierick, "Introduction" in *Forging a New Medium: The Comic Strip in the Nineteenth Century* (Brussels: VUB University Press, 1998), pp. 12–13.
3. Thierry Groensteen, "Topffer, the Originator of the Modern Comic Strip" in *Forging a New Medium: The Comic Strip in the Nineteenth Century* (Brussels: VUB University Press, 1998), p. 108.
4. David Kunzle, *History of the Comic Strip: Vol. 1, The Early Comic Strip* (Berkeley, Calif.: University of California Press, 1973), pp. 2–3.
5. Coulton Waugh, *The Comics* (New York, N.Y.: Macmillan, 1947), p. 14.
6. Quoted in E. Wiese, "Introduction" in *Enter: The Comics* (Lincoln, Neb.: University of Nebraska Press, 1965), p. xiii.
7. Herbert Johnson, "Why Cartoons—and How," *Saturday Evening Post*, July 14, 1928, p. 8; and Arthur Prager, *The Mahogany Tree: An Informal History of Punch* (New York, N.Y.: Hawthorne Books, 1979), pp. 88–89.

More History? Anyone wishing to dig deeper into the subject is referred to the following (arranged by date of publication):

Cartoon Cavalcade by Thomas Craven; Simon and Schuster, 1943.

The Comics by Coulton Waugh; Macmillan, 1947; reprinted by University Press of Mississippi, 1991.

Comic Art in America by Stephen Becker; Simon and Schuster, 1959.

The Comics: An Illustrated History of Comic Strip by Jerry Robinson; Putnam's Sons, 1974.

The Adventurous Decade by Ron Goulart; Arlington House, 1975.

The Encyclopedia of American Comics from 1897 to the Present by Ron Goulart; Facts on File, 1990.

Understanding Comics by Scott McCloud; Tundra, 1993.

The Art of the Funnies by Robert C. Harvey; University Press of Mississippi, 1994.

The Art of the Comic Book by Robert C. Harvey; University Press of Mississippi, 1996.

Forging a New Medium: The Comic Strip in the Nineteenth Century edited by Pascal Lefevre and Charles Dierick; VUB University Press, 1998.

Children of the Yellow Kid: The Evolution of the American Comic Strip by Robert C. Harvey; Frye Art Museum in association with the University of Washington, 1998.

The Comics Since 1945 by Brian Walker; Abrams, 2002.

The centennial year of 1995 saw the publication of several books that were produced expressly to celebrate the occasion:

The Yellow Kid, assembled by Bill Blackbeard; Kitchen Sink Press.

A Comic Strip Century, another Blackbeard production from Kitchen Sink Press in two volumes.

The Funnies: 100 Years of American Comic Strips by Ron Goulart; Adams.

"No Harm in Horror"

Ethical Dimensions of the Postwar Comic Book Controversy

—AMY KISTE NYBERG

Ten-year-old Lucy was an unwanted, mistreated child. Lucy's father, Sam, was an abusive alcoholic. Her mother, Mildred, had taken a lover, Steve, who visited the house when Sam was away. Mildred was planning to run away with Steve, leaving little Lucy behind. But Sam came home unexpectedly, and Mildred shot and killed Sam. She and Steve were found guilty of murder and executed in the electric chair. The orphan, Lucy, went to live with kindly Aunt Kate.

But there's more to this comic book story "The Orphan," published by EC Comics in *Shock SuspenStories No. 14*, dated April–May 1954. In the final panel, little Lucy gives the reader a knowing wink and confesses: "I shot daddy from the front bedroom window with the gun I knew was in the night table and went downstairs and put the gun in mommy's hand and starting the crying act. . . ."

On April 21, 1954, the publisher of that comic, William Gaines of EC Comics, faced off against the Senate Subcommittee on Juvenile Delinquency, which had come to New York City to conduct hearings on the comic book industry. Questions about "The Orphan" were coming thick and fast, from the committee's Chief Counsel Herbert Hannoch, from Herbert Beaser, Hannoch's assistant, and from committee member Senator Thomas Hennings Jr. of Missouri. Gaines was trying to explain that all his comic book stories had an "O. Henry" ending, a surprise for the reader, and that "The Orphan" was an example of that type of ending. But the committee was more concerned with how young readers would react to the fact a ten-year-old girl had gotten away with perjury and murder and emerged "triumphant."

"You think it does them a lot of good to read these things?" Hannoch demanded.

"I don't think it does them a bit of good, but I don't think it does them a bit of harm, either," Gaines replied (Hearings 103).

The next day, his answer became the front-page headline of the *New York Times* story on the hearings: "No Harm in Horror, Comics Issuer Says" (Khiss).

This exchange identifies the central element in the debate over comic books that raged in postwar America—the idea that somehow, comic books were harming their young readers. The notion of harm is at the core of many of the ethical questions raised about the mass media, both historically and in contemporary times. In the controversy over comic books, this harm is defined at two levels. First is the harm done to individual children, and critics of comic books relied on anecdotal evidence of children who modeled their own behavior after actions depicted in their comics. Second is the harm done to society, since comic books were implicated by some in the rise of juvenile delinquency in postwar America.

The "social harm" of juvenile delinquency prompted the formation of the Senate Subcommittee on Juvenile Delinquency in April 1953. Initially, the committee was to focus on the adequacy of existing laws in dealing with youthful offenders. What began as a specific inquiry, however, grew in scope, and one major task undertaken by the committee was to explore the link between juvenile delinquency and the content of mass media (Nyberg 1994, 353). As part of that investigation, the subcommittee conducted hearings on the comic book industry, hearing testimony on April 21 and 22, and on June 4, 1954. The senators called twenty-two witnesses and accepted thirty-three exhibits as evidence. Among the witnesses were four comic book publishers, four experts on the effects of comic books on children and seven people involved with some aspect of distribution (360).

In examining the ethical dimensions of the comic book controversy, this chapter will focus on those hearings for several reasons. First, the federal government's direct involvement in the investigation of comic book content reflects the ethical dilemma over how to balance the individual rights of the publishers—and freedom of expression—against society's interest in protecting its young citizens from harm. The need to resolve such conflicts is one of the reasons society needs a system of ethics, argues media ethicist Louis Alvin Day (23). Second, the hearings provided a national forum for the debate on comic books. Indeed, the chairman of the committee, Senator Robert Hendrickson of New Jersey, noted during the hearings, "We are trying to furnish some degree of leadership at the national level" (Hearings 203). And third, the hearings prompted action on the part of the comic book industry. The subcommittee's hearings produced a response—in the form of a self-regulatory code—where earlier criticism had not.

The work of the Senate subcommittee, however, must first be placed in the larger context of the controversy surrounding comic books. The federal government's investigation of the content and effects of comic books was the culmination of many years of debate, the origins of which can be traced back to the introduction of the modern comic book in the mid-1930s.

CONTROVERSIAL FROM THE START

Initially, the argument against comic book reading was made by the guardians of children's culture, teachers and librarians, who feared the contamination of children's culture by comic books. Educators from the beginning condemned comic books as undesirable reading material. Some objected to both the form and content of comics, whereas others saw no problem with the form, provided that comic book content was used to educate and enlighten. Their major concern was that comics lured young readers away from literature deemed more appropriate and worthwhile (Nyberg *Scorned Literature*).

This criticism was largely confined to the professional journals published for librarians and teachers, and the articles can be divided into three broad categories. First were articles written by professionals sharing personal observations and anecdotal information regarding comic books. The second type of article was the essay or opinion piece expressing the author's opinion about comics. The final type was scholarly articles based on research into comic books, usually written by a college or university professor. The distinction is important, because while the first two types of articles were generally negative, the research often did not support the assumptions made about comic books (Nyberg *Scorned Literature* 71).

Publishers responded to their critics in a number of ways. The most direct result of such criticism was the creation of the so-called educational comic. The leader in this area of publishing was *Parents' Magazine*, which brought out *True Comics* beginning in 1941, a series that offered biographies of "real life heroes." That same year brought *Classic Comics*, published by Albert Kanter, and renamed *Classics Illustrated* in 1947 (Nyberg *Scorned Literature* 178). These comics may have been popular with educators and parents, but their introduction did little to wean young readers away from the superhero comics that began to flood the stands after the success of *Action Comics* in 1938, featuring the now-familiar red-caped Superman. The popularity of superhero comics, however, waned in the years following World War II, and publishers turned to other genres in order to spark lagging sales. Many returned to the tried-and-true formulas that had served them so well in their days as publishers of pulp fiction—detective stories, crime, and horror. This shift helped to revive the industry, but it also introduced a new element into the debate over comic books (Nyberg 1994, 91).

Criticism of comics would take on an added dimension in postwar America, when comic books, and the mass media more generally, became linked to concerns over juvenile behavior, and in particular, the upsurge of juvenile delinquency. These critics, who included child psychiatrists, law enforcement officials and various civic groups, believed the content of comic books was a bad influence on children, who used the crime and horror comics popular in the postwar period as blueprints for their own criminal activity. The most influential of these critics was Dr. Fredric Wertham, a noted child psychiatrist who worked tirelessly to convince his colleagues in the medical field, civic groups and legislative bodies that comic books were harmful to children and should be banned. His attack on the comic book industry, *Seduction of the Innocent*, published in 1954 prior to the Senate hearings, was his final attempt to mobilize public opinion. He was a key witness in the Senate hearings.

Wertham, a native of Germany, came to the United States in 1922. He became known as an expert in forensic psychiatry, testifying in several sensational murder cases in the 1930s, and this emphasis fostered a lifelong interest in the causes of violence. It was also in the 1930s that Wertham began to fight for access to psychiatric care for minorities and the poor, and he established the Lafargue Clinic in 1945 in Harlem, where he focused on the treatment of children. It was there that he began to investigate the effects of comic books because so many of his young patients read them. Wertham's growing fears about the impact of comic books on juvenile delinquency was popularized in a 1948 article published in *Collier's* magazine on March 27, and he made his case to his medical colleagues in a symposium the same month (Nyberg 1998, 89–90). His work was widely quoted in both popular and medical literature, and he spoke to any number of civic and educational groups, as well as serving as an expert witness in the New York Legislature's investigation into comic books.

Even before Wertham's highly publicized attacks, publishers had become sensitive to the growing condemnation of comic books, and in 1947 they formed a trade association known as the Association of Comics Magazine Publishers (Nyberg 1998, 31). But it wasn't until after the *Collier's* article that the publishers made a concerted effort to address the criticism of comic books, and on July 1, 1948, the association announced the adoption of a six-point code to regulate the content of comics.

This code established a set of ethical guidelines for publishers, but it quickly proved unworkable. Implementing a pre-publication review process was unwieldy and expensive, and there was much disagreement among publishers about the interpretation and application of the code to their publications. It wasn't long before many publishers abandoned the trade association, and the remaining publishers were left to decide for themselves whether their comic books merited the seal of approval of the association (Nyberg 1994, 447–79). Henry Schultz, the general counsel for the trade association, testified before the senators that by 1954, the inclusion of the seal on the cover of a comic book had "no value" in determining whether the comic book adhered to the guidelines set forth several years earlier (Hearings 79).

The inaction on the part of the comic book industry made it vulnerable to the renewed criticism triggered by the publication of excerpts of *Seduction of the Innocent* in the *Ladies' Home Journal* in November 1953 and of the book in early 1954. The article's appearance coincided with the launch of the Senate Subcommittee on Juvenile Delinquency, which began to conduct hearings that month. Prior to the start of the hearings, the committee received thousands of unsolicited letters from citizens, and nearly 75 percent of those reflected concern over comic books, television, radio, and the movies. In the face of public pressure to investigate the mass media, including comic books, the committee scheduled a series of hearings on media effects and delinquency, including the New York City hearings on the comic book industry (Nyberg 1994, 351–52).

The next section of this chapter analyzes the arguments presented, both by the government itself in the course of the hearings, and of those witnesses called to represent the various constituencies seen as having an interest or expertise in the matter.

THE SENATE INQUIRY

Introductory remarks by Senator Robert Hendrickson of New Jersey, who was the chairman of the committee, attempted to set the limits of the debate in three significant ways. First, Henrickson noted that the purpose of the committee was to examine "the problem of horror and crime comic books." While he was attempting to narrow the committee's focus and exclude such material as newspaper comic strips and the more wholesome comic books, such as the funny animal books, he also defined comic books as "a problem" from the beginning, belying the insistence of the committee members that their investigation was a neutral examination. This was actually in keeping with the pattern of other Congressional investigations, where the committee perspective was determined before the actual work began and the investigation served as little more than a dramatization of the committee's point of view (Nyberg 1994, 361). Second, he noted that "freedom of the press is not at issue in this investigation," an effort to close off arguments against censorship that are often a central element in debates over media ethics. And third, he specifically identified the child reader as being central to the investigation: "We want to find out what damage, if any, is being done to our children's minds by certain types of publications which contain a substantial degree of sadism, crime, and horror" (Hearings 1–2).

The Senate subcommittee very carefully crafted the list of witnesses in order to support the senators' view of crime and horror comics as a problem to be solved. The subcommittee did include experts who testified either that comics were not, in their opinion, harmful or those who sounded a cautionary note about the lack of evidence to support that conclusion. However, these expert witnesses were discredited by the committee after they were shown to have ties to the publishers—many of these experts had been tapped by the comic book industry to provide guidance on content. Thus, argued the subcommittee, their opinions were tainted and could be disregarded.

In fact, Senator Estes Kefauver of Tennessee accused the Child Study Association of America of "flying under false colors" because two of the people who helped compile reports on comic book reading for the association were consultants for the comic book publishers (Hearings 133). The executive director, Gunnar Dybwad, retorted: "If you feel that we should have recommended censorship, police censorship of these, indeed we did not do so purposely because we do not think this is a good American method in the first place . . ." (145).

The critics of comic books did not share Dybwad's aversion to government censorship. Many hoped that the committee's work would yield federal legislation aimed at curbing what they saw as the excesses of comic book publishers. However, the committee members were familiar enough with the legal issues surrounding any governmental regulation of comic books to realize that it was highly unlikely that Congress could craft legislation that would withstand a Constitutional challenge. Indeed, municipal and state efforts at such legislation had failed precisely on those grounds.

An ordinance passed by Los Angeles County on September 21, 1948, prohibited the sale of crime comics to anyone under the age of eighteen. Some groups hoped that the ordinance would be a model for state legislation. However, the California Superior Court declared the ordinance unconstitutional. An attempt at similar legislation by the New York Legislature passed both houses, but Governor Thomas Dewey vetoed the bill in April 1949, arguing that it was unconstitutional. Subsequent legislation died in committee (Nyberg 1998, 41–42).

Despite Hendrickson's attempt to shift the debate away from censorship issues to focus on the possible harm done to children reading comic books, the two cannot really be separated. In fact, the legal justification for government censorship initially drew on this precept. The definition of obscenity in the United States was based on English law and its definition of obscenity: anything of possible harm to a child (Nyberg 1994, 156). As noted by Paul and Schwartz, this meant that enforcement of anti-obscenity laws was based on judging works using the possible impact on the minds of children as the basis for banning works intended for adults (27). This was also true of the work of the Catholic National Office of Decent Literature, which directed its attention at first against magazines, publishing a list of "Publications Disapproved for Youth" (Nyberg 1994, 177–78). The group later expanded its efforts to paperback books and comic books. Critics argued that such decency crusades censored not only material available to children, but adult reading material as well. The church's position was that while removal of such material might infringe on an adult's "right to read," good citizens should be willing to waive their rights in order to protect children (Haney 95).

The difficulty of arguing against this position is illustrated by an excerpt from comic book publisher William Gaines's opening statement to the Senate subcommittee:

> What are we afraid of? Are we afraid of our own children? Do we forget that they are citizens, too, and entitled to select what to read or do? We think our children are so evil, simple minded, that it takes a story of murder to set them to murder, a story of robbery to set them to robbery? (Hearings 98)

Gaines might have found himself on firmer footing if he had tried to argue that censorship efforts were too broad and that there was an adult readership for comic books. There were even figures that could have supported this argument: a market survey done in 1944 reported that of men ages eighteen to thirty, forty-one percent were regular readers, and for women in the same age bracket, twenty-eight percent were regular readers (Abelson 80). His insistence that children be considered "citizens" with the same rights as adults is a position that few media ethicists, even today, would support.

While the Senate subcommittee's concern for the welfare of children no doubt was genuine, focusing exclusively on the child audience for comics was also an excellent strategy for forestalling arguments regarding censorship. Day notes that most media ethicists adopt the view that media producers do have a special obligation to their youthful audiences, because juveniles do not have the same well-developed value systems of adult consumers and are more vulnerable to the influences of media (Day 326). Factoring in the child audience invalidates the argument often made, drawing on John Stuart Mill's essay *On Liberty*, that censorship issues represent a struggle between liberty and authority, and that while the state may restrict liberty in instances where action would harm others, it is an infringement on individual liberty to proscribe a behavior for the individual's own good.

Adult readers, then, can take full responsibility for what materials they select, and as long as they do not harm others as a result, the state has no business proscribing what they read. Mill himself writes, "It is, perhaps, hardly necessary to say that this doctrine is meant to apply only to human beings in the maturity of their faculties. We are not speaking of children . . . (t)hose who are still in a state to require being taken care of by others, must be protected against their own actions as well as against external injury" (Gray and Smith 31).

Children, then, require others to intercede on their behalf in restricting their exposure to certain kinds of media content. This is necessary, argues media ethicist Michael Kiernan, because children lack worldly experience and "may come to assume that the distortive nature of love, sex and violence portrayed do, in fact, manifest normal and morally appropriate behavior . . . (c)hildren learn their social and moral behavior primarily by example" (Kiernan 122). What sort of moral education did comic books provide? The answer to this question depends on whose viewpoint you adopt.

In his testimony, Wertham asserted comic books caused "ethical confusion" (Hearings 85–89). The psychiatrist was not particularly clear in his presentation to the senators what he meant by this phrase, but he alluded to the seductive nature of brutal images. He believed children are alternately repelled and attracted by such imagery and by stories of mayhem and murder, and eventually they become desensitized to the violence and accept it as normal, an argument he would make later against television as well (Wertham 51). This also was an answer those experts who suggested that comic book violence was cathartic and therefore served a positive function in children's lives, allowing them to work through their feelings of anger in a fantasy world. Wertham also refuted the claim that in crime comic books, good always triumphed over evil: "In many comic books the whole point is that evil triumphs; that you can commit a perfect crime . . . I want to make it perfectly clear that there are whole comic books in which every single story ends with the triumph of evil, with a perfect crime unpunished and actually glorified" (Hearings 86).

It is interesting to note that both Gaines and Wertham believed that comics provided children with instruction in values, but the two had vastly different ideas about how that was accomplished. Gaines insisted that many of his stories had direct social messages, spelled out clearly in the captions for his young readers. He cited the example of the story "The Whipping," published in *Shock SuspenStories No. 14*, 1954. In it, a Mexican family has moved into the neighborhood. Ed's daughter, Amy, begins to date Louis Martinez, and Ed stirs up the men in the neighborhood by telling them that Louis has tried to rape Amy. They break into the dark house, throw a sack over the person they find inside, and beat that person to death. In the end of the story, readers learn it is Amy, who secretly married Louis, whom they dragged from the house and killed. Gaines insisted the story clearly conveyed the dangers of racial intolerance.

But critics such as Wertham objected to the way the moral of the story was delivered. Rather than depicting "good" behavior being rewarded, these stories showed "bad" behavior, which was only punished in the very end of the story. Much better for children, critics argued, were positive role models, heroes whose behavior was above reproach. In addition, they disagreed with Gaines, who argued that while children picked up the "messages" deliberately incorporated into the stories, they were not picking up other, unintentional messages, such as the use of violence to solve problems. In his defense of the story "The Orphan," summarized at the beginning of this chapter, Gaines insisted, "No message has been spelled out there. We are not trying to prove anything with that story. None of the captions said anything like, 'If you unhappy with your [mother], shoot her' " (Hearings 101). Wertham, however, insisted it was the unintentional messages that had the most influence—messages about violence, the victimization of women and the making of criminals into heroic figures. He argued the exposure over time to the same types of messages built up a social context in which children learned to accept, if not to imitate, the violence (Nyberg 1998, 73).

If young readers were ethically confused, comic book publishers themselves were morally bankrupt because they were driven by the profit motive. That's the view taken by members of the committee. Senator Hennings, in an exchange with Richard Clendenen, the subcommittee's executive director, noted of comic book publishers: "(I)t is the business of making money and they do not seem to care what they do or what they purvey or what they dish out to these youngsters as long as it sells and brings in the money" (Hearings 59). Wertham, too, looked askance at the money to be made from such publications, noting: "Formerly to impair the morals of a minor was a punishable offense. It has now become a mass industry" (Hearings 87).

Gaines tried to argue that he applied standards other than the profit motive to his choices about what to publish. Beaser asked the young publisher whether he would limit content "because you thought a child should not see or read about it" or whether the "sole test of what you would put into your magazine is whether it sells." Gaines insisted, "My only limits are bounds of good taste, what I consider good taste." His remark sparked outrage from Senator Kefauver, who seized a copy of a comic book featuring a man with a bloody axe holding the severed head of a woman. "Do you think that is in good taste?" he demanded. Having just said he applied the standard of good taste to his choice of material to publish, Gaines had no recourse but to answer, "Yes sir; I do, for the cover of a horror comic." The exchange continued, with Senator Kefauver bringing up other examples of comics he thought to be in bad taste, until Senator Hennings put a stop to it by saying, "I don't think it is really the function of our committee to argue with this gentleman" (Hearings 103).

This exchange reinforced the belief on the part of the senators, and comic book critics more generally, that publishers cared only about making money and had no standards beyond what would sell. Although there was—and still is—no empirical evidence to prove that comic book reading harmed children, the committee members were clearly disturbed by the mayhem and monsters found in the pages of comic books. When all was said and done, they took the position that such fare simply could not be good for children. While the senators concluded their hearings in New York City by promising to study the material before them carefully before drawing their conclusions and making recommendations, Senator Hendrickson ended the three days of testimony by proposing a solution to the problem set forth earlier: "A competent job of self-policing within the industry will achieve much" (Hearings 310).

It wasn't until nine months later, in March 1955, that the committee issued its interim report. A draft was completed by November 1954, but a dispute over whether to include illustrations in the report delayed its publication (Nyberg 1994, 401–2). The report, written by Senator Kefauver, who had replaced Senator Hendrickson as chairman of the committee after the November 1954 elections returned control of the Senate to the Democrats, eventually was published without the illustrations. Kefauver, while noting that the evidence concerning the harm done by comics was inconclusive and further research was needed, called for immediate action, concluding the nation "cannot afford the calculated risk involved in the continued mass dissemination" of crime and horror comics to children. He added that the absolute right of the comics industry "to produce what it pleases unless it is proven 'beyond a reasonable doubt' that such a product is damaging to children are unjustified" (Interim Report 23, 27, 33).

The belief that comic books could possibly pose a threat to children provided the justification, ethically speaking, for some form of regulation. The senators, however, did not codify their ethical stance regarding comic books in recommendations for legal action, no doubt realizing that such legislation would never pass Constitutional muster. Instead, they endorsed self-censorship by publishers as a way to demonstrate the industry's recognition of its social responsibility for the material produced.

THE COMICS CODES OF 1948 AND 1954

The Senate Subcommittee on Juvenile Delinquency, of course, had no way to enforce its recommendations, but it did not have to. Shortly after the hearings, Gaines—alarmed at the way the investigation had gone—urged fellow publishers to band together to fight what he saw as the growing demand for comic book censorship from government and other critics (Reidelbach 28). The major publishers agreed to meet, but rather than developing a strategy to counter censorship pressure, they decided to form a new industry trade association and adopt a self-regulatory code. At an organizational meeting held August 17, 1954, the industry established the Comics Magazine Association of America and put into place a vigorous program of pre-publication review.

The Senate subcommittee was both pleased with and skeptical about the industry's efforts. The report noted that the association and its code "are steps in the right direction." But, it added, "since the association and the code authority have so recently been organized, it is still too early to form a judgment as to either the sincerity or the effectiveness of this latest attempt at self-regulation by the comic book industry" (Interim Report 32). The wait-and-see attitude of the committee was somewhat justified; the publishers' previous effort at industrywide self-regulation had been a failure. Still, this earlier attempt at self-regulation is worth closer examination because this 1948 code established a precedent, if not the framework, for what would follow eleven years later.

The introduction to the six-point code sets out the rationale:

The Association of Comics Magazine Publishers, realizing its responsibility to the millions of readers of comics magazines and to the public generally, urges its members and others to publish comics magazines containing only good, wholesome entertainment or education, and in no event to include in any magazine comics that may in any way lower the moral standards of those who read them.

It is significant that the comic book publishers were careful not to define their readership as made up wholly or even primarily of children. The statement "millions of readers" suggests no special consideration of content based on the age of the potential audience for comics. Whether intentional or not, it is an important distinction to make, because the argument of harm used by critics to suggest that publishers had crossed ethical boundaries was predicated on the notion of comic books as juvenile literature.

No one was suggesting that adult readers required protection from comic books, or that comic books might exert the same types of influence on adult readers. Nevertheless, the ACMP took the position that all readers of comics should be exposed only to "good, wholesome entertainment or education." This statement most likely was included in an effort to draw attention to the various highly touted "educational" comics on the market, but the claim about the educational function of comics opened up the industry to charges comics could educate their young readers in a less desirable way, as well. It is also important to note that there is no mention of "harmful" content anywhere in this preamble. Instead, the code states comics should not "lower the moral standards" of those who read them. This emphasis on morality rather than perceived dangerous effects might have been a good strategy for an industry that was understandably reluctant to associate its publications with the notion of "harm," but the use of the more ambiguous phrase "moral standards" actually led the industry to adopt far more restrictive guidelines than those dictated by desire to eliminate harmful materials.

Here are the six points covered under the 1948 code:

1. Sexy, wanton comics should not be published. No drawing should show a female indecently or unduly exposed, and in no event more nude than in a bathing suit commonly worn in the United States of America.

2. Crime should not be presented in such a way as to throw sympathy against law and justice or to inspire others with the desire for imitation. No comics shall show the details and methods of a crime committed by a youth. Policemen, judges, government officials, and respected institutions should not be portrayed as stupid or ineffective, or represented in such a way as to weaken respect for authority.
3. No scenes of sadistic torture shall be shown.
4. Vulgar and obscene language should never be used. Slang should be kept to a minimum and used only when essential to the story.
5. Divorce should not be treated humorously nor represented as glamorous or alluring.
6. Ridicule or attack on any religious or racial group is never permissible.

Only two points in this code deal specifically with crime and horror comics—point two, which forbids certain depictions of crime, and point three, which bans graphic images of torture. The other elements of the code go beyond concerns about violence, adopting standards based very much on the social values of the time: sexual propriety, respect for authority, avoidance of vulgar language and slang, portrayal of divorce as undesirable, and tolerance of religious and racial difference. These provisions impose a rather strict moral tone on comic book content. While this might, in fact, guarantee "wholesome" comics, it also guaranteed that comic books could not be used as a form of social critique, since stories questioning those in authority or exploring social issues such as racism or anti-Semitism would be interpreted as violations of the code.

However, these restrictions had little impact on comic book publishers and content because the 1948 code, adopted in July of that year, was never enforced. Many of the largest publishers refused to join the association because they felt their in-house codes were adequate and because they did not want to be affiliated with some of the more marginal publishers in the industry. Some publishers found the pre-publication review fees too steep and dropped their membership. Still others objected to the changes mandated by the reviewers. It was not long before the ACMP could no longer afford the staff necessary for pre-publication review, and the system was abandoned. The remaining members adopted a provision agreeing they would do their own censoring and decide for themselves which of their comic should carry the association's seal. By the time the Senate committee conducted its hearings on comic books, the ACMP membership had been reduced to three publishers (Hearings 72).

Although the 1948 self-regulatory code had proved unworkable, those drafting the 1954 version essentially expanded on the earlier attempt, also borrowing language from the Film Production Code adopted in the 1930s (a document that most likely served as a model for the 1948 code as well). Unlike its predecessor, the CMAA code had no introduction or preamble. It simply consisted of two sections, a "Code for Editorial Matter" and a "Code for Advertising Matter." While it was much more detailed—for example, twelve separate points were devoted to the handling of crime comics—it essentially imposed the same standards as the earlier ACMP guidelines, restricting the ways in which crime could be depicted (but eliminating the troublesome horror comics altogether), and stressing the values of the sanctity of family and respect for authority (including parents). This was precisely the response the senators had hoped for when they issued their report:

> Within the industry, the primary responsibility for the content of each comic book rests squarely upon the shoulders of its publisher . . . the publishers of children's comic books cannot discharge their responsibility to the Nation's youth merely by discontinuing the publication of a few individual titles. It can be fully discharged only as they seek and support ways and means of insuring that the industry's product permanently measures up to its standards of morality and decency which American parents have the right to expect. (Interim Report 29)

The portion of the 1954 code dealing with editorial matter was divided into three parts. The first, and most extensive, provided stringent guidelines for how crime could be depicted in comics. The second part, much shorter, effectively eliminated the horror comics altogether. The third part dealt with all other content deemed "offensive," under the general headings of dialogue, religion, costume, and marriage and sex.

"Part A" of the 1954 code reiterated earlier rules that forbid depicting crime in such a way as to create sympathy for the criminal or create desire for imitation, showing details and methods of committing crimes, or representing authority figures in such a way as to create disrespect. In addition, the 1954 version warned publishers against presenting criminals as "glamorous," showing methods of concealing weapons, depicting the deaths of law enforcement officers, or portraying the crime of kidnapping in any detail. Not only torture, but all scenes of "excessive violence" (defined as brutal torture, excessive and unnecessary knife and gun play, physical agony, and gory and gruesome details) are prohibited. As a final caution, the code also stated explicitly that "good shall triumph over evil and the criminal punished for his misdeeds."

The first provision of "Part B" of the code states: "No comic magazine shall use the word horror or terror in its title." If that weren't enough to discourage the publication of horror comics, the last provision prohibits "scenes dealing with, or instruments associated with walking dead, torture, vampires and vampirism, ghouls, cannibalism and werewolfism."

It is the specifications in "Part C" that move from content of crime and horror comics to more general guidelines that guarantee "good taste or decency." In addition to the prohibitions on sexually suggestive imagery and vulgar language, the code offers expanded guidelines on how to deal with depictions of sex and romance, specifying that "illicit sex relations" and "violent love scenes" are unacceptable, that the "value of the home and the sanctity of marriage" are to be emphasized, that such stories should not "stimulate the lower and baser emotions" and that "sex perversion or any inference to same is strictly forbidden," a veiled reference to any representations or insinuation of homosexuality. Finally, publishers are told that "respect for parents, the moral code and for honorable behavior shall be fostered." This part of the code was no doubt expanded in response to the increasing popularity of romance comics since the 1948 code was published. In fact, in 1950 , there were more romance comics on the newsstands than any other comic-book genre (Benton 167).

The CMAA announced the appointment of the code administrator, Charles Murphy, on October 1, 1954, and put the code into effect shortly afterward. The industry was able to enforce the code primarily through the cooperation of distributors and retailers, who agreed not to carry comics unless they bore the CMAA's "Seal of Approval." One immediate effect of the new comics code was that the crime and horror comics disappeared from the newsstands, thus helping to diffuse the anti-comic book sentiment among the public (Nyberg 1994, 407). This code remained in effect until changing social attitudes, coupled with a declining market, prompted the industry to rewrite the code in 1971 and relax the regulations that had governed comic book content for more than twenty-five years.

IMPACT OF THE 1954 CODE

The implementation of industry self-regulation as a solution to the ethical dilemma posed by comic books, however, is problematic. Day notes that formal codes of conduct are controversial; proponents argue that such codes are the "only way to avoid leaving moral judgments to individual interpretation; opponents view them as a form of self-censorship," and therefore undesirable (45). The American Civil Liberties Union opposed self-regulatory codes, arguing that they constituted a form of censorship against which there was no legal recourse (Hearings, Motion Pictures 71). The judgment of the CMAA reviewers was final. In fact, Gaines argued that the code was being used punitively against him and other publishers in an effort to drive them out of business (Stuart).

Knowing that retailers would refuse to carry his horror comics line, Gaines introduced six titles he labeled his "New Directions" comics and bowed to distributor pressure, joining the association (Jacobs 112–13; Reidelbach 30). Almost immediately, he clashed with the code administrator, over a story scheduled to run in *Incredible Science Fiction*, a title that had survived the implementation of the code (albeit with a name change, since *Weird Science-Fantasy* used the now-forbidden world "weird" in its title). The story, "Judgment Day," about a planet of robots segregated based on the color of the robot, was an obvious commentary on the practice of racial segregation. The hero of the story, a human, visits the planet and determines the robot society was not ready to join the galactic federation because of its policy of discrimination. He gets back in his spaceship and removes his helmet, revealing that he is black—just the type of "twist" ending that Gaines liked.

The code administrator rejected the story, although there are differing accounts of why he ruled against "Judgment Day." Gaines said that the final panel showed perspiration on the face of the astronaut, and that was deemed a violation of the portion of the code prohibiting "ridicule or attack on any religious or racial group." It was only after he threatened to take the CMAA to court that he obtained the "Seal of Approval" (Tebbel). Another account suggested that Gaines lost his fight to get the story approved but published the comic book with the code seal anyway (Benton 115). Gaines's business manager, Lyle Stuart, said that the story was rejected because in it, the robots think and talk, which violated the code administrator's belief that only man is endowed by God with a soul and the ability to think.

The dispute marked the end of Gaines's career as a comic book publisher. He focused his attention on *Mad* magazine, which was not published in comic-book format, so therefore was not subject to CMAA oversight. No other publishers stepped up to openly challenge the code until 1970, when Marvel comics published a three-part *Spider-Man* story about drug abuse in defiance of code guidelines. The code, which had been amended periodically in order to cover situations not foreseen by its originators, prohibited any mention of narcotics or their use. The CMAA rejected Marvel's request to be allowed to publish the story, but editor in chief Stan Lee decided to go ahead and publish the comics without the Seal of Approval (Daniels 152).

CONCLUSION

By defining the comic book as a form of juvenile literature and by emphasizing the potential for harm, both to individual children and to society as a whole, critics of comics put forth a compelling argument for comic book regulation. As a result, publishers adopted a self-censorship code, acknowledging the responsibilities of the media producers for the content. One ethical position lost in the rush to "solve" the problem of comic books, however, is the need to balance social responsibility with the preservation of freedom of expression. The comic book publishers were little concerned with the artistic or creative potential of the medium. For them, the code of ethics was a quick solution to the bad publicity generated by public attention to the content of comic books. In addition, they truly feared the implementation of government censorship and the possible impact it would have on their highly profitable industry. This attitude has its basis in system of comic book production common then (and to some extent even today), when comic books were produced in an assembly-line fashion, rather than being the work of a single "creator." The publishers owned the rights to the characters. As a result, there was no creative "voice" to speak on behalf of the medium.

This failure to strike a balance between social responsibility and freedom of expression has had some far-reaching consequences. Comic book historians have argued that forcing the comic book creators into such a narrow range of possibilities ensured the industry would publish only banal and formulaic material that severely arrested the artistic development of the medium. The publishers' inability to deal with adult themes relegated comic books to the fringes of juvenile literature, a marginalization from which they have never fully recovered (Williams 60; McAlliester 61).

The comics code today has much less impact on content and distribution, due to the defection of one major publisher—Marvel Comics—and the fact the other major publisher, DC Comics, which does adhere to the code, publishes non-code imprints that circumvent code restrictions. The legacy of the code, however, is that in their rush to address the ethical questions raised by critics of comic books in the 1950s, publishers failed to recognize their own ethical responsibility to the medium.

Truth Be Told

Authorship and the Creation of the Black Captain America

STANFORD W. CARPENTER

TRUE

The world is permeated by images and stories that convey notions of Black identity. Many of these images and stories circulate in the form of artifacts. Artifacts—in this case comic books—are more than the images, texts, representations, or discourses that they seem to contain. Artifacts should not be "read" as text. To do so denies the fact that artifacts—as "things"—are part and parcel of a vast array of cultural, economic, political, and social relationships. In looking at comic books as artifacts, in configuring my investigations as an ethnographic enterprise, I am acknowledging that images, texts, representations, and discourses of Black identity are the end result of processes in which human agents—people working together and alone—make decisions about which images, which texts, which representations, and which discourses will be used to construct Black identities and stories about Black people. It is within these contexts that the construction of Black identity and stories about Black people is at once a negotiation, a vocation, and a creative enterprise.

The 2003 comic book miniseries titled *Truth: Red, White, and Black* reexamined the origins of Captain America and established that the first man to wear the red, white, and blue uniform and go by the name of Captain America was Black . . . a move that enraged fans and impressed mainstream audiences all the while adding to the bottom line of Marvel Enterprises by increasing the corporation's portfolio of license-able properties.

This paper looks at *Truth* through the eyes of three members of its creative team, each of whom came to the project with different intentions, skills, experiences, histories, and a variety of creative archives—in order to address the simultaneous construction of identity, reworking of myth, and the maintenance and development of property.

Comic books do not have a single author or creator; rather, they are made by teams of people, usually consisting of an editor, assistant editor, writer, penciler, inker, letterer, and colorist, create most comic books. Of the seven aforementioned named positions only two, the editor and the assistant editor, are employed by the comic book publisher. The remaining members of the creative team are hired as freelance workers with contracts ranging from months to years. The creative team works in an assembly line fashion in which each person works on a few pages at a time and passes them on to the next person. For example, once a script is complete it is sent to the penciler who, upon drawing a predetermined amount of pages in pencil, sends them on to the inker who applies ink and so on.

Like the surrealist game, exquisite corpse, in which participants contribute elements to a picture, the lack of a single author in comics doesn't eliminate individual intentions, nor does it resolve creative negotiations. Rather, comic books are the end results of a process by which individual intentions are executed at one stage in the process, only to be added to or altered in latter stages . . . a process that does not require that negotiations be resolved or disagreements settled.

Comic book fans regard comic book characters such as the White Captain America as the product of a text. They read the White Captain America's adventures within the context of his continuing story. Marvel Enterprises, the corporation that owns the Captain America likeness, regards Captain America as property and view his adventures within the context of the development, maintenance, investment in, and improvement of the property.

Once assembled, creative teams focus on the task of satisfying the often-contradictory audience and corporate desires. This task is complicated by the fact that there are no discreet lines that distinguish comic book creators, comic book audiences, and their corporate owners.

Comic book creators read comics, and in many cases they grew up on comics just as their fans did. As a result, comic book creators shape and are shaped by the very transnational flows of stories and images that they play a role in creating. And while many of the established properties that the members of creative teams work with have histories that are problematic in terms of race, gender, ethnicity, and a myriad other representational concerns, these concerns must be reconciled within a production process that includes creative teams that have only recently seen an influx of creators from the very same racial and ethnic groups that these established properties demeaned.

AUTHORSHIP AND THE CREATIVE TEAM AS AN ETHNOGRAPHIC SUBJECT

My ethnographic emphasis on creative teams, archives, and processes emerges out of my own experiences as a cartoonist that manifest themselves in debates about the authorship and ownership of creative work. In the mid 1990s I wrote and illustrated a weekly comic strip retelling "African" folktales for the *Skanner*, a Black newspaper with circulation in Portland, Oregon, and Seattle, Washington. While comic strips employ imagery similar to comic books, comic strips emerge out of a different type of production and method of circulation. Briefly, comic strips tend to be owned and created by an individual who may or may not employ various assistants. Unlike comic books where the comic book exists for the characters, comic strips are inserted into newspapers or magazines to alongside other, lengthier content. Comic strips can be distributed to periodicals by the creator/owner but for the most part, comic strip artists prefer to enter into an arrangement with a syndicate that has the ability to sell a strip to tens or hundreds of newspapers or magazines. My comic strip appeared as part of an arrangement that was negotiated between the publisher and me. I was not represented by a syndicate.

My original intent was to a do comic strip featuring folktales from around the world titled *Tales Retold*. I solicited it to a variety of newspapers and syndication services. When the publisher of the *Skanner* saw it he said, "looks interesting, we'll take the Black ones." The editor gave it a new title, *African Tales*, and asked that I use an undifferentiated "African looking" background. Many readers and academics assumed that its "pan-African" images, title, and stories were a direct reflection of my politics. I may have been the "author" of this comic strip—in a legal and creative sense—but

I still worked within a social, economic, and political context. It was truly jarring to have that context read back on to me.

The scholarly emphasis in works dealing with comics on thematic content, textual analysis, cultural historical significance, and readership can best be understood within the context of trends in cultural studies. In separate essays Jason Toynbee and Graham Murdock trace the emphasis in media and cultural studies on audiences, readership and textual analysis to Roland Barthes influential essay, *The Death of the Author*, in which he argues that authorship is built on the romantic idea that "great works" are the exclusive product of the "author's" imaginative resources and fail to account for the pre-existing work upon which "great works" are based. This essay led to the development of cultural and media studies scholarship emphasizing audience readings, interpretations, and consumption patterns of texts. I experienced the problem of this line of inquiry firsthand as my cartoon was deconstructed, explained, and interpreted without regard for my intentions, source material, editorial restrictions, and a working life intimately bound to copyrights and trademarks.

A later article by Michel Foucault titled, *What Is an Author*, argues that the author is a discursive function of the text. Legal scholars have further developed this idea in order to address the legal author as a subject position that is a precondition for the establishment of an entertainment industry in which the ownership of stories and characters—that include images of race—can be centralized in corporate hands. James Boyle argues that this phenomenon is rooted in society's desire to "romanticize a notion of subjective control of private information," that the creation of a legal author requires that ideas be convertible into a property form and then attributed back to an author as the property holder.

While the legal definition of the author is built on "the romantic [notion of the] author whose original transformative genius justifies [the creation of] private property," what it really designates is the line of ownership. Jane Gaines argues that comics are no different from any other entertainment industry. In the earlier years of the industry copyright laws designed to protect stories necessitated that the roles of artists, editors, and writers be downplayed or regarded as small contributions to a larger story in order for corporations to retain their proprietary rights. The move away from copyright to trademark protections shifted the industry away from an emphasis on the ownership of stories to the likenesses or images of the characters. This paved the way for a greater recognition of the contributions of creative teams, without a concomitant loss of proprietary rights, thus setting the stage for today's comic book industry in which individual members of creative teams acquire their own fan bases. Comic book creators with large fan bases are able to negotiate more lucrative contracts with better terms than lesser-known counterparts. Creators with large fan bases can also exert greater influence within the creative process. In essence, they are more likely to get their way. Ironically, the scholarly emphasis on thematic analysis and reading the comic book purely as text has continued. This is in sharp contrast to fanzines, the comic book press, and the mainstream media outlets that have tended to focus on individual creators and business concerns.

Still, whether it is *African Tales* or *Captain America*, analyses of race in terms of images and text overlook the role of proprietary concerns, publishers, divisions of labor, creative negotiations, and the acquisition and deployment of transnational flows of artifacts, images, and stories by creators. For this reason, I have conducted ethnographic research among comic book creators to explore the interlocking issues of authorship, intent, and ownership that cut to the heart of racial representation in comics and a variety of other realms.

Captain America in Black and White

Yes, they made a Black Captain America, a man of a different hue than his fair-skinned counterpart that symbolized America in all its glory . . . and shame. And the truth is, that in the eyes of many fans a Black Captain America, especially a Black Captain America that is revealed to have preceded the White super powered patriot they have become accustomed to, doesn't so much add too the mythos as it tarnishes his fair-skinned counterpart.

The White Captain America was created in 1941 by Jack Kirby and Joe Simon—employees of Timely Publishing—an earlier incarnation of Marvel Enterprises. The White Captain America's story begins when 98 lb. weakling Steve Rogers volunteers to be injected with the top-secret super soldier serum. The serum transforms him, giving him the strength, agility, and constitution of ten men. Tragically, the creator of the serum is assassinated before the serum can be mass-produced. The newly powered Steve Rogers is given a red, white, and blue uniform; an indestructible shield; and the moniker Captain America.

In three separate interviews the *Truth*'s respective editor, writer, and artist had the same comment about the White Captain America's premise: *the military would never have performed the super soldier experiments on a blonde haired, blue eyed, White guy . . . at least not the more dangerous initial trials.* And they cited the Tuskegee Syphilis experiments to support their contention. These experiments, conducted in Tuskegee, Alabama, from 1932–72 involved the intentional misdiagnosis of African America men with syphilis in order to give researchers an opportunity to see what the disease would do if left unchecked. The end result was a seven issue comic book miniseries titled *Truth: Red, White, and Black* that introduced the Black Captain America.

The *Truth* miniseries opened with a dapper young African American couple, Isaiah and Faith Bradley walking arm and arm at the 1940 World's Fair. "That day was pretty much our honeymoon," says Isaiah in a voiceover, "We had our picture taken on the corner of Rainbow Avenue. The World's Fair had declared 'Negro Week.' A whopping seventy-five cents admission could buy you the dream of equality for a whole day . . . that is, until somebody decided it didn't." WW II begins and Isaiah Bradley along with hundreds of soldiers are selected as test subjects for the Super Soldier Serum.

The soldiers' friends and relatives are told that they died in training accidents. Meanwhile, the soldiers are subjected to horrifying experiments designed to create the perfect warrior. The survivors are packed into the steerage of a ship headed across the Atlantic to Europe. As the men, bodies deformed from rapid muscle growth, play cards and listen to stories about post-WWI race riots, one of the soldiers begins to sweat, slips into unconsciousness, and dies amidst visions of Africans that have come to take him with them. The unit's numbers dwindle to just one, Isaiah Bradley, as they are sent on a series of missions behind enemy lines. While in the hospital Isaiah Bradley ordered to prepare for a suicide mission by Colonel Price.

"Soldier," says Colonel Price, "at this moment, you may not think there's much difference between the Germans and us, but if we win the war, your family will live."

The story of the suicide mission continues. In an installment titled *The Math* Isaiah Bradley, now the Black Captain America, raids the Schwartzabita concentration camp. All the pieces come together as the Black Captain America uncovers Nazi experiments, not unlike the ones that he experienced. His mission near complete, the Black Captain America unwittingly enters a gas chamber . . . just before the valves are opened. By the end of the installment, the unseen narrator is later revealed to be Faith Bradley. The mission was successful on all but one count: Isaiah Bradley did not die. The listener is revealed to be the White Captain America, on his own personal quest to uncover the true stories behind both the Super Soldier Program and the "urban legend" about a Black Captain America.

It doesn't take long for the White Captain America to get to the truth. It is later revealed that the Super Soldier Program was originally conceived as part of joint German/U.S. eugenics program that was begun long before WWI!

Isaiah Bradley, the Black Captain America, escaped and was smuggled back to the U.S. by a loose confederation of Black soldiers and European Resistance fighters. He resides in Faith Bradley's Bronx apartment, physically young but with few remaining mental faculties. His wall is papered with photos of himself with a veritable who's who of Black history since WWII. The story comes to a bitter sweet end, as Faith Bradley takes a picture of Isaiah Bradley—in the tattered remains of his Captain America uniform—and the White Captain America arm and arm.

AXEL ALONSO ON EDITING *TRUTH*

Axel Alonso has been in the comic book industry since the mid 1990s. Of mixed Hispanic and English origins, Alonso grew up in the San Francisco Bay Area. He received his B.A. in journalism from U.C. Santa Cruz and M.A. in journalism from Columbia University. He is currently the executive editor for Marvel Comics, a division of Marvel Enterprises. When *Truth* was published he was a group editor with responsibility for various Hulk, Spider-Man, and X-Men related comic book series. He was also *Truth*'s lead editor and one of the prime movers behind the project.

I originally met Alonso in 1999 when he was an editor for the mature readers Vertigo Line of comics published by Marvel's cross-town rival, DC

Comics. He was lured from DC after he had built a reputation for developing new freelance talent and turning forgotten, and even embarrassing, comic book properties into critical and market successes. Many of these successes dealt with racial themes. For example, he created a miniseries based on the Human Target, a White male character who assumes the identities of people in trouble. The miniseries focused on the Human Target's identity crisis, prompted in part by his decision to impersonate a Black preacher so effectively that even the preacher's wife couldn't tell them apart. This was followed by a *Congo Bill* miniseries. Congo Bill was a White male character, created in the 1950s, who goes to Africa and acquires a ring that gives him the ability to exchange his consciousness with a gorilla. He used *Congo Bill* to retell Joseph Conrad's *Heart of Darkness* from the perspective of Glass, a Black mercenary haunted by the memories of the innocent lives that he has destroyed. Glass is sent into the Congo to put down the now mentally unstable Congo Bill. Alonso is most known for developing *100 Bullets*, a comic book about an international conspiracy that seeks out individuals and gives them a briefcase with a gun, 100 untraceable bullets, and a reason to kill. Most of the characters in *100 Bullets* are, at best, deeply flawed. But the world of *100 Bullets* is incredibly diverse. One of the first projects that Alonso created for Marvel was *Luke Cage: Hero for Hire* miniseries with *100 Bullets* writer Brian Azarrello. Luke Cage was a Shaft knock-off from the 1970s. According to Azarrello, his intent was to recast Luke Cage as the superhero version of criminal rapper Suge Knight.

In one of our early conversations in 1999, Alonso was put off by my suggestion that the work was about any kind of overt identity politics. He argued that comics are genre medium, he described the political and the racial elements as necessary "high concept story elements" that were mixed in with "enough explosions to sell the books."

Moving up the ladder has been a double-edged sword for Alonso. In his current position he has greater power to green-light projects but a lot less time and a lot more worries. The sales of his monthly books are tracked and it is expected that they continually rise. His desk is littered with proofs and proposals, the walls are papered with covers for upcoming comics in the order that they were due out, the phone rings constantly, and people are popping their heads in his office every few minutes with questions.

According to Alonso, the *Truth* miniseries started as an offhand comment by then Marvel publisher, Bill Jemas. Jemas never intended to follow through but the idea the "inherent of politics of wrapping a Black man in red, white, and blue" intrigued Alonso as he played out the possible consequences of a WWII Super Soldier Program in his head. The Tuskegee Experiments immediately came to mind.

"I thought it would be a really interesting way to use the character to tell a larger story, a chapter of American history. [We used] *Captain America* as a metaphor for America itself."

With Alonso pushing the idea and Jemas open to it, it wasn't difficult to get the necessary internal permissions to solicit a proposal from Bob Morales.

"Bob [Morales] bought the premise . . . and from there it was all a part of an ongoing dialogue . . . Bob came up with the ensemble cast. And most importantly . . . that ending is purely his. It's Bob's story. [But it's his] story based on concepts that were initiated internally."

BOB MORALES ON WRITING *TRUTH*

Bob Morales has been in and out of the comic book industry for about a decade. Of mixed Black and Hispanic origins, Morales grew up in the Williamsburg section of Brooklyn, New York. Throughout the mid 1990s, Morales wrote a comic strip with *Truth* artist Kyle Baker for *Vibe Magazine* where he eventually became the arts editor. The strip featured one page musical and cultural satires that included *Nirvana Can Wait* in which Curt Cobain is sent back to earth to live as a Black man; *Hip Hop Wampum* in which gun for cash programs evolve to the point were guns become currency, and the self explanatory *Old School Retirement Home*. While the strip was short lived, it established that Morales and Baker as comic creators that could appeal to a Hip Hop audience.

Morales's initial reaction to the idea of a Black Captain America was laughter. Then he heard the premise. He thought it was depressing . . . so depressing that when he finished the proposal he couldn't even look at it for several weeks.

Then came the negotiations. At issue were three elements. Morales had lifted the idea for Faith and Isaiah Bradley, a strong marriage with a proactive woman at its core, from a previous unsuccessful proposal for a Luke Cage miniseries, the one that would be written by Brian Azzarello. Morales also wanted Isaiah to be a young science prodigy working on the project, a nod the Marvel's tradition of scientists such as Reed Richard—a.k.a. Mr. Fantastic—and Bruce Banner—a.k.a. the Hulk—who are victims of their own experiments. And Morales wanted Isaiah to live into the present in a brain-damaged state. But Marvel didn't want Isaiah to be a scientist. Instead they wanted the story to adhere more closely to the Tuskegee Experiments and have an ensemble cast of possible Captain Americas. At different times Marvel wanted Isaiah to come home to a parade or die a tragic death. Morales won out as far as keeping Isaiah and Faith as a couple and having Isaiah suffer from brain damage. Alonso and Morales both remarked that this intentional nod to Mohammad Ali was a greater tragedy than any of the other proposed endings.

While he was disappointed in having to get rid of his idea for a Black scientist, Morales felt that the single most important element of his proposal was to have a strong Black marriage at its core.

For Morales, much of the actual writing of *Truth* consisted of toggling between his original proposal, continual editorial suggestions, and his own research into the period. He described the medium of comics as a "reductionist form." A continual challenge to figure out what can be crammed into a few panels. Citing a Kurt Vonnegut essay, Morales continued, "the important thing to do . . . is to always have your character want something and at the end he either gets it or he doesn't." He described the scenes in which the families are notified of their loved one's deaths as an example of this.

Morales decided to start the story at the World's Fair when he stumbled on a reference to Negro Week at the New York public library. He continued his research at the Schomberg center where he came across letters and papers describing Negro Week, Black soldiers experiences during WWII, and pre-WWII race riots. He also spent a lot of time tracking down urban legends about mass killings of Black soldiers. In the end, according to Morales, "reality supplies you." With the opening scene established, the proposal in hand, and a sense of what Marvel was looking for, the script itself was a logical progression. Looming over all of this was the fact that the actual story of the Black Captain America in uniform was going to take about three and a quarter issues. This meant that he had to kill all but one of the test subjects—299 men—by issue four, page seventeen in such a way that the readers will identify with the characters and ramifications for their families.

This also meant that a unit of Super Soldiers had to be in Europe by issue four and since this was a top secret program it made sense to have the soldiers transported in steerage. He didn't want all of issue three to take place at the base so something had to happen on the ship. The reverse middle passage sequence grew out of these considerations. Making the Super Soldier Serum Project a joint U.S./German endeavor was one of the first things that Morales added to the concept. Having the project splinter during WWII and building up to a confrontation in a German concentration camp was a natural progression. But the "sequence with the women in the gas chambers, not understanding what the hell [was happening when Isaiah showed up] . . . that was in the original proposal."

For Morales there is a real downside to doing the research in that it leaves him feeling torn between his desire to be true to the facts and write an exciting story.

"This is a story about people getting fucked and its only incidental that they're getting fucked because they're Black. They're getting fucked because that's what happens in war. [Still], there's a racial reality to the way Blacks were [treated] during the war that people can forget now."

"People were sacrificed. Was it worth [it to sacrifice] a group of Blacks for the rest of society? [When] you get inducted into the Army, you're property whether you're Black or White, Italian [or] Irish. It doesn't matter. You're there for somebody to throw you at something . . . And if you don't go, people will shoot you . . . that's the greater reality."

"[Then] there's the ambiguity of whether or not somebody can make an argument that a *Super Soldier Program* as it's depicted in this book is a good thing . . . I'm not making that argument [but] I left room in there for that argument to be made because it's basically the argument of war."

KYLE BAKER ON VISUALIZING *TRUTH*

Kyle Baker's first experiences in the comic book industry were as a high school intern at Marvel Comics in the 1980s. Baker grew up in the Jamaica Queens section of New York and identifies himself as Black. He has worked on both DC and Marvel characters; written and illustrated his own graphic novels; created cartoons for *Vibe Magazine*, the *New Yorker*, and *New York Magazine*; and worked in Hollywood as a writer and animator. Like a growing number of comic book artists, Baker does much of his art on computer, allowing him to do triple duty as the penciler, inker, and colorist.

A recent thirty-two page feature article in the *Comics Journal* by Kent Worcester about Baker's career focused on his comic projects and his musings about the comic book industry but never broached the subject of race. Some might use this to argue that Baker has transcended race but my interview raises a different set of questions. During our interview Baker spoke in racialized terms, leaving me to wonder whether Worcester omitted the topic, avoided it altogether, or if the topic came up because I am African American.

In trying to create the visuals for *Truth*, Baker was caught in the middle of a series of contradictory expectations. The idea was simple: make a Black Captain America that would appeal to comic book fans and non-comic book readers (particularly Hip Hop consumers). The problem was that not only do these audiences have very different ideas about what good comic art is but the concept itself—an exploration of the gruesome underbelly of the American Dream in a time of war—didn't necessarily sit well with the established notion of what the White Captain America is in the eyes of his fans.

According to Baker, when he was approached to create the art for *Truth*, the proposal had already been accepted but the script was still in progress. When Morales first mentioned the idea of a Black Captain America, Baker was skeptical. He wondered aloud if this decision was about using Black characters to show White audiences that Marvel is cool or trying to expand Marvel's market share. "Anytime you make a decision like that it's a financial thing."

Still, in spite of his initial cynicism, Baker felt that it was a good starting point and he liked the angle that Morales settled on.

When Baker created the art for *Truth*, he consciously tried to develop a look that would appeal to the Hip Hop market . . . a market with an aesthetic that he identified as being urban and Black.

"I used the style that I used for my *Vibe Magazine* [comic strip], which is . . . very graffiti inspired stuff, a lot of magic marker, very loose sketchy drawings, a lot of action and a lot of bright colors . . . It's a very pop, poppy, pop art type of thing."

However, Baker's pursuit of the Hip Hop consumer was not without its drawbacks, "[*Truth*] got really good press in the *New York Times*, CNN, [and] MTV. It did really well with people who don't normally read comics and it did really poorly with comic book fans."

"I think my favorite part of the story was when [the Black Captain America] was killing all of the Nazis [at the Schwartzabita] concentration camp."

But even as Baker asserted his preference for action, he made an historical argument for much of Morales's more subdued storytelling and the negative reactions among comic book fans. "The trend in super hero books . . . is less fights . . . when I started, the business had been mostly for children and [comics were around] 50 cents and sold at 7–11s and candy stores."

Now comic books are sold at specialty stores at much higher prices to collectors. In the effort to tailor their products to collectors, Baker feels that the industry has painted itself into a corner.

"What I find is that a lot of the people who read that stuff are 30 to 40-year-old men who are sort of embarrassed about the fact that they're 30 or 40-years-old and still reading *Batman*. So [creators] try to make [the comics] appear more sophisticated by getting rid of all the fights and all the color . . . [I worked on *New Mutants* and] that book had no fights for a year. The year that I worked on it, it was just them sitting around talking . . . what's the point of being able to shoot rays out of your eyes if you're not going to ever do it!"

Baker believes that this and the current trend toward photo realistic rendering of superheroes, typified by the work of Alex Ross, has created a comic book industry incapable of selling comic books to children and, in many cases, non–comic book collectors.

"It just seems that anything comic booky is looked down on by the readers and by the critics," remarked Baker.

In addition to incorporating a Hip Hop aesthetic, Baker had a lot of problems solving what to do around the issue of skin tone. Comics are a medium that tends to use earth tones and shadows in the backgrounds in order to create atmosphere.

Yes, there are times when the stories will call for the heroes to skulk in the shadows or blend into the crowds, but dramatic moments and fight scenes—of which there are many—work best when the heroes stand out.

For Baker, this meant rethinking a lot of his color choices, an issue that he had encountered on the project that he did just before working on *Truth*: a graphic novel retelling the story of David from the Bible.

In *King David*, he intentionally used shades of black and brown to reflect the African and Middle-Eastern origins of the story's characters. "If the person is dark-skinned, the only way to make him separate from the background is to make the background light. People are just not used to seeing this because there aren't very many Black people in comic books."

According to Baker, a lot of comic book fans wrote to him to complain about the color. Some blamed Baker and others blamed the printer. In most of the cases, when Baker responded to the letters, explaining that the characters were Black, the fans didn't believe him!

"They absolutely [thought] there was something wrong with the color!" exclaimed Baker.

While Baker used a lot of the coloring conventions from *King David* in *Truth*, he didn't receive color-related complaints. The complaints about his visuals for *Truth* were directed at the pop art style.

"The reason I wanted to do *Captain America* was because it was a positive Black character. The reason I did *King David* is he's a positive hero."

Baker followed up by describing the rules that he goes by when he creates a comic book. "I don't like stupid Black characters and I don't like criminal Black characters. I won't do it."

For example, in the graphic novel *You Are Here*, which he described as a book where all of the lead characters were "stupid criminals" he assigned all the lead roles to White characters. The supporting characters, however, were much more diverse. Ironically, he did get mail complaining about the lack of diversity of the cast.

Baker continued, "When you're watching *Cops* or you're watching the news, every time it's a criminal it's a Black guy. Look at the [crime] statistics. If you break [them] down by race, it has no resemblance to what you see in the media."

"You never see Black people in church. We go to church more than anybody . . . I know more people who go to church than sell drugs. [Laughs] You know. I don't know any gangsters or drug dealers. I know tons of Black churchgoers."

"Yes," I thought to myself in agreement.

FINAL THOUGHTS

I privileged discussions of authorship early on in this paper because they highlight the ways in which creative teams work with pre-existing material and how legal and romantic notions of authorship establish divisions of labor, editorial control, proprietary rights throughout the production process. Essentially, Barthes's assertion that texts are built on the works that precede them is dead on. Foucault's argument that the author is a discursive function of the text is correct. But neither of these statements necessarily lead me to believe that the reader should hold a privileged position in scholarship. Rather, both of these statements highlight a series of cultural, economic, and social constructions that can be teased out through ethnographic research.

Comic book creators use existing works, identifiable images, and story elements that lack specificity to "draw in" or "connect" with the reader in order to create a connection between the comic book page and the reader's world. This continual movement between general and specific images and story elements—as well as the introduction of visual elements with no connection to the narrative—opens the door to the juxtaposition of conflicting imaginaries while giving the "world" of comics its sense of depth. Comic books are group-authored texts by individuals, working within a series of editorial, production, and proprietary constraints. While each individual has a primary responsibility to the task for which they are credited, they routinely influence and even alter each other's contributions. The waters are further muddied by the co-presence of romantic and legal notions of authorship.

The truth of the matter is that ethnographic research into the intersections, the places where legal notions of authorship, intent, production processes, creative negotiations meet can help to make sense of how ideas about war, patriotism, heroism, and race take on a form that circulates in the market place (in this case as a comic book!) and eventually find its way into public discourse and the archives from which people construct their world views.

The irony is that, within this configuration, the differences of opinion and intention between Alonso, Morales, and Baker don't have to be resolved. Each of them performs their allotted task and sends their work to the next person in the process.

As members of the *Truth* creative team, Alonso, Morales, and Baker bring different skills and desires to the process. They each provide different elements. But their views on race and its representations are not commensurate. Alonso was the catalyst. His position within Marvel Enterprises made him much more sensitive to bottom line concerns than his colleagues. Alonso's take on the Black Captain America had more to do with broader political concerns and gritty realities of everyday life, a perspective that is carried from his previous work developing the *Human Target, Congo Bill, 100 Bullets*, and *Cage*. These projects featured worlds with diverse protagonists who, while having heroic elements, are deeply flawed. He sets the premise—that the government would never develop the Super Soldier Serum on the backs of White men—and determines who will execute it.

Morales develops the story and creates the characters through his exploration of Black history and urban legends. Though Morales thought the idea of a Black Captain America, as Alonso put it to him, was depressing he saw it as an opportunity tell a story about good Black characters who make choices in the ethically murky fog of war. His idea for a Black scientist never saw the light of day but he gets to keep a Black marriage at the story's core.

Baker turns the stories into images. He takes on the job because he has worked with Morales in the past and is interested in telling the story of a positive Black hero. He tailors his style to Hip Hop consumers. Baker was cynical about the prospect of creating a Black Captain America. I don't think he would have done the project if not for the involvement of Morales. Baker is ardently opposed to creating Black characters in a negative light for the simple reason that he doesn't want to add to the existing archive of negative images. And while this may gel with Morales's world of good people making bad choices in complicated times, Alonso's emphasis on gritty realities, anti-heroes, and deeply flawed characters are simply not something that Baker has an interest in.

Truth be told, the stories of both the Black and White Captain Americas are quintessentially American stories. What is most interesting about *Truth* is the way in which it scratches below the surface of the White Captain America's origin to reveal the gritty realities and ethical complexities of a World War that is usually looked back on in such simplistic terms as good vs. evil. The truth is that the story of Captain America has always been about how far America is willing to go to win, what sacrifices are acceptable, creating the perfect man, creating the perfect warrior, creating the perfect symbol of its ideals. The dirty little secret, the ultimate irony, is that the answer to these questions undercut the very ideals that the idea of the White Captain America stands for. And the story of the Black Captain America, aptly titled *Truth*, puts the nightmarish underbelly of the America's ideals in high relief.

While this story could be looked at as a chapter in the never ending saga of Captain America, a cautionary WWII story, or an allegory of the African American experience, *there could be no Truth without Congo Bill, Nirvana Can Wait, King David, or many other of Alonso, Morales, or Baker's works.* There would be no Black Captain America without the White Captain America created by Jack Kirby and Joe Simon. Alonso, Morales, Baker, Kirby, and Simon are credited in accordance with the tasks they performed but they are not considered to be the "authors."

The kicker is that the role of author, and all of the proprietary rights that come with it, are reserved for Marvel Enterprises. Even after all of its referents, metaphors, allegories, negotiations, debates, and intentions are sorted out, the *Truth* comic book miniseries is brought to its readers by Marvel Enterprises, an imagined entity that pays dividends to people who may or may not ever flip through the pages of the comic books upon which their fortunes are based.

But one truth remains—that it's so much easier to discuss the *Truth* comic book miniseries as a chapter in the continuous story of a legendary figure as opposed to a commentary on the lack of Black role models, casualties of war, or the failure of America to live up to its ideals. In fact, that's the magic of the medium of comics—taking uncomfortable truths and putting them into a familiar, less abrasive form.

Plato, Spider-Man and the Meaning of Life[1]

—JEREMY BARRIS

To see a World in a Grain of Sand
And a Heaven in a Wild Flower
Hold Infinity in the palm of your hand
And Eternity in an hour

—WILLIAM BLAKE, "Auguries of Innocence"

"Is there a form, itself by itself, of just, and beautiful, and good, and everything of
that sort?"
"Yes," he said.
. . .
"And what about these, Socrates? Things that might seem absurd, like hair and
mud and dirt, or anything else totally undignified and worthless? Are you doubt-
ful whether or not you should say that a form is separate for each of these too . . . ?"

—PLATO, *Parmenides*

"Who *was* that masked man?"

—*THE LONE RANGER*

Some versions of mysticism have taught that the ordinary world around
us is sacred and wonderful, that the meaning of life is to be found not
through some extraordinary knowledge or awareness, but in appreciating
what already surrounds us. I believe that both *Spider-Man* comics and Plato's
dialogues offer exactly this deep vision, and that they introduce us to it in

63

some remarkably similar ways. I cannot do any kind of justice here to the richness of either set of works, or to the variations of style and meaning within each of them. Instead I shall focus only on four interconnected themes they share. Both sets of works foreground sexual aspects of life. They both emphasize the inadequate, shadowy dimensions of our lives and a need to get beyond those limitations. Both prominently include a great deal of self-trivialising humour. In Plato this humour is typically ironic, in *Spider-Man* it is typically flippant, and both connect with more serious ironies. And they both present their themes centrally and incompletely through sensory images.

I shall try to show that these themes illustrate the meaning of life through their very close interconnections. Human insight is limited by our dependence on our bodily senses, our particular perspectives, our biasing and blinding desires. These dependencies also seriously limit our ability to see what is right and fair, to see the need to follow it, and to behave rightly even when we see the need. But we only *have* a need for truth and rightness because we are flawed and limited. As Plato puts it in his *Symposium*, "none of the gods loves wisdom or wants to become wise—for they are wise" (204A). Without our inadequacies, following truth and rightness would be automatic, already accomplished before we started needing anything. In fact, both Spider-Man's and Plato's characters' heroism emerges exactly in their working *with* their limitations—their senses, their desires, their biases, their flaws—to get beyond them. And, as their self-trivialising ironic humour shows, they love flaws and bodies as well as ideals. They both pursue the ideals they love *for the sake of* the faulty human persons and societies they are and live with. Spider-Man seeks justice for the sake of the citizens of New York, and for the sake of his family, friends and lovers, with all their notable faults and eccentricities. Socrates, Plato's hero, seeks truth for the good of his particular city-state, Athens, for the good of the boys and men he loves, and for the good of his own soul.

In other words, both heroes struggle to get beyond their flaws precisely by means of and for the sake of what is loveable about human flaws. And in the end, as I shall try to show, the irony that is their means of dealing with life describes the nature of life itself. The shadowy inadequacies of life are the source of striving for fully adequate light beyond them, and, since the shadows are therefore, in the end, the source of the light's presence, light turns out to be part of what the shadows already embodied in the first place.

Marvellously, our own experience as readers of *Spider-Man* comics and Plato's dialogues illustrates exactly the same wonder of the ordinary. We are fascinated by these images, these characters, drawn to them by their flaws and humour, inspired to their ideals by their human accessibility and their struggle with their human limitations. And this fascination, this inspiration, this wonder of the limited adequacies of our world, is exactly what the comics and dialogues are about. They show us the wonder of who we are, just as we are, even as we read them.

1. SEX, SHADOWS, AND WISDOM IN PLATO

I shall devote this first section mainly to Plato, since his direct and elaborate focus on philosophy makes it easier to develop a philosophical framework to approach *Spider-Man* as well as Plato. Sexuality plays a large role in each set of works, both in its unsettling and confusing dimensions and its inspiring, eye-opening sides. Peter Parker has many erotic loves, and most of them are structured by the conflict between his obvious athletic attractiveness and personal appeal, and the unappealing false appearances that result from the hidden truths of his life. Even Spider-Man is often preoccupied with trying to figure out how he should feel about himself, and what kind of person he truly is beyond how he appears. Is he really perhaps an uncaring person, a bad nephew, a bad friend, just another kind of criminal? As I shall try to show, this very commonplace tension between beauty and worthwhileness on the one hand, and inadequacy and falsehood on the other, in fact contains the meaning of lust, love, and our relation to truth. To say this more accurately: beauty, genuineness and meaning *are* one kind of tension and even mixture with their opposites. If this is true, then our very ordinary emotional engagement with Peter Parker's love life, and with his person and body, is itself already an expression of the meaningful structure of life and our relation to truth.

But first: Plato.

Plato has traditionally been understood as rejecting the body and its senses, seeing them as obstacles to finding truth, the real goal of life. Hence, of course, the expression "Platonic love," love separate from physical desire. There is an important element of truth in this view of Plato. Plato's *Phaedo*, for example, shows Socrates describing the body with its desires and senses as a prison for the soul, "chained hand and foot in the body, compelled to view reality not directly but only through its prison bars" (82E).[2] Our senses and desires, says Socrates, blind us to truth. "So long as we keep to the body and our soul is contaminated with this imperfection, there is no chance of our ever attaining satisfactorily to ... truth" (66B). Observation "by means of ... the senses is entirely deceptive" (83A). "Pleasures and desires and griefs" mislead us, since "when anyone's soul feels a keen pleasure or pain it cannot help supposing that whatever causes the most violent emotion is the plainest and truest reality, which it is not" (83B–C). The soul should trust "nothing but its own independent judgment upon objects considered in themselves, and attributing no truth to anything which it views indirectly [i.e., through the senses] as being subject to variation, because such objects are sensible and visible but what the soul itself sees is intelligible and invisible" (83A–B, insertion added).

In the *Republic* the philosopher is described as loving pure truth, which, again, cannot be seen. "The lovers of sounds and sights" are "incapable of apprehending and taking delight in the nature of the beautiful itself" (476B). The pure truth of a thing is always one and the same, but each thing we experience through our senses is seen in many different ways. The "just and the unjust, the good and the bad ... in itself each is one," but "by virtue of their communion with actions and bodies and with one another they present themselves ... as a multiplicity of aspects" (476A). Justice itself is one "thing," but there are many different just actions, which are just in many different ways. And each of these will be more or less just depending on differences in context and on what they are compared to, just as an object is heavy in comparison with a lighter object and light in comparison with a heavier one. "Is there any one of these many fair and honorable things that will not sometimes appear ugly and base? And of the just things, that will not seem unjust? ... And likewise of the great and small things, the light and the heavy things ..." (479A–B). Unlike the single truth of each thing, each of these multiple sensory things "*is not*" as much as it "*is* ... that which one affirms it to be" (479B, translator's emphasis). The nature and truth of movement, for example, does not lie in this moving thing or that moving thing, in which that "truth" would change depending on context, but in movement itself, independently of any of the examples we might see.

Similarly for the nature and truth of beauty, or goodness, or of "being-one-thing," or "being-a-horse." What is generally true about horses is, clearly, true independently of any particular horse. These separated, unified, consistent truths are what Plato calls the Ideas or Forms.

But then, how do we understand how truth works, when the truth *of* the things we experience through our bodily senses is independent of, separate from *those same things*? Differently put, how does the secret identity relate to the mask, if the private identity is the identity *of that public mask*? As Plato understands it, the bridge across this strange gap between sensory experience and its own truth happens to be sexual desire. In other words, it is *also* true that Plato regards bodily experience as *essential* for truth.

His *Symposium*, for example, insists that the road to seeing truth begins with the love of bodies: first a single young man, then all young men, and from there to non-bodily things like social laws and the principles of truth. "A lover who goes about this matter correctly must begin in his youth to devote himself to beautiful bodies" (210A). Through "loving boys correctly" and "starting out from beautiful things and using them as rising stairs" (211B–C), one comes to see "the divine Beauty itself in its one form." And "only then will it become possible for him to give birth not to images of virtue . . . but to true virtue (because he's in touch with the true Beauty)" (211E–12A). And Plato's *Phaedrus* explains that the only reason we get moving along the road to truth is that beauty inspires us to explore the thing that has it, and it does so by first inflaming us with physical lust for particular sensual bodies. Of all the true realities, "beauty alone" is "most manifest to sense" and draws us to recognise truth (250D). When one sees "the person of the beloved" (253E), the lust in one's soul "leaps and dashes" to "the delights of love's commerce." Restraint, and the driver or "charioteer of the soul," struggle against lust but "at last . . . yield" to "him": "and so he draws them on, and now they are quite close and behold the spectacle of the beloved flashing upon them. At that sight" the driver is filled with "awe and reverence" (254A–B), and lust takes a back seat. But it is only because lust struggles successfully that one gets close enough to "the person of the beloved" for the truth of beauty itself to dawn on one, and only then to put lust back in its place.[3]

Let me remind the reader here that part of the appeal of Spider-Man is his muscular and beautifully proportioned body. The villains, by contrast, are usually physically much cruder or just unalluring: the Rhino, the Green Goblin, the Kingpin. Part of what we (or many of us) as readers are attracted to and/or identify with in Spider-Man is his physical grace and beauty. What Plato and, with his help, our thinking about *Spider-Man* should help us appreciate is that this ordinary, shallow pleasure is in fact already our participating in the depths of the meaning of life, and that we only need to recognise and value it in the right way.

Now, the conflict between this emphasis on the essential role of our senses and desires in approaching truth, and on their forming an obstacle to achieving that same goal, is not simply a contradiction. In fact the key is to see how these two opposed views go together. We can approach this most easily and helpfully through Plato's discussions of goodness. In his *Charmides*, for example, he shows Socrates interviewing a beautiful young man, Charmides, on the topic of self-control. As Socrates begins to talk to the boy he is momentarily overwhelmed by lust, almost losing his own self-control. "I caught sight of the inwards of his garment, and took the flame. Then I could no longer contain myself . . . " (155D–E). Plato is surely telling us something by placing this obvious irony here: perhaps, that lust must be taken into account in considering self-control. Clearly, there would be no need for self-control without the desires and irrationalities that oppose it. The very idea of self-control would have no meaning without that struggle. In other words, self-control is both opposed to irrational desire and partly *composed of* it. Self-control *is* the struggle, or rather a successful version of it.

We can find the same insight that good qualities work together with their opposites in *Spider-Man*. For example, "Spider-Man versus Doctor Octopus" begins with Spider-Man's thinking, "It's almost *too* easy! . . . I'm too powerful for *any* foe! I almost *wish* for an opponent who'd give me a run for my money!" (Lee, et al., *Amazing Spider-Man* No. 3:2). (More on this episode later, loyal fans!) Without a struggle, there is no virtue, no achievement in doing good. The effects of the good actions are good, but the actions themselves, requiring very little, do not count for much as a moral achievement.

Generally, then, being a good person is both opposed to being a bad person *and* partly composed of *being* a bad person. Plato's famous allegory of the cave makes this generalisation. The allegory describes human life as imprisonment in a cave, where all one sees are shadows of the truth, cast by firelight behind one. Even the light is only a poor relation of sunlight. In order to see the truth, one has to turn one's soul so as to leave the cave and its shadows, and see the true world in true sunlight (*Republic* 518C). This is an allegory: the true world is the world as "seen" without the senses, and the cave and its shadows are the world as experienced through our bodies. "The ascent . . . is the soul's ascension to the intelligible region" (517B). But, the allegory continues, one has to return to the cave: "down you must go then. . . . So our city will be governed by us and you with waking minds, and not . . . ruled darkly as in a dream by men who fight one another for shadows." This necessity is "imposing just commands on men who are just" (520C–E). Turning one's soul away from the world of bodily experience is not enough. Being a good person requires both turning away from the world of the body so that one can see what is good with a "waking mind," *and* turning back to the world of the body so that one can make use of what one sees, as goodness by its nature requires one to do.

More precisely, goodness requires a turning back to the bodily world *because of* the turn away from that world: once the turn away from the bodily world allows us to see the nature of goodness clearly, part of what can then be seen is that goodness itself requires its being put to use in the world. And, vice-versa, goodness requires a turning away from the bodily world in the first place *because of* the commitment to that world: it is the failings of the bodily world that make goodness necessary, make it an issue at all. So these two opposed movements in fact go together by requiring each other.

Now, already implicit in all this is that what is good is closely connected to what is true, our real topic here. For a start, we need to see the truth in order to know what is good. More directly, we need to see the truth *of* goodness if we are to be good. In fact, for Plato, it is really the other way round: what is good is the basis of what is true. "The idea of good" is what we must come to see as "giving birth in the sensible world to light, and . . . being the authentic source of truth and reason" (*Republic* 517B–C). The *Republic* insists that the very truth of reality, the source or ultimate truth of truth itself, *is* what is good. If this is really so (and we shall return to why it may be), then truth requires the same things that goodness requires. That is, commitment to the truth would require, like goodness, bodily experience *as well as* a turning away from it. More exactly, again, as with goodness, commitment to truth would require both bodily experience and the turn away from it each *because of* the other.

The essential role of the senses in finding truth, and the conflicting obstacle they form to finding truth, would go together by requiring each other.

In fact, even if goodness and truth were not connected, Plato still shows that truth requires the body. Some "reports of our perceptions . . . provoke thought to reconsideration . . . when the perception no more manifests one thing than its contrary" (*Republic* 523B–C). For example, as we have already seen, the same thing is big in relation to a smaller thing but small in relation to a bigger thing. So, to the senses, size is contradictory, being opposites at once. This provokes our intellect to consider the nature of largeness and smallness themselves, independently of the sensed things. Sight sees

> the great and the small . . . not separated but confounded. . . . And for the clarification of this, the intelligence is compelled to contemplate the great and the small . . . as distinct entities, in the opposite way from sensation. . . . And is it not in some such experience as this that the question first occurs to us, What in the world, then, is the great and the small? . . . And this is the origin of the designation *intelligible* for the one, and *visible* for the other. (524C)

It is only because of a conflict experienced through our senses that our intellect is first made to consider the truth independently of our senses. Just as it is only the force of bodily lust that motivates us to start making the effort of pursuing truth beyond bodily experience.

But, returning to the relation between goodness and truth, why is what is good not merely connected to, but the source of and even the *same* as the truth of reality? Let me suggest a tentative answer. A life in which nothing is either good or bad is a life in which nothing makes a difference. No goal is worth pursuing over any other. There is no point to anything. In such a life, there is no point in searching for truth itself, either: the search for truth, and truth itself, are meaningless. They play no role. The *words* might have a meaning; but even that kind of meaning loses its sense. That is, at a certain point "meaning" in the sense of "what we understand" coincides with "meaning" in the sense of "value" or "significance for life." What meaning can the word "truth" have if it refers to something that makes no difference whatsoever? As we said earlier, we only need truth *because* we are inadequate, because it makes a difference. Further, what meaning can *any* word have if even the *concern for* meaning has no point? Consequently, if there is truth at all, then something in life matters, something makes a difference. And if that is the case, then there is good and bad. In other words, the very nature of truth itself already involves the difference between good and bad, between what is worthwhile and what should be avoided. And while this difference involves both the good and the bad, the good is nonetheless what is worth aiming for, and the bad is nonetheless what should be avoided.

The truth of reality, then, is already built up out of, as its most basic building blocks, an establishing of what is good and its difference from what is bad. And let us not forget the ironic other side of this nature of truth, given that it really involves the bad as well as the good. As I argued previously, what is good is partly composed of what is bad, what should be avoided, so that in establishing what is good, the truth of reality also establishes, and so is also partly built of, what is bad.

In short, for Plato, bodily lust and what our senses show are essential to draw us to what is worthwhile, the good and the true. More than this, lust and what our bodily senses show are *part* of truth all along, and so must be returned to as well as moved beyond. But it also remains true that lust and our bodily experience, the very things that draw us to truth and are part of truth, must be overcome in order to get truth, since they are *also* limited and blinding. In other words, the movement is away from ourselves, but in order to find ourselves where we have already been all along.

As Plato's *Apology* expresses it, we must be concerned with human truth, truth as it includes and joins with the truth of who we limited beings are, not truth as we might imagine it to be in unlimited beings like gods. In the *Apology* Socrates insists that he is wise only in the "limited sense" of "human wisdom," which is built exactly on the recognition that it is wisdom only *because* of its limits (20D). Beyond those limits it does not become greater, but stops being wisdom at all. "These ... experts ... claimed a perfect understanding ... I would rather be ... neither wise with their wisdom nor stupid with their stupidity ... real wisdom is the property of God" (22D–23A).

2. SEX AND SHADOWS IN PLATO AND SPIDER-MAN

In *Spider-Man*, sexual love is present both as a theme of the comics and as a reaction invited from the reader/viewer to Spider-Man himself. Peter

Parker is obsessed with beautiful girls, like Betty Brant, Gwen Stacy and Mary Jane Watson. He is also handsome, and as Spider-Man is typically shown in a way that emphasises his beautiful muscularity. And in addition to his physical appeal he has a variety of other sexy qualities. As both Peter Parker and Spider-Man he is intriguingly mysterious. As Spider-Man he is brave, witty, and dashingly rescues one at great personal risk, when almost no one else could or would, and asks for nothing in return. And he is troubled in hidden ways, so that many of the people he appeals to want to be the special person who can share the deep things he keeps so private. The interested reader, of course, is already in that special position, and already feels with Peter Parker against the hard facts of life. We are already his "significant other," and already enjoy the privileges of that position.

While Spider-Man's sexual attractiveness is a pleasure in its own right, it ties in to the comic books' significance as a whole. Spider-Man struggles to live out certain ideals, principally goodness—most obviously in the form of justice—and love or nurturing. His major commitments are stopping criminals, protecting innocent people, and taking care of those he loves, like Aunt May. Now, his personal attractiveness is central in that it draws us to sympathise with those ideals—in exactly the way Plato says beauty draws us to seek truth and goodness. As I have mentioned, the villains, by contrast, are generally ugly: Doctor Octopus, for example, or the Rhino or the Green Goblin. We usually do not experience their commitments as worthwhile, but rather as something to avoid.

There is an interesting difference here between *Spider-Man* and Plato's dialogues. Where the hero of *Spider-Man* is beautiful, Plato's usual hero, Socrates, is famously ugly. In the *Meno*, for example, he is said to look "exactly like the flat sting ray" (80A). The beauties in Plato are those the hero tries to help. Like Spider-Man himself, these are adolescent young men, that is, importantly for philosophical concerns, people at the point of coming to grips with life and their place in it. But, in fact, Spider-Man and Plato's young men are not simply beautiful, and Socrates is not simply ugly. As I have mentioned, sexuality in Plato is generally linked with the shadows of human bodily limitation and inadequacy. And we find the same thing in *Spider-Man*. The hero is, after all, *Spider-Man*: an ugly, eerie and frightening comparison. And his movements are typically both graceful *and* awkward, inelegant. His legs get splayed in all sorts of undignified postures as he swings. He often pauses in a flattened, eerie crouch. And sometimes his body hangs comically upside down, absurdly suspended by a finger from a single thread, as he peers coyly at his opponents from the shadows.

But, conversely, in Plato bodily limitation is also linked with the light of truth and goodness. And we find just this in Socrates: although he is ugly— as I shall suggest, partly *because* he is ugly— the boys are mad about him. The source for the story of the *Symposium*, for example, "was obsessed with Socrates ['*Sōkratous erastēs*': 'a lover of Socrates']—one of the worst cases at that time" (173B). But, again, the maddening, blinding physical desires are not just an obstacle to seeking truth. Socrates claims that the "the only thing I say I understand is the art of love" (*Symposium* 177D–E). That is, love *is* what he has to teach, if anything; it *is* his wisdom. And it is desire for his wisdom that is expressed in the lust of these boys. As Alcibiades, Socrates' beloved, explains, "I thought . . . all I had to do was to let him have his way with me, and he would teach me everything he knew" (*Symposium* 217A).

In both *Spider-Man* and Plato the bodily limitations and inadequacies of human existence, most especially our most mindless drive, lust, are exactly what lead us to true beauty and goodness. But, more than this, beauty and goodness *are* those limitations and inadequacies, properly appreciated, done justice to, and nurtured. Desire, born of need and limitation, is what Socrates has to teach, and it is what he has to teach as *fulfilling* our needs and transcending our limitations. Socrates' homely presence, too, is *part* of his charm. Similarly, part of what makes Spider-Man attractive *is*, for example, his frequent awkwardness.

The list of Spider-Man's sexy qualities I gave earlier in fact already included inadequacies and limitations: for instance, that he is troubled, and that the truth about him is inaccessible. In fact, he is troubled partly because he himself is unsure about the truth of who he is. But this ignorance of the truth is already part of the truth about him. Further, it is also part of what equips him to seek truth (one cannot seek truth without recognising one's ignorance of it), and part of what makes him appealing. These inadequacies, then, are part of these heroes' adequacies. And these inadequacies, including the vulnerability that causes Spider-Man to keep his truths inaccessible, are also part of what makes these heroes accessible, makes their splendid qualities human-sized. In other words, their inadequacies are part of what allows us to appreciate them. But, as we have discussed, what is to be appreciated, what is worthwhile, *is* what is good and true. The awkwardness and homeliness that give us the experience of appreciation are therefore part of the very truth of what is good and true themselves. Our heroes' particular attractiveness and beauty *is* in part their contrasting limitations, and not simply lessened by them.

By way of analogy, and more generally, the presence of shadows is part of what makes light, light. Light that cast no shadows could not be part of any world we could understand. And as we have argued, truth is ultimately the truth *of* and therefore *in* the inadequate world from which we seek it, and true goodness and true beauty are also the goodness and beauty *of* the world around us, *in* all its variations from the ideal.

Presented together with the theme of sexuality as the medium of goodness and wisdom, then, is another theme common to Plato and *Spider-Man*: that human life is filled with inescapable shadows and imbalances, and that its meaning lies partly in wrestling with those shadows, but in order to find the grace and light that is already in them.

3. IRONY

The theme of shadows as the source of light echoes another theme present in both sets of works: the theme of irony. Things unexpectedly tend to involve their opposites. Even the idea that the shadows turn out to have contained the light all along has its reverse, that light also inevitably casts shadows.

Central to *Spider-Man*, in contrast with most comics, are such ironies as, for example, that the hero is often undignified at his most heroic moments, or, more seriously, that his moments of victory are often also moments of another kind of defeat. A typically undignified moment takes place in "Doc. Ock Wins!" When Doctor Octopus asks, "How can your feeble *spider powers* possibly compare with the shattering *impact* of my hydraulic *tentacles?*," Spider-Man, reeling from the impact of those tentacles, says, "I—was hoping—you wouldn't *ask!*" (Lee, et al., *Marvel Tales* No. 40:16). On the more serious level, in "Spidey Saves the Day!" Spider-Man defeats the Green Goblin permanently, but he has to stay away from home so long to do it that his newly fragile Aunt May collapses from worry. "Why must I *hurt* everything

I touch?" he asks (Lee, et al., *Amazing Spider-Man* No. 40:19). Again, he makes great personal sacrifices for the sake of New York, but he is vilified by powerful social forces, often exactly *because* of his heroic efforts. As Spider-Man himself comments in "Enter: Doctor Octopus!," the *Daily Bugle* editor J. Jonah Jameson "writes the story as if *he's* the hero and *I'm* the heavy!" (Lee, et al., *Marvel Tales* No. 38:1). In "How Green Was My Goblin!" one of the victims Spider-Man is busy rescuing from thugs says, " 'cordin' to what I read in the *Bugle*, he's as bad as *any* of them!" (Lee, et al., *Amazing Spider-Man* No. 39:8). And Spider-Man thinks to himself that, if a bystander got hurt, "No matter *how* it happened, *I'd* be sure to get the *blame!*" (9). Again, in "The Tentacles and the Trap!" a bystander watching him fight criminals exclaims, "Anyone who can fight like *Spider-Man* should be *locked up*! He's a *menace!*" (Lee, et al., *Marvel Tales* No. 39:15).

As Peter Parker he is a kind of social outcast both as a result of his secret heroism and in contrast with heroic figures. "Spider-Man versus Doctor Octopus" ends with a schoolmate saying to him about the Human Torch and Spider-Man himself, "Why don'tcha . . . see what a *real* man is like, bookworm?" (21). His friend Harry Osborn turns cold to him since "he acts like he's in his own private *world*—and everyone else better keep *out!*" (Lee, et al., *Marvel Tales* No. 38:5). And "puny Parker" is described by his fellow students as "the original *cold shoulder kid.*" (Lee, *Amazing Spider-Man* No. 39:5). Of course it is because he is trying to do good as Spider-Man that he is preoccupied and unavailable as Peter Parker. He constantly gives the girls he likes the impression that he is not interested or that he is in some way lacking, again because he needs to rush off to save situations as Spider-Man. In "Vengeance from Vietnam!" Gwen Stacy exclaims, "Whenever there's *danger*—whenever there's *trouble*—you always *leave* and run off! Ever since I can remember—Flash, and the others, have called you—a *coward*! I've tried to *ignore* it . . . but . . ." (Lee, et al., *Amazing Spider-Man* No. 108:21).

Another variety of this irony consists in Spider-Man's, and his opponents', setting themselves up or being set up for falls and reversals. The issue which begins with his wishing for a real opponent ("it's almost *too* easy!") introduces Doctor Octopus—who badly shakes his confidence by easily defeating him (Lee, et al., *Spider-Man vs Dr. Octopus*). He moves from "I can do almost *anything!*" (6) to "I—I never had a *chance!*" (10). But Doctor

Octopus is also overweening, in fact in a largely parallel way. Doctor Octopus boasts, "Though others fear radiation, I alone am able to make it my *servant!*" (3), just before being damaged by the radiation run wild. He is also impressed that he can "do anything" (10), and of course he is ultimately defeated by Spider-Man. Again, in "The Tentacles and the Trap!" Spider-Man gives up trying to find Doctor Octopus—"Wherever he *is* . . . I guess he's *safe* for now! So I might as well head *home* and grab some *shut-eye!*" (3)—only to find that the villain has taken lodgings in Spider-Man's own home, with his Aunt May. And in "How Green Was My Goblin!," just as Aunt May's health takes a turn for the worse and needs protection from shocks, the Green Goblin succeeds in unmasking Spider-Man.

In Plato's dialogues, Socrates, "of all those whom we knew in our time, the bravest and also the wisest and most upright man" (*Phaedo* 118), is put to death by the city of Athens for corrupting its youth. The charge is that he taught the very kind of knowledge he in fact devoted his life to disclaiming, and which he disclaimed precisely for the sake of justice, so as not to mislead people or allow people to mislead themselves and one another (*Apology* 20Dff.). Like Spider-Man, he has always been suspected of being the menace he in fact opposes. "I have . . . been accused . . . by a great many people for a great many years, though without a word of truth" (18B). Both heroes, though they embody a fight for the light of justice and truth, are subjected to varieties of deep injustice and falsehood. And this is all the more poignant in that it is often their very struggle against injustice that contributes to bringing about the injustice towards themselves.

Like Spider-Man and his opponents, Socrates and his conversational partners also often set themselves up for a fall. Socrates frequently finds that he has overlooked something which brings all his efforts to nothing. At the end of the *Protagoras*, Socrates says, "the present outcome of our talk is pointing at us . . . the finger of . . . scorn," since Socrates, "having said at the beginning that virtue is not teachable, now is bent upon contradicting himself by trying to demonstrate that . . . virtue *is* teachable" (361A–B).[4] And his partners in discussion often boast about what they know but end up having to admit that they are lost. "I have spoken about virtue hundreds of times, . . . and very well too, or so I thought. Now I can't even say what it is," says Meno (*Meno* 80A–B). Euthyphro considers himself "far advanced" in wisdom, but when, at the end of the discussion, he sees that "we must go back again, and start from the beginning," he runs away. "Another time, then, Socrates, for I am in a hurry, and must be off this minute."[5]

On the other hand, both heroes also deliberately approach their lives by ironically undercutting their achievements. The attitude with which Spider-Man and his authors deal with his life is often an ironically flippant, self-trivialising humour. In "Spider-Man versus Doctor Octopus," for example, when Doctor Octopus recognises Spider-Man, calling out his name, he replies, "Well, I sure ain't Albert Schweitzer!" (7). In "Enter: Doctor Octopus!," when the versatile villain takes him by surprise, Spider-Man makes wry mid-fight comments like "*No fair* raising yourself up to *my* height!" (10). Again, in "Spidey Saves the Day!," Spider-Man describes his spider speed as "so *sublime*, I'm surprised no one's written a *sonnet* about it!" (16). In another issue, Spider-Man (and his ironically self-celebrating authors!) thinks to himself, while battling the Rhino, "I wonder if I *really* do this to preserve justice and to safeguard the human race—or, is it just that I love to hear the crazy *sound effects*?!" (Lee, et al., *Amazing Spider-Man* No. 41:17).

Similarly, in Plato's *Republic*, Socrates consistently presents his arguments for the necessity of pure, absolute knowledge as themselves limited, inadequate opinions: surely a means of *not* persuading an attentive audience. "If I could, I would show you . . . the very truth, as it appears to me—though whether rightly or not I may not properly affirm" (*Republic* 533A). When he describes the Idea of the Good, which, as we have seen, "gives their truth to the objects of knowledge and the power of knowing to the knower" (508D–E), Socrates is asked for his own view of it. He answers, "do you think it right to speak as having knowledge about things one does not know? . . . opinions divorced from knowledge . . . are blind" (506B–C). Again, although he condemns drama that imitates bad and uncontrolled characters (394Dff.), this kind of imitation is a frequent practice of his own and of his author's, even in this very dialogue. For example, the *Republic* begins with Socrates' report of a conversation he had with the intemperate and rude Thrasymachus: "Tell me Socrates, have you got a nurse? . . . Because she lets her little snotty run about driveling . . ." (343A). And while Plato's dialogues insist that we must seek to know, many if not all of them end in puzzlement, leaving the issues under discussion even more mysterious than when the dialogue began.

Plato starts the *Symposium* with characters who insist that philosophers are mad and so not worth listening to. We are told right at the beginning that Apollodorus, our narrator and a follower of Socrates, is known as "the maniac," and he himself says, "Of course . . . it's perfectly obvious why I have these views . . . it's simply because I'm a maniac, and I'm raving!" (173D–E). Socrates himself typically trivialises his own abilities and comments. In the *Protagoras*, for example, "There is just one small thing holding me back, which Protagoras I know will easily explain. . . ." (*Protagoras*, 328E) And in the *Cratylus*, if Socrates had "heard the fifty-drachma course of the great Prodicus . . . I should have been at once able to answer your question. . . . But, indeed, I have only heard the single-drachma course, and therefore I do not know the truth about such matters." [6] Alcibiades, who as Socrates' beloved has spent a great deal of time with him, insists that Socrates' "whole life is one big game—a game of irony" (*Symposium* 216E).

The message in both sets of works, I suggest, is twofold. On the one hand, the way to deal with reality truthfully and justly is by approaching it ironically, going towards it by heading in a different direction from it. And the reason for this is that reality itself is ironically organised, being itself by being different from itself. We have already encountered several examples of this ironic organisation. One is that our inadequacies are what make it meaningful to seek adequacy, so that goodness itself is not only opposed to but also partly composed of badness. Another is that the truth of particular things is separate from them *in being* the truth *of* them. An example we have met of the need to approach truth and justice ironically is that our desires and bodily senses are what motivate and allow us to move beyond our desires and bodily senses. And, more, that the way to adequacy and light is by grasping the worth *of* the inadequacies and shadows.

This is exactly what both Socrates and Spider-Man do: they embrace their limitations, and in the very act of doing so—*as* the very act of doing so—transcend them. This irony is so thorough that at bottom it undercuts even itself. We land up with both characters being utterly sincere in their ironic self-presentation. They really are limited by their inadequacies, just as they say. *And* they do successfully transcend them. *And* they transcend them *by*, ironically, being limited by them.

What is more, we, the reader/viewers, are drawn into the appeal of their ideals by the very ironies of their obvious limitations and absurdities. The erotic theme we have discussed is also a dimension of these ironies, just as the ironies are a dimension of the erotic theme.

There is another shared stylistic theme, which also ties the experience of the reader/viewer into the content of the two sets of works, and is also connected to sensual appeal as well as to the theme of human inadequacy: the theme of both works' central and incomplete reliance on sensory images.

4. IMAGES: WHAT WE SEE

In *Spider-Man* sensory images are of course the medium in which the comics are presented. But these images are inadequate, in at least two ways. First, they need the verbal language in the balloons and captions to achieve their specific messages, since otherwise they are too ambiguous and approximate. Second, they are obviously unreal: they are cartoon images. The authors even draw explicit attention to this invented unreality. "The Horns of the Rhino!," for example, contains captions like, "After struggling through the last panels, you can be sure . . . our story can't possibly move any *slower* from now on!" (2), and "Notice the sneaky way we change our scenes? Using Pete's last thought as a springboard, let's visit . . ." (10).

But the unreal, homely pictures in *Spider-Man*, partly *because* of their obvious lack of real correspondence to reality, are part of the attraction the work offers. And this attraction, as we have seen, is what allows us to appreciate what is worthwhile about the ideals the work presents. As Geoffrey O'Brien puts it, the "boxy little frames . . . have a quirky vigor and caricatural grace that let us know a live hand is tracing them, and when those scrawny miniature figures are forced to contend with moral dilemmas they acquire a quixotic stature. Such is the odd intimacy that comics can command" (O'Brien, 8). The unreal pictures, then, are part of the erotic appeal we have discussed. Their unreality gives us experience of the worth of the ideals that world presents.

We are drawn in to what is worthwhile partly by the continuing evidence of the unreality of the presentation: the cartoon pictures, the written-in sound effects, even the smell of the ink and the smudgy paper, all of which continuously connect our thoroughly human reality with the ideals which organise the story. Readers/viewers of the comics can testify that these sensory

experiences really are part of the delight in reading them. And Plato can testify that delight, like anything else, only happens for a reason. Even if we are
reacting to an illusion or to something which is really not delightful, that reaction can only happen because we grasp *what it is to be* delightful. Without that
grasp, we could not even react with delight by mistake. Delight happens, then,
because we grasp the idea of delight itself: the idea of goodness itself.

In reading the comics we take it for granted that what our senses are
reacting to is not the truth, but also that there is something worth reacting
to that the unreal images represent. In fact, the images are *so* unreal that we
cannot take them seriously at all, and consequently we really react, in a
sense, completely independently of them and their crudeness. We do not
even begin to believe that Spider-Man is really battling Doctor Octopus:
what we are reacting to is the presentation of struggle in a way abstracted
from what the pictures show. *Because* the pictures are clearly unreal, we
react to very pure "abstractions" separate from the pictures: victory itself,
justice itself, suspense itself. In Plato's language, we react to the separate
truth itself, ironically in and through our love for the sensuous and varying
appearances we experience *as untrue appearances*. And while it is true that
the reader/viewer is interested in no especially deep way in the suspense,
battles, satisfying violence, and is perhaps just entertained by them, *what it
is that* just entertains the reader is in fact all the deep "essences" of these
things, not any immediately experienced particular examples of them.

Less obviously than in *Spider-Man*, images are also central to Plato's dialogues. For one thing, Plato uses images to express his points extensively
throughout the dialogues. The allegory of the cave is one example, and the
charioteer of the soul another. But more strikingly, the dialogues themselves *are* images: they are presentations of various characters in imaginary
conversation. So, in fact, images are also the medium in which Plato's works
are presented. And these images are also inadequate, in two ways.

First, they are explicitly said to be inadequate to deliver the truth, in contrast with "lasting and unalterable" words (*Timaeus*, 29B). Socrates says, for
example, that "if I could, I would show you, no longer an image and symbol
of my meaning, but the very truth" (*Republic* 533A). The *Timaeus* explains
that images arise from the changing, becoming world of our senses, and so
will only allow "probabilities as likely as any others," not truth (29C–D). For
"that which is conceived by opinion with the help of sensation . . . is always

in a process of becoming and perishing and never really is" (27D–28A). In fact, the very world we experience through our senses "has been framed in the likeness of that which is apprehended by . . . mind and is unchangeable, and must therefore . . . be a copy of something"(29A–B). The natural world itself is only an image that "never really is," an inadequate image of the truth, so that what our senses experience, and words and ideas tailored to our senses—that is, images—are also inadequate.

Second, the images in which the dialogues consist, like those of the comic books, are unreal fictions. The dialogues themselves, again like the comics, also typically draw attention to their own unreality and unreliability. Their events may be reported, for example, through a chain of people who told people, or they may contain details from impossible combinations of dates. The "maniac" who narrates the *Symposium*, for instance, tells us he heard it from someone else who witnessed it about twenty years before (173B). And the characters in that dialogue refer to things which only occurred after their deaths, like the existence of a Theban army of lovers (178E). Even Socrates' own arguments, at the very time he makes them, are frequently a tale he heard, or perhaps a dream. In the *Theaetetus*, for example, he introduces an argument by saying, "Listen then to a dream. . . . In my dream . . . I thought I was listening to people saying . . ." (201D–E).[7]

For Plato, the true reality to which images, including everything we immediately experience, are inadequate, is found in the eternal, unified, self-consistent "separate forms." This is the famous Platonic ideal reality. But, as we have discussed, love of the ideal, of truth and justice, is love of the truth *of the temporal and sensual,* for the sake of the temporal and sensual. It is love truly of this person here, this city here. The truth of which we experience images through our senses is the truth *of those images,* of what we immediately experience. And both sides of this contradiction are true. The images are *also* still inadequate images: they are not the whole story of themselves at any given time. The side of the tree that we see is not the whole tree. In fact, *as* just the side we see it does not present *itself* accurately either: it is not really a two-dimensional surface. But—it also *is,* in fact, *the tree* that we are seeing as this side of it. The whole tree really *is* the truth of the side as which we are seeing it.

Putting these opposite things together, truth itself *is* in the particular things that do not fully coincide with it. Truth is divided from *itself,* separate from itself, at a distance from what it itself is. If one wants to express truth and reality with full accuracy, then, one has to do so by pointing partly away from it, by not capturing it fully. And this is exactly what images do. Images, in being *only* images, express the truth while not coinciding with it, while specifically *not* being it. And in that way they express truth *exactly*, down to its nature of not coinciding with itself. Ironically, images and sensory experience present truth and reality directly by noticeably not presenting it directly. Their inadequacy is in fact their perfect splendour.

In the end, then, it is *Spider-Man* that gives us the framework in which to read Plato and the meaning of life. The obvious unreality of the comics expresses what we easily miss in reading the "serious" philosophical dialogues, but which, I suggest, is really the central part of their message about truth and the sense that life makes.

Intuitively, it seems right to say that the reality and truth of the world around us is never complete, is at a distance from its complete version. There are always more possibilities of how things can be, and of what things there can be, always more in any particular thing to understand, always more aspects of things to take an interest in. But this "incompleteness" is not added on to reality as an extra piece. It is precisely the way the world we live in always is: reality *is what it is* partly *with* the always present possibility of more and new aspects and things. This "incompleteness" *is* a dimension of reality. It is, then, part of how reality is when it is fully itself, when it is in fact "complete."

Another intuitively clear example of the "separation" in reality itself lies in our sense of ourselves. When we reflect on ourselves, we take a distance from ourselves: and then we are what we are reflecting on, *and* what is doing the reflecting, *and* the distance between them. But this is not simply an activity we perform: as self-conscious creatures it is something we *are*. It is the reality of our consciousness. We can describe consciousness itself as that kind of awareness of itself, distance from itself.

Since reality does not simply coincide with itself, our relating to the unreality of images and of immediate experience *is* our fully experiencing the truth of reality. And not as what is beyond those images and that experience, but *as* their combination of reality and unreality itself. Differently expressed, recognising the separation of truth from itself, and struggling with that separation (since that struggle is what it requires, as a separation from the truth that we want to get to), and accepting and delighting in it (since as part of truth it *is* the truth we want to get to): all of this is our fully experiencing the sense of the world.

The evident unreality of Plato's dialogues and *Spider-Man* comics, then, their presence as made up here and now, is part of the sense of reality we need if we are to relate to the truth of reality. In a sense, *that* we react *as* we react to the comic books and to Plato's dialogues in all their unreality and appeal, that they are made up and that nonetheless we relate to them in the ways we do, is the theme of the comic books and the dialogues. It is what the books are about. And in its wonderful absurdity and meaningfulness, it is part of what reality is about.

NOTES

1. I am grateful to Jeff McLaughlin for his suggestions as to how to improve this essay. For any remaining faults, of course, the responsibility rests with gremlins.

2. A nice detail here is that "person of the beloved" translates "*idōn to erōtikon*": "the look or visual appearance of the love-worthy." "*Idōn*" is a version of "*idea*," the word Plato uses to mean the true reality (the Idea or Form), so that this passage is beautifully (!) ambiguous as to whether the true reality is in what one sees or separate from it. Harold Fowler translates it as "the love-inspiring vision." Plato, *Euthyphro, Apology, Crito, Phaedo, Phaedrus*, trans. Harold North Fowler (Cambridge: Harvard University Press, 1914) 253E.

3. Similarly, by the end of the *Meno* Socrates realises he has been overlooking something obvious: "absurdly enough, we failed to perceive . . ." (*Meno* 96E). And Socrates in the *Theaetetus*, "So, after going a long way round, we are back at our original difficulty." *Theaetetus*, trans. M. J. Levett, revised by Myles Burnyeat (Indianapolis: Hackett Publishing Company, 1992) 200A.

4. Plato, *Euthyphro*, trans. Lane Cooper, in *Collected Dialogues* 4B, 15C, 15E. Similarly, Ion begins by boasting that "I, of all men, have the finest things to say on Homer," but by the end Socrates observes, "you assure me that you have much fine knowledge about Homer, . . . but you will not even tell me what subject it is on which you are so able." *Ion*, trans. Lane Cooper, in *Collected Dialogues* 530C, 541E.

5. Plato, *Cratylus*, trans. Benjamin Jowett, in *Collected Dialogues* 384B–C. Similarly, in the *Euthyphro*, "It would seem, I must give in, for what could we urge who admit that, for our own part, we are quite ignorant about these matters?" (6B). In the *Meno*, "I'm a forgetful sort of person, and I can't say just now what I thought at the time" (71C). In the *Apology* Socrates insists that it will become "obvious that I have not the slightest skill as a speaker" (17B).

6. And in the *Meno*, "I have heard from men and women who understand the truths of religion . . ." (81A).

Modernity, Race, and the American Superhero

—ALDO REGALADO

"Faster than a speeding bullet! More powerful than a locomotive! Able to leap tall buildings in a single bound!" Although first broadcast over the radio in 1940, these three simple phrases continue to introduce millions of readers, listeners, and viewers to Superman, the first modern superhero (Daniels 54). By measuring Superman's powers against those of the bullet, the train, and the skyscraper, however, they also offer clues that hint at the cultural, social, and historical origins of this uniquely American phenomenon. Bullets, and the guns that fire them, conjure images not only of speed, but also of violence and power; violence and power employed in imperialist ventures both on the North American continent and abroad, as well as in urban crime and in law enforcement. The train, instrumental in conquering the West, essential to the expansion of American commerce, and a testament to the vast industrial capacity of the nation, became for many Americans of the late nineteenth and early twentieth centuries the ultimate symbol of modernity. Similarly, the skyscraper transformed American society, dwarfing the residents of already populous cities and housing within their walls a growing number of office workers who, according to many social critics, found their opportunities for personal freedom curtailed by the realities of mass market capitalism. Considered in this context, Superman, and the hundreds of superheroes that come after him, can be seen as affirming the primacy of a besieged humanity by transcending these forces of modernity.

Modernity, however, is far more ambiguous a challenge than the standard comic book supervillain. Indeed, its parameters have been defined and redefined by many scholars, including Jackson Lears, Robin Blackburn, Clark Kerr, Wilbert Moore, Arnold Feldmen, E. P. Thompson, Herbert Gutman, Walter Rodney, and Daniel Rodgers. As used in this essay, modernity refers to an on-going centuries long process involving the restructuring of humanity's relationship to nature, society, and the self. Enabled by the ascendance of increasingly impersonal global economic systems, the rise of industrial culture, and the movement of goods, people, and information resulting from innovations in communications and transportation technology, this process destabilizes pre-modern social systems, with their ties to place, religion, and local culture. In so doing, modern forces threaten to atomize communities and individuals, reducing human thought and action to quantifiable and manipulable objects harnessed to engines of production and profit. Scholars like Michel de Certeau, however, argue that despite the ubiquitous nature of modern social systems, the human will to resist these forces persists, and the cultural apparatus of modern culture itself provides a means for affirming the primacy of individual and communal identities.

Produced through the mass market, comic books can be counted among the cultural apparatus of modern culture, and the four-color marvels appearing in their pages arguably express popular longings to challenge and overcome the potentially atomizing, rationalizing, dehumanizing, and oppressive forces of urban industrial life. In this way, comic book superheroes can be seen as challenging modernity's claim that technological and economic progress equates moral progress. Comic book superheroes challenge the primacy of industrial technology over nature. They resist attempts to limit and scientifically manage personal conduct and other human action for the sole benefit of corporate capitalism, and they acknowledge, albeit in the spirit of carnival and laughter delineated by Mikhail Bakhtin, the corruption and violence that often enable the development of modern societies.

Such a reading of the social meaning of comic book superheroes, however, meets a strong challenge from critics who point to the conservative voices that often resonate in superhero fiction. Indeed, many might argue that in their efforts to turn a profit, the producers of superhero comic books are far from being agents of rebellion against western capitalism or established social orders. Instead, writers, artists, industry executives, and audiences have historically, although often unconsciously, employed an often divisive, exclusionary, and oppressive vocabulary of themes and images in the creation of characters, landscapes, and narratives that sell the dream, but not the reality, of individual liberation and social transgression. Of these discourses, none is more insidiously prevalent than that of race, as is evidenced by the overwhelming majority of white, muscled, male heroes that populate the genre, as well as by the negative stereotypes of Asians, Native Americans, African Americans, and other ethnic groups that often manifest in the face of comic book villainy.

How, then, should the transgressive potential of superhero fiction be understood in light of the genre's often racist underpinnings? The problem is complex, especially when one considers the foundational role played by racism in enabling modernity in America. Racism in America, after all, reached its most mature expression in the nineteenth-century, when it became a codified tool for legitimating slavery, the slaughter of Native Americans, westward expansion, exploitative labor practices, imperialist ventures overseas, and many more of the violently oppressive processes that made possible the accumulation of wealth and power that ultimately produced modern America (Blackburn 1–20). How, then, can creators and audiences possibly employ the racially defined figure of the superhero towards subversive ends? The answer lies in viewing race not as the essence of modernity, but rather as a language employed in defining and navigating its contours. Comic book creators and audiences engaged the language and imagery of race, either consciously or unconsciously, because it existed (and continues to exist) as part of their lived experience. Appropriating this racial language, comic book creators manipulated its contours, and employed it in giving voice to their own desires, fantasies, and longings. This process of appropriation, which has been explored by such scholars as Michel de Certeau, Janice Radaway, and Mikhail Bakhtin, brings with it the potential to subvert as well as to reaffirm traditional values, but always preeminent is the drive to affirm the humanity of individuals and groups in the face of restrictive and often violent social realities. Historically, however, this process of individual or group affirmation has often entailed an objectification or vilification of ethnically or racially defined others. This essay then endeavors to examine the possibilities and limitations of these life-affirming efforts, by tracing the historical interactions between super-hero fiction and changing notions of race in America, as influenced by the economic, political, and cultural changes wrought upon the nation by the rise of industrial modernity in the late nineteenth- and twentieth-centuries. In so doing, this study aims to offer insights that will help us understand not just the meaning of American superheroes, but also the social dynamics of popular culture, and the significance of race in America.

In order to grasp the relevance of race to American superhero comic books, one must first understand the significance of early American mass-market fiction, which largely established the themes and heroic paradigms later used in imagining the modern American superhero. Starting with mid-nineteenth-century dime novels, and continuing with early twentieth-century pulp magazines, the creators of cheap stories used themes of imperial expansion, industrial technology, revolutionary politics, and American blackface, employing them in expressing what was often a critical response to the realities of American modernity (Denning 1–5). While the list of cheap fiction writers who joined in this chorus is rather extensive, among the most popular and influential was Edgar Rice Burroughs, whose life is vividly chronicled by biographers Irwin Porges and John Taliaferro. In creating Tarzan, his most enduring character, this failed rancher and Indian fighter, who at the age of 35 found himself working as the frustrated man-ager of pencil sharpener salesmen, transformed himself into a successful and wealthy writer, while simultaneously creating a heroic paradigm that transcended the limitations that modern society placed upon him (Burroughs, *Autobiography*). Burroughs accomplished this by creating a character that touched on sensibilities he shared with millions of Americans, and thus Tarzan became a national sensation, appearing in magazines, books, and film. He also appeared in comic books, becoming one of the first adventure heroes translated to the sequential art form in the early 1930s. Key to the character's success was a creative strategy that com-pletely removed Tarzan from the offending presence of urban life. Attributing what Burroughs considered Tarzan's physical, intellectual, and moral perfection to his being raised in a fictionalized African jungle environment, Burroughs leveled a sharp criticism against modern urban

civilization, which he saw as a breeding ground for powerless and ineffectual men. This becomes evident in the following excerpt:

> With swelling breast, he [Tarzan] placed a foot upon the body of his powerful
> enemy, and throwing back his fine young head, roared out the awful challenge of
> the victorious bull ape. The forest echoed to the savage and triumphant paen.
> Birds fell still, and the larger animals and beasts of prey slunk stealthily away, for
> few there were of all the jungle who sought for trouble with the great anthropoids.
>
> And in London another Lord Greystoke was speaking to *his* kind in the
> House of Lords, but none trembled at the sound of his soft voice. (Burroughs,
> *Tarzan of the Apes* 135)

This juxtaposition of the savage Tarzan and his more genteel cousin accen-
tuates the ape-man's power, freedom, and competence, at the expense of
urban and civilized man, who is seen as soft, powerless, and effeminate.
Thus Burroughs engages the early twentieth-century "crisis in masculinity"
outlined by scholars Anthony Rotundo, Michael Kimmel, and Brenda Gail
Bederman, challenging the notion that modern man, with his access to
technology and modern economic, political, and cultural systems, is somehow inherently superior.

Although the Tarzan stories affirm the primacy of humanity in the face of
modern civilization, they do so, in part, by employing traditional racial
stereotypes. Having provided his hero with the ferocity, aggression, physical
prowess, and manliness that, in his estimation, was too often denied the desk
clerk of his age, Burroughs goes about defining Tarzan's moral qualities, by
contrasting him with the fictional African tribe led by Mbonga. Indeed, the
only thing separating these fictional natives from the great apes that raised
Tarzan is their agriculture and their use of weapons. Otherwise, like the great
apes, their defining cultural practice is that of cannibalism. It is on this basis
that Burroughs most clearly elevates Tarzan at the expense of the African.
After murdering the killer of his ape mother, Tarzan approaches the body
and, having been raised as a great ape, prepares to eat his kill. However,
before he can do so, he hesitates, and Burroughs gives us this fascinating
glimpse into the character of the ape-man.

> Did men eat men? Alas, he did not know. Why, then, this hesitancy! Once more
> he essayed the effort, but of a sudden a qualm of nausea overwhelmed him.

He did not understand. All he knew was that he could not eat the flesh of this black man, and thus hereditary instinct, ages old, usurped the functions of his untaught mind and saved him from transgressing a world-wide law of whose very existence he was ignorant. (Burroughs, *Tarzan of the Apes* 116)

If Tarzan is saved from committing this heinous act against humanity by a genetically transmitted morality, then by implication every man, woman, and child of Mbonga's village is not only morally inferior to Tarzan, but also sub-human.

Surprisingly, in his private life Burroughs seems to have been relatively tolerant in regards to race and ethnicity. In his unpublished autobiography, Burroughs reflects on his short stint in the U.S. military, noting the professionalism of the African American soldiers of the 24th Infantry and commenting that "their colored sergeants" were "without exception ... better to work under than our white sergeants" (Burroughs, *Autobiography*). In private letters he reflects on the interactions between his children and their Jewish and Catholic playmates, hoping that this inter-ethnic contact would contribute to overcoming the social intolerance evident in his day (Burroughs, *Letter to Harry*). In what was perhaps his most dramatic stand against racial and ethnic intolerance, Burroughs also spoke out publicly against the concentration-camp policy leveled at Japanese Americans by the U.S. government during WWII (Burroughs, *Hawaii Magazine*). Nevertheless, when constructing the heroic image of Tarzan, Burroughs tapped into the popular discourses on race evident in the minstrel shows, dime novels, and pseudo-scientific journals of his day (Denning 1–5; Horsman 1–6; Lott 78–88). Although he constantly stated that the only purpose of his writing was to entertain and to make money, the vocabulary of images most readily available to him for achieving these goals betrayed a broader insensitivity towards marginal individuals in American society, and resulted in a heroic icon that was expressly empowered by his genetic inheritance. Indeed, although Burroughs cried out against the very systems that legitimated a racially divided society, he remained largely uninterested in challenging racism itself. Instead, he appropriated the discourse of empire, transforming colonial spaces into literary playgrounds wherein fantasies of white power could be imagined and enacted. Furthermore, Burroughs treated the black bodies that inhabited such spaces with a strange mixture of awe and revulsion. Sensing something powerful and liberating in the stereotyped images of African savagery that appeared in both the elite and popular culture of his day, Burroughs largely defined Tarzan through an act of literary blackface, allowing the ape-man to appropriate the perceived savagery of black Africans. At the same time, Burroughs employed Tarzan in destructive fantasies, where the newly empowered white hero proves his superiority over the very blackness that he appropriates. Despite his unease with American imperialism and industrial modernity, then, Burroughs's fiction amounts to a form of literary empire, which perpetuates traditional notions of race in America.

Burroughs's creative voice, largely shaped by Anglo-Saxon, middle-class, masculine values and sensibilities, reached an expanded audience, as Tarzan made his way into film, and then into the flourishing comic book industry of the 1930s. The comic book industry, however, also allowed new voices to engage in the business of imagining American superheroes. Although similar to Burroughs in their efforts to transcend the restrictions of modernity, these new voices demonstrated subtle yet significant differences.

Such was the case with Jerry Siegel and Joe Shuster, the creators of the aforementioned Superman. Born to Jewish parents in 1914, Siegel and Shuster enthusiastically consumed and admired Burroughs's brand of science fiction and fantasy (Goulart 333). In many respects, they also felt the consequences of modernity far more acutely. While Burroughs's ethnic background granted him a socially and economically advantaged position from which to confront the modern world, Siegel and Shuster had to contend with the prevalent anti-Semitism evident in their day. Such prejudice must have exacerbated the difficulties these young men and their families faced during the Great Depression. Indeed, Siegel recalls that he grew up "knowing what it meant to be poor," and "knowing what it meant to be at the bottom and in need of help." "Superman," he continues, grew out of his "personal feelings about life," and from the need or desire to imagine someone "who would help the folks at the bottom. Superman came from the heart and not from the pocketbook" (Siegel, *San Diego Comic Con*).

If Superman came from the heart, then Siegel's creation betrayed his creator's frustration with modernity. Pitted against common criminals, corrupt politicians, violent husbands, and unruly foreign countries that threaten peace in the world, Superman transcends the restrictions of a corrupt and unsympathetic society, dispensing justice by dint of his amazing powers. Leaping over buildings, outrunning trains and automobiles, and bending steel in his bear hands, Superman also affirms his humanity in the face of a sprawling metropolis, whose very structures and massive size threaten to render the individual insignificant. Indeed, a cursory examination of the first year of Superman stories reveals a pervasive theme of human triumph over modern technology and urban architecture. The famous cover of *Action Comics* No. 1, for instance, portrays Superman hefting a car over his head, and smashing it to pieces against a rock. Although this image figured into the plot of the story within the comic, Superman often appeared in similar poses, completely divorced from the tales featured in the magazines. This is the case on the first page of *Action Comics* No. 7, which features the Man of Steel casually lifting a passenger filled trolley over his head. Similarly, the first page of *Action Comics* No. 8 presents a dramatic scene wherein the red and blue clad vigilante leaps over a moving bus as passengers marvel at his incredible abilities. Sometimes, the images are more overtly violent. In another instance completely unrelated to story, Superman triumphs over the instruments of mechanized warfare, as he crumples a tank to pieces, and in *Action Comics* No. 12, Siegel and Shuster gave us a glimpse of a more needlessly destructive Superman who, for no apparent reason, is pictured on the outskirts of a thriving metropolitan center, tearing down a suspension bridge by one of its main cables.

Superman, however, did not merely embody humanity's triumph over mechanized urban society. In addition, Superman evinced and reaffirmed the spirit of New Deal politics, with its ideals of social justice. Far from being an extension of official authority and culture, Superman often worked at odds with authority figures, fighting political and urban corruption. Although a consistent theme throughout Superman's early run, the Man of Steel's New Deal values manifest most clearly in *Action Comics* No. 11, when Superman investigates the death of a man who commits suicide after buying phony oil stock from a pair of unscrupulous businessmen named Meeks and Brosnon. Angered by this injustice, Superman dons the guise of investor Homer Ramsey, and buys a significant amount of stock in Meeks and Bronson's oil company. Then, using his abilities, he causes their once phony drilling operation to erupt with newly discovered oil. When Meeks and Bronson try to have Ramsay killed in order to maximize their own profits, Superman easily dispenses with their henchmen before suddenly agreeing to sell his stock back to the businessmen for one million dollars. Upon collecting the money, he returns to the oil derricks and tears them down, bankrupting Meeks and Bronson. At this point, Superman admonishes the businessmen, telling them "quit selling stock, or I'll pay you another visit!—From now on, stick to selling shoe-laces!" Issues later, Superman demonstrates the proper way to use capital when he donates the million dollars he swindled from Meeks and Bronson to Kidtown, a rehabilitation camp for wayward boys. Thus, Superman directly engaged the terms of modernity in America, embodying popular longings to challenge the inequities of its systems of corporate capitalism.

However, Siegel and Shuster's Superman defied anger, tackling oppression and affirming his identity with unbridled optimism. "Superman," Siegel reminds us, "was always having fun, even when he was kicking airplane squadrons from here to there" (Siegel, *San Diego Comic Con*). Although Siegel and Shuster never called for a new world order, and never styled themselves social revolutionaries, their Superman stories did tackle the realities of the world, transforming fear into hope, hate into laughter, and otherwise dispelling realities that loomed over the heads of these two creators and millions of their readers.

Although Superman shares Tarzan's concerns over the consequences of modern technology and culture, the two differ in one very significant way. Tarzan is a genetically pure Anglo-Saxon, and Superman is not. Rocketed to Earth as an infant from his home planet, Krypton, Superman is an immigrant. As such, he discreetly challenges the notion that only racially pure Anglo-Saxons could be powerful symbols of masculine prowess and human perfection. While phenotypically Superman meets American standards of whiteness, he successfully broadens its definition to include foreign-born immigrants, as long as they make an effort to assimilate into American mainstream culture and use their talents to contribute to society. Given the ethnic prejudices held by many Americans of their day, the creative voices of Siegel and Shuster, who were themselves the children of immigrant Jews, contributed a subtle but significantly different sensibility to the construction of superhero images.

A few years later, a young Jewish man named Jacob Kurtzberg, working under the name Jack Kirby, lent his voice to the creation of superhero images with similar results. Like Siegel and Shuster, Kirby grew up reading, and was deeply influenced by, the fiction of Edgar Rice Burroughs (Goulart 219). Also like Siegel and Shuster, Kirby faced anti-Semitism and the scarcity of the Great Depression. For Kirby, however, the ugliness of the world seemed compounded by the urban violence he witnessed while growing up in the lower East Side, by his knowledge of the German Jewish fate at the hands of Hitler, and by intimations that the U.S. would become involved in the Second World War. Once the latter happened, Kirby's perspective on the world was further influenced by his experiences on the battlefield. In 1940, Kirby and his collaborator, Joe Simon, tackled these issues by inventing Captain America (Goulart 219–20). Although at the time comic book writers shied away from specifically condemning Nazi Germany, preferring instead to make vague references to unspecified foreign aggressors, Kirby and Simon pitted their star-spangled superhero against Hitler on the cover of their first issue (Simon and Kirby, *Captain America* front cover). In so doing, Kirby and Simon led the charge for the dozens of similarly clad superheroes that emerged during the war, and thus significantly shaped wartime propaganda. Despite its social and political commentary, Kirby's fiction was designed primarily to entertain and to transform an otherwise dull, dangerous, frightening, and violent world into one that is exciting, optimistic, and empowering. Kirby enunciated this when he addressed the issue of comic book violence in a 1976 interview for the fanzine *Nostalgia*:

I know there's violence but I like to show violence in a graceful way, a dramatic way, but never in its true way. I just don't like to look at it that way. There is something stupid in violence as violence. There's something stupid about jealousy; there's something even stupider about love. In other words, we have to take a basic mineral and make something out of it. Now basic violence is stupid because I was in war and I saw the results of it.... I used to walk around and watch the dead bodies in the field and the dead cows and the dead kids and the dead houses and the dead fields and that dead sky. There was smoke all over and you couldn't see the sky. It was just stupid. It got to the point where I couldn't walk in that kind of atmosphere anymore. I feel that we shouldn't degenerate to that level. I can't. I won't take violence in that form even if it is the truth.... I feel what I'm doing in my comics is violent, but my kind of violence. I feel dancing is a kind of violence. I feel any kind of movement is violence in a lesser degree. But violence, basic raw violence in which violence is inflicted in a mindless terrible way, I can't see. I won't look at it and I won't tolerate it and I won't put it in my drawings. I'll show a reaction. I'll show a splat or a bang. Now you'll see a guy flying and you'll see him go through a house, but you'll never see him hurt or you'll never see the house completely destroyed. You'll notice there is no realism in anything I do because they are things as I like to see them. I just like to see them that way; that's my bag and it's my fantasy. You want to sue me, great. (Kirby, *Nostalgia* 26)

Just as Kirby's creative voice echoes the cry to transform the world into one that is decent, safe, and that otherwise dignifies the human condition, it also has a specific resonance in regards to racial discourse in America. Like Tarzan and Superman, Captain America's alter ego, Steve Rogers, is phenotypically white. Unlike Tarzan and Superman, however, the specifics of his ethnicity are left ambiguous. All we know is that he is an American. Since names are mutable, as evidenced by Jacob Kurtzberg/Jack Kirby, even Captain America's seemingly Anglo-Saxon name reveals little of the character's ethnicity. Also unlike Tarzan and Superman, Steve Rogers is not possessed of a hereditary manly prowess. Instead, Rogers is born so weak and fragile that he is rejected for military service. However, impressed by his patriotism, government officials offer to enroll him in a secret super-soldier program, and, after being injected with the super-soldier serum, Rogers is transformed into the paragon of human physical and mental perfection. In so doing, Kirby and Simon broaden the concept of what it means to be an American superhero by suggesting that allegiance to nation, not ethnic origins, is the source of masculine empowerment.

Kirby's influence continued to be felt. Starting in the 1960s, Kirby became among the most influential artists and writers in comic books. Co-creating such characters as the Fantastic Four, the Silver Surfer, the Incredible Hulk, the Mighty Thor, and the Avengers, Kirby helped lay the foundation upon which Marvel Comics was built (Goulart 219–20). However, comic books, like all popular culture, are not only influenced by the voices of individual creators. They are also influenced by the innumerable voices that resonate in society as a whole, and starting in the 1950s, a powerful chorus rose up in America and commingled with the individual voices of Jack Kirby and co-creator Stan Lee, resulting in one of the most innovative characters in all of comic book history. The chorus was that of the Civil Rights Movement, and the character is the first African superhero, the Black Panther.

Given that the Black Panther was a response to the outrage voiced against centuries of racial oppression, and that popular culture was increasingly the target of this public outcry, the inversion of the Tarzan image evident in the Black Panther's origin story should come as no surprise. Like many Tarzan movies and most Tarzan novels, the first Black Panther story features an unscrupulous white man coming to Africa in search of exploitable resources only to be stopped by a self-styled "King of the Jungle." In this case, the white adventurer is American Ulysses Klaw. The resource is vibranium, a fictional extra-terrestrial ore found only in the equally fictional African country of Wakanda. In his efforts to obtain the vibranium he desires, Klaw kills the reigning Wakandan king. The King's adolescent son, T'Challa, avenges his father's death by vanquishing Klaw and securing the safety of his people, the sovereignty of his nation, and his own kingship. T'Challa then studies at the best European and American schools, returns to his homeland with a degree in physics, and, after completing a series of trials that culminate in his obtaining a secret heart-shaped herb that grants him great physical abilities, prepares to lead Wakanda to greater industrialization and wealth. In constructing the Black Panther, Kirby and Lee drew heavily from the heroic formula popularized by Burroughs, yet they altered it significantly, presenting their readers with a Black character that matches Tarzan in physical ability, and arguably surpasses him as an intellectual and as a leader of men. In the Black Panther's first appearance, which took place in *Fantastic Four* No. 52, Stan Lee implicitly connects T'Challa to the legacy of Burroughs's famous ape-man, by having the character of Ben Grimm refer to the Wakandan King as "some refugee from a Tarzan movie." Indeed, this first issue possesses more than a hint of the noble savage stereotype so common in popular literature from the nineteenth and early twentieth centuries. Nevertheless, such images are rapidly inverted, and by the following issue the Black Panther emerges as a powerful ally to the Fantastic Four, proving every bit the equal to the white heroes. Interestingly, what largely signifies the Black Panther's worthiness and sophistication is his scientific and technological acumen. Unlike Superman and Tarzan, whose original expressions embody longings to either escape or defeat technology, the Black Panther uses technology, employing it to create:

> . . . A world of sheer wonderment! . . . It's a strange new land . . . hidden from above by a concealing cover of giant trees. It's truly a jungle . . . but like nothing ever spawned by nature! It's a man-made jungle! . . . The entire topography and

flora are electronically-controlled mechanical apparatus! The very branches about us are composed of delicately constructed wires . . . while the flowers which abound here are highly complex buttons and dials! Even bolders can be heard to hum with the steady pulse of computer dynamos! (Lee and Kirby, *Fantastic Four* 39)

Thus T'Challa creates a social environment that is technologically advanced, yet respectful of both tradition and nature.

As evidenced in the above passage, Kirby and Lee use technology as a signifier of T'Challa's sophistication, but in so doing they embrace modern notions of civilization that conflate technological innovation with an individual's or a people's worthiness. Thus Kirby and Lee obscured the legacy of Western culture, which brought slavery and colonialism to the African continent. Furthermore, as the Black Panther continued to make appearances in Marvel Comics' line of superhero titles, T'Challa's ties to Wakanda became secondary, and he increasingly served as companion or sidekick for white heroes and superhero teams, such as Captain American and the Avengers. Despite such portrayals, the Black Panther's subversive potential remained.

Although the character receded into obscurity in the early 1990s, Marvel Comics revived the Black Panther in 1998 with a new monthly title written by Christopher Priest. In this series, Priest adds new dimension to the critique of modern society evident in superhero comic books since their inception. Whereas earlier stories featuring the character obscured the connections between forms of racial oppression and modern economic and political systems, Priest weaves a complex story of international intrigue that blends the two themes in poignant ways. In so doing, he creates a narrative that presents the potentially destructive, predatory, and ruthless nature of global capitalism, hints at the legacy of Western colonialism in the African continent, and demonstrates the connections between these global systems and American domestic society and culture.

In his first story, for instance, Priest introduces Everett K. Ross, a new character who establishes the casually racist attitude held by many Americans towards Africa and her people. A young white officer from the U.S. State Department, Ross is assigned to serve as liaison to T'Challa during the King's visit in the United States. Over the course of the first issue, he quickly betrays his ignorance of things outside his privileged existence. Driving through an inner city neighborhood on his way to meet T'Challa at the airport, for instance, he comments, "Oddly enough, nobody was singing, which really disturbed me. I mean, on TV, there was all this SINGING in the ghetto. I was made to believe people sang here, and that singing would often spin out into these big production numbers. I'd been lied to" (Priest 2). Ross's pop culture understanding of inner city life also emerges in his speech, which is peppered with popular hip-hop terms that he employs to structure his understanding of the world, as well as his own sense of identity. The limitations of his pop culture education lead Everett K. Ross, the self proclaimed "Superfly," "Midnight Warrior," and "Emperor of Useless White Boys," to underestimate T'Challa's importance (Priest 3–4). Reasoning that T'Challa merely "hangs out at the Avengers Mansion" and "orders up some ribs," Ross dismisses his assignment, and arrives at the airport in his Miata woefully unprepared to handle the King's entourage (Priest 28). Ross's casual racism serves to illuminate the ways in which both popular and official culture work together in the West to misinform readers and audiences about African and African American communities, and their place in the world. Priest, however, presents Ross as a likable character, and maintains him as the series' narrator, an everyman who vindicates his initial racist ignorance by growing through his contact with the Black Panther.

These themes quickly manifest more prominently in the series as Priest explores the place of Wakanda in the fictional world of the Marvel Universe. Situating the African nation in the context of Western colonial and post-colonial policies regarding Africa, Priest imagines Wakanda as a nation on the defensive, constantly guarding against the modern and global forces that threaten its sovereignty. Not only do these forces threaten the internal stability of Wakanda, setting up corrupt African governments, causing ethnic skirmishes, and creating divisions between city-dwellers and rural tribesmen, but the Black Panther's homeland also becomes the target of American national security forces, backed by multi-national corporations, who attempt to takeover the Wakandan government. Highlighting these themes, Priest reinvents the Black Panther's past in issue No. 30 of the series, using retroactive continuity to reveal that the Black Panther originally allied with the Fantastic Four, Captain America, and the Avengers as a means of spying on potential threats to his sovereignty. His themes thus established, Priest opens the door for questioning global economic systems, the nature and consequences of American foreign policy, and the social dimensions of those systems, which underpin often invisible or unspoken assumptions based on race.

Nevertheless, the genre of superhero comics resists becoming a vehicle for unmitigated political or social commentary, and despite its dealing with such diverse social issues, the Black Panther is just as often employed in reaffirming human freedom in the face of social constraints and official authority. Although Priest's T'Challa grapples with the aforementioned issues more than any other incarnation of the character, his Black Panther is just as often involved in the carnivalesque adventures that define the superhero genre. Even those stories, however, seem to evince an emancipatory impulse that pervades superhero comics in general. The following quote, taken from an earlier but equally weighty incarnation of the Black Panther, demonstrates this effectively:

> For one moment, he is free! For one moment, there is only the molten dawn sun lighting the sky a poet red and the air racing coolly past him as he drops in free form flight. For this one moment, he does not have to be the Black Panther! As he leaps, with graceful precision, a human paragon of the animal he is named after, he does not have to be T'Challa, King of the Wakandas, either—and as he flexes and springs fluidly from one rocky outcropping to the next, the burdens of nobility are fleetingly lifted. And then he lands at the bottom of the precipice . . . and the moment ends . . . and he is once more all those things. (McGregor 1)

It is in this way that the Black Panther shares most in common with Captain America, Superman, and even Tarzan. All of these characters allow creators and readers alike to confront harsh realities and contentious issues, such as racism, violence, war, drudgery, and poverty, elevating them to a plane where they can be understood, dissected, disarmed, and rethought through laughter, enjoyment, pleasure, and honest dialogue. Superhero comics, like most comics, playfully challenge the world to be different, without necessarily seeking to subvert established social realities through politics. Instead, they present new ideas for consideration, but they do so in an often-contradictory fashion. Although issues such as race should be acknowledged as active discourses within the genre, superhero comics should not be understood as a medium concerned only with such issues. More often than not, superhero comics are more concerned with satisfying the need for humanity to laugh in the face of adversity and to imagine an optimistic future. This laughter is a human chorus that resonates with the voices of all that participate, and its history is as vast as its audience. To properly understand this laughter, it is necessary to take a historical approach, searching for the nuanced changes that it undergoes as new voices join in the chorus overtime. By doing so, we begin to untangle the multiple and ever changing meanings evident in super-hero comic books, and thus come closer to understanding the nature of American popular culture.

Deconstructing the Hero

—IAIN THOMSON

Obviously, if you're going to be doing something new, then to a degree you're destroying—[Laughs]—whatever preceded it.

—ALAN MOORE (Kavanagh, 2000)

But by my love and hope I beseech you: Do not throw away the hero in your soul! Hold holy your highest hope!

—FRIEDRICH NIETZSCHE (tr. by Kaufmann, 156)

Our identities as individuals and as groups are shaped, in ways both subtle and profound, by our heroes. If our enemies (and the other "villains" in our psychic narratives) help give us a sense of who we are *not*, of what we stand *against*, then, conversely, our heroes help tell us who we *are*, what we stand *for*.[1] Indeed, as Heidegger recognized, the heroes we choose focus our common sense of what is most important in life, shaping our feel for which battles we should fight as well as how we should go about fighting them. Thus those who chose Martin Luther King Jr. as their hero, for example, pursued very different goals, and pursued them in a very different manner, than those who heroized Adolph Hitler.[2] Despite the obvious differences, however, in both cases the chosen hero functioned like a mirror, reflecting back to the group an idealized image of itself, an ideal concentrated and so given an almost *superhuman* form. What happens, then, when we *shatter* these mirrors? What does it mean when we seek not just to destroy our heroes—to gleefully expose their feet of clay, their human, all-too-human failings—but to *deconstruct* the very idea of the hero?[3] Does this deconstruction of the hero argue for—or against—the historical dispensability of the hero? Why do Enlightenment thinkers, existentialists, and postmodernists give such different answers to this question? What is at stake in their disagreement?

In pursuit of these questions, we will follow a perhaps surprising itinerary, one which leads back to the masterworks of the great existentialists by way of a postmodern comic book.[4] Written by Alan Moore and illustrated by Dave Gibbons, *Watchmen* is best known as the comic book with which comic books "grew up."[5] *Watchmen* helped accomplish this coming of age, not—as in the romantic *Bildungsroman* tradition which stretches back to *Beowulf* and Homer's *Odyssey*—by celebrating the *development* of its heroes, but rather by developing its heroes precisely in order to *deconstruct* the very idea of the hero, overloading and thereby shattering this idealized reflection of humanity and so encouraging us to reflect upon its significance from the many different angles of the shards left lying on the ground.

I. SHATTERING: FRAGMENT OF A *BILDUNGSROMAN*

With *Watchmen*, comic books came of age, and, in a sense (a coincidence which is not merely coincidental), we grew up together. During 1986–87, while *Watchmen* was being published, I was an 18 year-old freshman at UC Berkeley, living in overcrowded dorms and working part-time at the Best of Two Worlds, a once great but now defunct comic book store on Telegraph Avenue, right around the corner from the legendary "People's Park". Although I tried to play it cool, this was a dream job for me, as some of my most memorable childhood pilgrimages had been to this very store. To get there, my younger brother and I had to convince one of our parents to drive us (sometimes with a lucky friend or two) from Davis (ninety long minutes away) to Berkeley, where, after being dropped off (always for too brief a time), we hurried past pan-handlers, drug-pushers, mentally-ill homeless (quite obviously off their medications), street artisans and performers, plus a wide assortment of colorful locals (I later learned some of their names—the

Bubble Lady, Polka-Dot Man, Hate-Man—they sounded like tragically fallen heroes and were embraced by the counter-cultural Berkeley community as anti-heroes), all of whom seemed completely unlike anyone we had ever seen before. As a result, the Best of Two Worlds felt like it was located in the eye of a slightly threatening and deeply intriguing storm called "Berkeley." [6]

The owner of the Best of Two Worlds—despite being, as comic collectors might say, "a few issues short of a complete run"—knew exactly what he was doing when he hired me; like most of the core staff I took much of my salary in comics, which meant (because of the difference between wholesale prices and employee discounts) that we were actually paid very little, and the store benefited from the combined expertise of a group of hardcore comic book fans. Growing up, I was the kid that the owners of the local comic book shop called when they were unable to answer some customer's question; now I was surrounded by comic experts who knew at least as much as I did. (It was here that I first found that concentration of intellectual talent I had expected from UC Berkeley itself, but did not encounter there until I started taking advanced political theory and philosophy courses.) We employees each had our areas of particular expertise; as befitted a small-town boy, mine was superhero comics. One of the older employees—a diffident artist who exuded that air of bitter superiority any fan of *The Simpsons* would recognize from Matt Groening's grotesque but knowing caricature ("Worst. Episode. Ever.")—took a perverse pleasure in turning me on to *Watchmen*, which was then coming out each month.

To begin to imagine the impact of *Watchmen* on die-hard superhero comics fans like me, visualize a train-wreck taking place in twelve monthly installments. I may not then have recognized *Watchmen* as a deconstruction of the hero, but certainly I realized (with that combination of horror and fascination known to rubberneckers everywhere) that here my precious heroes were being *shattered* before my very eyes, taken apart from the inside-out, in the pages of the medium that had always loved and cared for them, and in a style that demonstrated an obvious mastery of this medium that it now set out to implode. As I sift once again through the rubble, it is, moreover, clear to me—for to reread *Watchmen* is to be stunned once again by the brutal clarity of this masterful deconstruction of the hero—that Moore and Gibbons knew exactly what they were doing.

II. REREADING, RETROACTIVE DEFAMILIARIZATION, AND THE UNCANNY

Perhaps the first thing one realizes upon rereading *Watchmen* is that it *requires* rereading. *Watchmen* was written to be reread; indeed, it can only be read by being reread.[7] That may sound paradoxical, but upon rereading *Watchmen* it becomes painfully obvious that the meanings of almost every word, image, panel, and page are multiple—*obviously* multiple.[8] In *Watchmen*, the meanings are primarily multiplied by the fact—and this is painfully obvious when one finishes the series and then rereads it—that, from the first panel (a blood-stained smiley-face, looking like a clock counting-down to midnight, floating in a gutter of blood), the parts all fit into a whole one grasps only in the end (although in retrospect the hints are everywhere).[9] Because that end is so unsuspected and surprising (I will spoil it in the next section), the parts are given a new and different meaning by their place in it. This new meaning, moreover, immediately strikes home as the true meaning of the work, thereby subverting and displacing the first reading.

Rereading *Watchmen*, we thus undergo the same kind of *retroactive defamiliarization* we experience when, rereading Aeschylus's *Oresteia*, we blushingly realize that on our first reading we had been taken in, along with King Agamemnon himself, by the beautiful duplicity of Queen Clytemnestra's early speeches, for now we recognize that her artful words, seductive on a first reading, drip with venom on a second. Or, to use a more recent example, we experience the same kind of retroactive defamiliarization when, viewing M. Night Shyamalan's *The Sixth Sense*, we share the protagonist's stunning realization that he himself is a ghost, a realization which displaces and reorients our entire sense of the film. (Of course, one does not need actually to re-view *The Sixth Sense*—to view it twice—since Shyamalan, apparently not trusting his audience, embeds a reviewing within it, in the form of a series of flashbacks. Thanks to this rather heavy-handed move—which, to be fair, only Aeschylus never condescends to make—to view *The Sixth Sense* is already to re-view it.) In Moore's *Watchmen*, Aeschylus's *Oresteia*, and Shyamalan's *The Sixth Sense*, rereading effects this retroactive defamiliarization by undermining and displacing the familiar sense that emerged from and guided the first "reading," changing our minds about what we thought we understood by leading us to recognize that in fact we had not understood what we thought we understood.

With such retroactive defamiliarization, we experience what Heidegger called the "uncanny" (*unheimlich*, literally, "unhomelike"). Although this is often overlooked, we can only experience this uncanniness (this *Unheimlichkeit* or sense of "not-being-at-home") somewhere that we have first been at home. One's *first* reading of a new text, like one's first visit to a new city or one's first date with a new person, might be strange, different, disorienting, even anxiety-provoking, but it cannot be *uncanny*. The uncanny emerges only with "rereading," when what seemed familiar suddenly becomes strange—and *estranging*; it is as if we are gripped by that upon which we have lost our grip. (Here I am using "rereading" in the broad Derridean sense, which applies to the lives we lead as well as the texts we more literally "read," since, as Derrida provocatively put it, "there is nothing but text.") When rereading uncanny works, we find ourselves no longer at home in our first reading; we realize that the first reading was not a "reading" properly so-called, since (we now realize) we had not yet understood the text on that first reading, although we assumed, of course, that we did understand it, and so we learn (or at least are encouraged to learn) to become more reflective about the course that we have been following with unreflective self-assurance. Shattering this self-assurance—with the realization that we were ignorant of our own ignorance—has been, since Socrates at least, one of the first pedagogical steps (and stumbling blocks) of the philosophical education.[10]

Uncanny works, moreover, in that they must be reread in order to be *read*, teach us something fundamental about reading itself, namely, that at least some of the great works survive and perpetuate themselves not by statically maintaining eternal truths, or even simply by offering successive generations the same experience again and again, but rather by being deep enough—that is, resonant enough, *meaningful* enough—to continue to generate new readings, even those revolutionary rereadings which radically reorient our original sense of the work. It was by helping to effect just such a revolutionary reorientation of the entire genre of superhero comic books that *Watchmen* established itself as a great work, a work of postmodern deconstruction. This means that *Watchmen* is not only a work of rereading, a work that we have to reread simply in order to read, but that *Watchmen* itself has to be understood as a rereading of the history of comic books.

Watchmen gives us a revisionary history that asks (as one astute observer put it), "What would have happened to us if costumed heroes had appeared in reality around the same time they appeared in the American pop consciousness?" [11]

III. DECONSTRUCTION, THE UNHAPPY REALIZATION OF FANTASY, AND NIHILISM

The animating idea in the background of *Watchmen* is as simple as it is compelling: What if superheroes were real? What would it *really* be like if comic book heroes walked among us? By taking this question with deadly seriousness, *Watchmen* shows that previous comics in fact failed to do so. Yes, Peter Parker had his share of personal problems, but he (let alone his impact on his world) only seems real until one reads *Watchmen*. If, moreover, the *Spider-Man* movie did a surprisingly good job of seeming real (and so helping to suspend the disbelief of its audience), this was thanks not only to the inspired casting of the main character (Tobey Maguire had already established a Peter Parker—like screen persona in *The Ice Storm* and *Wonder Boys*), it was also because the movie seems to have been influenced by a recent re-telling of *Spider-Man* which is itself part of a series of deliberately *realist* reprisals (namely, Marvel's "Ultimate" versions of its most famous comics), a series inspired in large part by the dark realism of *Watchmen*. (Thus, however ungenerous the sentiment, Moore is not entirely wrong when he denigrates such work as *Watchmen*'s "deformed bastard grandchildren.")[12]

In effect, *Watchmen* makes the case that if our superhero fantasies were realized, our world would be radically altered, and not for the better. In this way it asks us, "Which world would you rather live in?" [13] In the alternative reality which forms the backdrop for *Watchmen*, America won the Vietnam war (with the help of the earth's only super-powered hero, "Dr. Manhattan"); Nixon was never impeached, since an especially right-wing hero ("The Comedian") killed Woodward and Bernstein; there are no longer any superhero comics (apparently no one wants to read about them in a world with actual superheroes; in fact, many ordinary people hate these heroes, who they perceive, correctly in most cases, as right-wing pawns of a repressive government); instead, very dark Pirate comics now dominate the market (in this reality, unlike our own, no censoring "comics code" was ever imposed because the government protected the genre which had spawned the heroes upon whom it became politically dependent); the cold war is being won by America, thanks to our super-powered being (Dr. Manhattan); unfortunately, this American "superman" (or "God") has Russia terrified about its chances of survival, so when Dr. Manhattan decides to leave the earth (humanity having become no more interesting to this him than ants are to us), an atomic world war (and planet-destroying nuclear holocaust) seems imminent.[14] It is a bleak vision, to be sure, but one made entirely compelling by the unprecedented wealth of background detail Moore and Gibbons deftly weave into the story.

Moore did not need Jean Baudrillard (perhaps the greatest of the post-modern philosophers) to tell him that "the idea is destroyed by its own realization," that the "extreme" development of an idea (which takes that idea beyond its own limits, end, or terminus, into "a state of ex-termination") can thereby destroy it—as, for example, sex is destroyed by "porn," which is "more sexual than sex"; the body by "obesity," which is "fatter than fat"; violence by "terror," which is "more violent than violence"; information by "simulation," which is "truer than true"; time by "instantaneity," which is "more present than the present," and as, in *Watchmen*, the hero is destroyed by the superhero, who is more heroic than any hero, but whose extreme "heroics" are no longer recognizable as *heroics*.[15] Moore seems instinctively to know (or else he has, like *Watchmen*'s Ozymandias, studied "a hundred different philosophies") that one of the most powerful deconstructive strategies involves provisionally accepting an idea, thesis, position, or worldview, then working from inside it to extend it beyond its limits until it is eventually made to collapse under its own weight, like a plant forced to bear fruit too heavy for its own branches.[16] I would call this strategy *hypertrophic deconstruction* (after Nietzsche, who recognized that "a hypertrophic virtue . . . may bring about the decay of a people as much as a hypertrophic vice." Preuss 8). *Watchmen* deconstructs the hero by developing its heroes—extending traditional hero fantasies beyond their limits—to the point where the reader comes to understand that these fantasies, realized, become nightmares.

Watchmen begins, tellingly, with the hero "Rorschach," a hypertrophic development of the Batman archetype. Batman himself, of course, was

already a later version of *The Shadow*, a character drawn from the notoriously gritty, "detective" genre of pulp fiction.[17] With Rorschach, however,
Moore gives us such an extreme version of the archetypal "hard-nosed
detective" character that not only Bogart but the entire *film noir* genre (even
such John Woo films as *The Killer*) look squeaky clean by comparison.
Watchmen's intentionally shocking first words establish this dark and violent mood: "Rorschach's Journal. October 12th, 1985: Dog Carcass in alley
this morning, tire tread on burst stomach. This city is afraid of me. I have
seen its true face."[18] As this notion of "seeing" the "true face" already hints,
Rorschach takes his name (and his mask, which he views as his own true
"face") from the famous "ink-blot test" in which a psychiatrist asks an
analysand to interpret an image that has no meaning of its own, in order to
gain access to the analysand's unconscious as it is revealed in the meanings
the analysand *projects* onto the image (*Watchmen* V. 18 .vi–vii). By opening
(and "closing") the comic with Rorschach, Moore implies that comic book
heroes are projections of the fantasies of their readers—as well as their
authors.[19] *Watchmen*'s development of Rorschach as a character makes
clear Moore's contention that these wishful superheroic fantasies of power
stem not just from a deep fear that we are powerless to live up to our own
ideals, but also from an even deeper fear that these ideals themselves are
mere *projections* with which we cover over and so conceal from ourselves
"the real horror" that "in the end" reality "is simply an empty meaningless
blackness."[20] Thus we learn, for example, that Rorschach was driven to
become a "masked hero" by the neglect, abuse, and abandonment he suffered as a foster child, that his right-wing ideology is itself a construction
with which he tries in vain to please a father he never knew, and that the real
evil he encountered soon after putting on his mask led him to reject his
humanity for his mask and so become empty, a blank onto which others
would project their own fears—becoming, in philosophical terms, a *nihilist*.
(As Rorschach puts it, "Existence is random, [it] has no pattern save what
we imagine after staring at it for too long. No meaning save what we choose
to impose"). Although Moore presents us here with one of *Watchmen*'s brilliantly twisted versions of the "secret origins" device common to all superhero comics, Rorschach's *nihilism*—his defining conviction that reality is
ultimately meaningless—cannot simply be dismissed as a symptom of the
personal psychological traumas that led him to become a "hero."

Instead, Moore presents nihilism as a psychological state shared by almost all the heroes in *Watchmen*. Initially, Moore suggests that, given the black-and-white, all-or-nothing mentality of the kind of person who would become a hero (a person who wants to believe in "absolute values" but encounters only "darkness and ambiguity"), nihilism is a natural fall-back position.[21] It is as if, rebounding from an inevitable collision with moral ambiguity, such a hero precipitously concludes that, since our values are not absolute, they must be relative—their absolutism having led them falsely to assume these alternatives to be exhaustive. Later, however, Moore deepens this explanation by suggesting that such nihilism is the natural complement of a thoroughly scientific worldview. As I mentioned earlier, "Dr. Manhattan" is *Watchmen*'s only truly super-powered being; he is a hero of the "Superman" archetype, but his seemingly omnipotent power over matter comes from his own advanced scientific understanding of—and consequent control over—the physical world. In Dr. Manhattan, Moore embodies our near-deification of science—and its dangers. Thus *Watchmen* tells us not only that Dr. Manhattan "symbolized mankind's problems," but that his name was itself chosen for its "ominous associations," namely, the government-controlled scientific project that produced the first atom bomb, and so, more broadly, science's god-like power to control nature and its perilous consequences (*Watchmen* XI. 22.ii and IV. 12.viii). *Watchmen* thus says that: "We are all of us living in the shadow of Dr. Manhattan"; this "shadow" is the dark side of science—the nihilism of a thoroughly objectified and thereby disenchanted world, a world science takes to be intrinsically value-free, and so ultimately meaningless (a meaninglessness which nuclear annihilation threatens to realize).[22] Hence, when told about the murder of another hero, Dr. Manhattan's revealing reply is: "A live body and a dead body contain the same number of particles. Structurally, there is no discernible difference. Life and death are unquantifiable abstracts. Why should I be concerned?"[23]

In the end, *Watchmen* not only deconstructs the motivations of its individual heroes (who become heroes to please their mothers, because of traumatic childhoods, repressed homoerotic urges, naively absolutist worldviews, fetishes for costumes, equipment, night-patrols, and so on). By presenting nihilism as the simple, unvarnished truth about life in a godless universe, Moore seeks to deconstruct the would-be hero's ultimate motivation, namely, to provide a secular salvation and so attain a mortal immortality.[24] If there is no God, who will save us? This is the basic question to which *Watchmen*'s heroes seek to respond. (Thus the old hero implores the young, would-be heroes who had briefly gathered before him, even as they walk away: "Somebody has to do it, don't you see. Somebody has to save the world." *Watchmen* II. 11.vii.) The hero rises above normal human beings by *saving* them, and, through this secular salvation, he or she lives on in their memory. Ozymandias, the hero who most lucidly realizes all this, unapologetically seeks to put himself in the place previously thought to be occupied by God (*Watchmen* II.9.ii–iii; XII.27.ii.). His ability to shoulder this superhuman responsibility—by choosing to sacrifice millions of innocent lives in a bid to save the world from nuclear annihilation—not only makes him a hero with which most of us cannot identify, it also puts him above, and so alienates him from, humanity in general.[25]

Although *Watchmen*'s heroes all subscribe to the nihilistic belief that reality is ultimately meaningless, they are *heroes* precisely in so far as they embrace this nihilism and nevertheless seek a path leading beyond it.[26] By suggesting that all such paths may be either hopeless or horrific, and that the heroes' motives for seeking them are either dangerous or else unworthy of our admiration, *Watchmen* develops its heroes precisely in order to ask us if we would not in fact be better off without heroes. In order to suggest a response, I will now examine the perhaps surprising conceptual roots of *Watchmen*'s postmodern cynicism in the Enlightenment, then show that the existentialists too deconstructed the hero, but that their deconstructions suggest very different conclusions.

IV. FRAMING THE FRAME: SHOULD HISTORY DISPENSE WITH THE HERO?[27]

Does the apparent paucity of real heroes in our culture suggest that we are living in a post-heroic age? If not, *should* we seek to dispense with heroes? Isaiah Berlin famously maintains that Romanticism's tendency toward hero-worship helped spark the flames of fascism, and so he suggests that, after the terrible conflagration of the Holocaust, for one human being to heroize another is a dangerously childish refusal of "Enlightenment," and thus an historically retrogressive resistance to what was for Kant the "essential destiny" of "human nature": We human beings must grow up, emerge from our "self-imposed immaturity," and have the "courage" to think for ourselves.[28] Have we indeed reached the point in history when, in pursuit of autonomy, we need to put away such childish things—as heroes? Or is the intense cynicism of the times perhaps merely a burnt shell that hides (and thereby also shelters and protects) an inextinguishable human need for something better: Hope, ideals, a future worth pursuing, and heroes to lead us there? If one takes the history of the West and subtracts all the stories of its heroes, what remains? Can there even be a *meaningful* history—a history worth living—without heroes?

These are fateful questions, for history concerns the future at least as much as the past. We "exist" (from the Latin, *ek-sistere*, to "stand out") historically. As Heidegger saw, we enact the life-projects which render us intelligible—to ourselves and to others—only by projecting the past into the future and so constituting the present. History is a congealing of this basic temporality; it is time made thick. Indeed, without the historical dimension of intelligibility, our existence would be desiccated, massively impoverished; the temporal frame through which we live would be too transient to sustain the thick worlds of meaning that make us who we are. We cannot meaningfully be without history; so, can history be meaningful without its hero stories? If the West began to confront such fateful questions as the last millennium drew to a close, this was due not only to the eschatological despair that drives millennialism and thereby betrays our (more or less conscious) belief that *history is over*, a thanatological belief which has been haunting the cultural unconscious of the West for almost two thousand years but which, as our technology becomes ever more destructive, is in increasing danger of being self-fulfilling.[29] This fateful questioning of the hero emerges even more directly in those philosophical counter-movements to millennial despair (post-modernism, post-colonialism, post-imperialism, and the like) which seek to get us beyond our destructive desire to get beyond (our limits, borders, finitude, and so on).

In *Watchmen*, a text now widely regarded as a major work of postmodern literature, the imminence of just such a self-fulfilling apocalypse is one of the major points of departure for the plot. Recall that *Watchmen*'s signature image (which appears on *Watchmen*'s first cover as well as its first and last panels) depicts a blood-stained happy-face, the blood transforming the smiley into a millennium-clock twelve minutes (that is, twelve issues) away from midnight (*Watchmen* I.1.i and XII.32.vii). Ozymandias—the heroic "world's smartest man" who uses his intelligence to avert nuclear holocaust in the shocking culmination of the story—tells an interviewer earlier: "I believe there are some people who really do want, if only subconsciously [*sic*], an end to the world. . . . I see the twentieth century as a race between enlightenment and extinction."[30] If Ozymandias sounds like Isaiah Berlin here, however, we need to recall that Ozymandias intentionally kills millions of innocent people—"half of New York"—in his successful bid to convince cold-warring nations on the brink of a nuclear war that they are being attacked by an alien species and so must put aside their differences and band together in order to survive.[31] This is no mere triumph of consequentialist reasoning over the deontological ethics of the Enlightenment. Read carefully (which, I have argued, is the only way it can be *read*), *Watchmen* clearly calls Ozymandias's "less obvious heroism" into question along with the more traditional "schoolboy heroics" of the other heroes, who proved incapable of resolving a world crisis of such magnitude.[32] Thus, in all the ways we have seen (and more), *Watchmen*'s deconstruction of the hero suggests that perhaps the time for heroes has passed, and this, as we will see next, distinguishes this postmodern work from those deconstructions of the hero contained in the existentialist movement that preceded postmodernism.[33]

V. EXISTENTIAL DECONSTRUCTIONS OF THE HERO

Existentialism, that philosophical tradition previously best known for radical questioning (the tradition which, with Heidegger, gave us the very concept of *deconstruction*), questioned, but did not overturn, the great importance Western history has *always* accorded to the hero. ("Always," here that means—since we are talking about Western history—beginning with our own beginning: Our founding myths are hero stories all.) Indeed, of the three greatest existential philosophers, Nietzsche and Heidegger both found it easier to give up their own devout Christianity than to stop believing in heroes.[34] The third, Kierkegaard, transformed Christian faith into an heroic act, heroizing faith in provocatively contemporary terms: Kierkegaard's "knight of faith" is essentially a secret identity, an identity "the public" can never see. Wrapping this existential riddle inside the enigma of his own authorship, Kierkegaard permitted himself to describe his hero (which is also an obvious attempt at self-heroization) only while masking his own authorial identity with various pseudonyms.[35] This doubly-secretive strategy for self-heroization is repeated by Rorschach (the hero and anti-hero—really, he is both—who initially occupies the shifting center of *Watchmen*), when he chronicles, and so seeks to justify, his own (would-be) heroics in "Rorschach's Journal," which serves as both an homage (ironic or not) to the tradition of the detective's voice-over in *film noir* and, more importantly, as a symbolic stand-in for the projected fantasies of the comic-book as such, and one with which *Watchmen*, tellingly, not only opens but closes—and "closes" precisely by leaving *open* (however seemingly pessimistic its suggestions on this score) the question of whether or not comic books have any future.[36]

Why, then, do the three greatest existentialists so vehemently resist the Enlightenment suggestion that the time for heroes is past? It is important to understand that these existentialists inherited two great but conflicting traditions: On the one hand, the Enlightenment revolution (which celebrated Reason *über alles* and so stripped the holy halos from the heads of earlier saints and saviors, leaving only a "de-auratized," halo-free world), and, on the other hand, the Romantic counter-revolution (which sought to resacralize the world by recognizing that the sources of meaning always exceed humanity as it currently exists. See Horkheimer and Adorno, 1988). Kierkegaard, Nietzsche, and Heidegger recognized that the Enlightenment yielded powerful and important insights into the "transcendental" structures that make existence as we know it possible, but they also believed that the possible *should* always "transcend" existence as we know it, and so they held that human beings, in order to lead lives worth living, need to celebrate the romantic *imagination* that creates the possible as well as the enlightened *reason* that discovers the actual.[37] It is, however, precisely this Romantic current in the existentialists' work (succinctly expressed by Nietzsche's anti-Enlightenment quip, "not only light but also darkness is required for life by all organisms") that renders existentialism vulnerable to criticism coming from those neo-Enlightenment movements which seek to move us historically beyond our need for heroes.[38]

This vulnerability can be seen most clearly in the fact that Kierkegaard's *heroization* of faith stands or falls along with the fate of the hero in general. Put simply, if there can be no *heroes*, then there can be no *heroizations*.[39] This same vulnerability holds, albeit in a more complex way, for Nietzsche's own heroic struggle against historical nihilism, the existential mission which animates Nietzsche's work as a whole and which is at the heart of his magnum opus, *Thus Spoke Zarathustra*. *Zarathustra*, of course, is the text that gave us the very idea of the "superman" (*Übermensch*), Nietzsche's personification of the neo-Darwinian idea that *history is not over*, since humanity too "is something that shall be overcome."[40] Indeed, Nietzsche equates belief in the hero with hope for the future (as the epigraph over this chapter indicates: "But by my love and hope I beseech you: Do not throw away the hero in your soul! Hold holy your highest hope!"). Those individuals who would participate in the creation of a more meaningful future need to be inspired by the great heroes of the past, Nietzsche thought, ultimately so as to overcome these heroes and thereby become "overheroes"—or, better, "superheroes"—that is, even greater heroes for the future. The "superhero" (another Nietzschean conception) is someone who becomes a hero by superceding the hero who inspired him or her. (As *Zarathustra* says: "For this is the soul's secret: Only when the hero has abandoned her, is she approached in a dream by the superhero [*Über-Held*]" Nietzsche, 231.)

Under the influence of the comics Nietzsche unintentionally helped inspire, we tend to think of *Superman* as a type of superhero, but on Nietzsche's view, it would be more accurate to say that all superheroes are variations of the superman archetype. (Applied to the history of comic books, this overly-reductive view can be surprisingly revealing.)[41] The "superman" personifies Nietzsche's idea that the creation of a future worth living requires the continual supercession of the past, while his "superhero" symbolizes the component claim that in order to help create that future, we must supercede even the *heroes* of the past. (Thus, in the fourth and final book of *Zarathustra*, Zarathustra himself finally becomes the superman only by superceding the greatest heroes of the past, "the higher men," each of whom represents a different peak of past human achievement.) One of the lessons Nietzsche drew from Darwin was that to survive in a competitive environment organisms cannot remain static but must grow and develop. By helping us supercede even our greatest past achievements, the Nietzschean superhero serves the "constant overcoming"—or "will to power"—whereby "life" keeps itself *alive*.[42]

Nietzsche thus believed that without the continued emergence of new heroes, "superheroes," we will have no *future*—whether the absence of a future means, as it does in *Watchmen*, a literal annihilation of human civilization, or, as in *Zarathustra*, the endless repetition of an old value system which becomes increasingly worn-out and meaningless to us. Since, for Nietzsche, only a superhero should dare undertake the dangerous venture of questioning the heroes of the past, this means that past heroics may be questioned only for the sake of future heroics; Nietzsche's deconstruction of the hero never calls into question the idea of the hero as such. It is Moore who uses *Watchmen*'s two main "superhero" candidates—Ozymandias and Dr. Manhattan—to demonstrate the dangers of this Nietzschean ideal. As we have seen, Ozymandias succeeds, where even his hero Alexander the Great did not, in unifying the world, but at the cost of alienating himself from humanity by rising so far above them. Thanks to a more extreme version of this alienating transcendence, the superficially more Superman-like Dr. Manhattan becomes a "god" rather than a human being (as *Watchmen* makes clear), eventually abandoning our world in order to create one of his own.[43] Nevertheless, Nietzsche himself maintains that, however dangerous the idea of the superhero, we cannot give it up without risking the future itself.[44]

Heidegger, the last and most complex of the three great existentialists, explicitly chose Nietzsche as his own philosophical "hero" and so, as a faithful Nietzschean, sought to overcome Nietzsche—with all the paradox (and hermeneutic violence) this notoriously involves.[45] In other words, Heidegger's attempt to supercede Nietzsche follows from an acceptance (and critical appropriation), not a rejection, of Nietzsche's conception of the hero. In fact, with *Being and Time*'s notion of "authentic historicality," Heidegger formalizes an idea he learned from his appropriation of Nietzsche (and Kierkegaard), namely, that the true heritage of an otherwise stultifying tradition is best kept alive via "reciprocative rejoinders," sympathetic but critical appropriations of the "heroes" of the past in which we develop and update our chosen hero's mission or example so that it will be capable of meeting the changed demands of our contemporary world.[46] Not surprisingly, then, Heidegger supercedes Nietzsche and Kierkegaard (even as he critically appropriates their views) when, in 1927's *Being and Time*, he deconstructs the hero, seeking to describe the structural features of the process whereby individuals and social groups constitute fundamental aspects of their own identities by "choosing their heroes."

In Heidegger's view, although the heroes we choose fundamentally shape our sense of self, initially we choose our heroes without even being aware that we are choosing them, and, moreover, we tend to choose from the same predetermined array of heroes as everyone else. By simply taking over a hero society has pre-packaged for us, we are doing what Heidegger calls choosing "the anonymous anyone" for a hero (*Being and Time*, 422). Whether the hero unreflexively embraced is Michael Jordan, Albert Einstein, or Marilyn Manson, such conformist (or "inauthentic") heroization helps perpetuate the status-quo sense of what matters in life, be it athletic excellence, scientific genius, or a route to rebellion already mapped out by the status-quo— and so a rebellion which, like those contemporary political protests which accept their confinement to "pre-determined protest areas," tends unintentionally to reinforce the very order it rebels against.[47] Nor am I necessarily any closer to owning my own identity simply in virtue of having chosen a more marginal figure—such as John Muir, Ansel Adams, or Julia "Butterfly" Hill—as the hero who inspires my defining existential projects (here, say, "deep-ecological" environmentalism) and so my sense of self. In terms of *authenticity* (*Eigentlichkeit*, more literally "ownmostness"), what matters is not the *type* of hero chosen so much as the *way* that hero is chosen and so made my own.

For, Heidegger believed it possible, in a "moment of vision," to step back from the heroes we have "always-already" chosen, adopt a second-order perspective on those choices, and choose again, in full awareness that we are choosing a hero, and that doing so *lucidly* can help us own our own lives in a way that will restore our sense of the meaning, weight, and integrity of our actions.[48] With such "authentic" heroization, what is crucial is the "reciprocative rejoinder" mentioned earlier, whereby we critically appropriate our heroes by interpreting and updating their "mission" so that it speaks to the changed demands of our own world. In this way we keep alive what our hero stood for in our own lives, rather than simply admiring our hero from afar, worshiping them from a safe distance. When we choose our heroes *inau*-thentically, we do not really have to do much (to "Be like Mike," apparently

I simply need to drink Gatorade), and, moreover, our society will subtly reassure us that we have made the right choice (since, sticking with this example, our society continually reinforces its ridiculous overemphasis on athletic excellence).[49] When we choose our heroes *authentically*, however, we take more upon ourselves (here, I would actually dedicate myself to *being* like Mike, and I would also have to take responsibility for my interpretation of what that demands), and the result is much riskier (for I am likely to *fail* to be like Mike).[50] If we choose our heroes authentically, we, like Ozymandias at the end of *Watchmen*, will not be able to find any reassurance outside ourselves that we have made "the right choice," and like Heidegger himself (when he chose to believe in the initial promise of Hitler's "revolution"), it is always possible that we are making a horrible mistake.[51] Authentic heroics require learning to live with this uncertainty. Following in the footsteps of our heroes thus encourages us to follow Nietzsche's exhortation to "live dangerously," to risk an absolute commitment (a commitment in which our very identity is at stake), since only such a risk, Kierkegaard argues, can give existential weight and meaning to our lives.[52]

VI. SPARKS IN THE DARKNESS

> If we look for people who made no mistakes, who were always on the right side, who never apologized for tyrants or unjust wars, we shall have very few heroes and heroines.
>
> —RICHARD RORTY (45)

In the end, *Watchmen*'s postmodern ambivalence concerning the hero places it somewhere between the Enlightenment rejection of, and the existentialist commitment to, the idea of the hero; and in this, *Watchmen* reflects a tension underlying our own age. For, even if one believes that there is something admirable in the desire to live without heroes, the problem remains that we have not woken up and walked with our eyes wide-open into the clear light of a post-heroic tomorrow. Instead, we as a culture have simply discovered the decadent pleasure of destroying the heroes we create. Indeed, building up sham heroes only to destroy them the next week or month—once the fare only of the tabloids—seems to have become our most popular national pastime. Concealed, however, behind this spectacle of a "star-studded" popular culture saturated with "malicious joy" (*Schadenfreude*, a German word for an increasingly American disposition) is the fact that we not only degrade our sham heroes (in whose company I would include not only Joe Millionaire, American Idol, and their ilk, but almost all our precious "stars"), we also ignore or quickly forget the real heroes who emerge despite it all (Julia Hill, Rachel Corrie, Mark Bingham, to name but a few), heroes with the capacity to disrupt our cynical complacency, realign our felt-understanding of what matters, and so give focus to our guiding sense of self. When greatness as such is suspect, and quickly subjected to vicious persecution, in the end we are left with only conformity, cultural banalization, and the triumph, by default, of sad mediocrity. Although I look forward to a dawn beyond our twilight of the idols, our dusk of "stars" made mostly of paper-thin tinsel (easily torn and foresworn), I do not believe we are entering into—or *should* seek to enter—a time without heroes, a post-heroic age.

I would suggest instead that when a genre seems to commit suicide—as philosophy did (with Kant, Heidegger, and Wittgenstein) and as the superhero comic did (with *Watchmen*)—this apparent suicide is usually better understood as an attempted martyrdom, that is, a sacrifice with a redemptive intent, a would-be rebirth (even if in a different form). When the greatest representatives of a genre seek to end it, this is perhaps because they sense (on some level) that no field can long survive without being periodically revitalized by such sacrifice and rebirth. It is no coincidence that many of the comics which followed *Watchmen* sought to respond to its challenging deconstruction of the hero, and that the result greatly enriched the comics medium as a whole. More than fifteen years later, mainstream comics continue to occupy a post-*Watchmen* landscape, one in which *Watchmen*'s ambivalence about the hero has become nearly ubiquitous.[53] Even in the darkest of contemporary comics, however, a careful reader can still recognize the sparks from that ongoing struggle to imagine and create the kinds of heroes who will prove themselves capable of inspiring the denizens of this complex and morally ambiguous world,[54] a struggle which seeks to keep alive (as the dream of the hero, with all its risks, has always done) our hope for a better future. This hope (which, really, is hope itself) we can deconstruct but never destroy.[55]

NOTES

1. This functional definition of the hero suggests that one of the dangers of a society with enemies but not heroes—a society we sometimes seem to be becoming—is that such a society will only define itself negatively, in terms of what it is *against*, and so become ever more empty, hostile, and closed-in upon itself.

2. Between 1933 and 1938, this latter group included Heidegger himself. On this issue, see below and my "Heidegger and the Politics of the University," *Journal of the History of Philosophy*, 41:4 (2003), pp. 515–42.

3. It is important to realize that "deconstruction" (*Destruktion, Abbau*) is not the same as "destruction" (*Zerstörung*). I will discuss the particular deconstructive strategy employed by Moore below, but for a broader philosophical discussion of "deconstruction," see my "Ontotheology? Understanding Heidegger's *Destruktion* of Metaphysics," *International Journal of Philosophical Studies* 8:3 (2000), pp. 297–327.

4. In referring to what may well be one of the great works of postmodern literature, I shall nevertheless avoid the embarrassed euphemism, "graphic novel"; Moore himself rejects this term as a ploy meant to help market comic books to adults. Still, it is difficult to ignore the embarrassment to which such marketing responds. (Michael Chabon, in what is basically a graphics-free "graphic novel" about comic books, *The Amazing Adventures of Kavalier & Clay* [New York: Picador, 2000], recognizes "the opprobrium and sense of embarrassment that would forever . . . attach itself to the comic book" [p. 75], but also describes the truly American art form of the comic book as "something that only the most purblind of societies would have denied the status art" [pp. 574–75]; see also *Unbreakable*, in which Shyamalan makes his case for comics.) A few words about the philosophical study of comic books may thus be in order here, as a maximally unapologetic apology for what follows. As the great sociologist Pierre Bourdieu observes, academics are the dominated members of the dominant class. Owing to this position in the field of cultural capital, we tend unconsciously to turn our backs on our humbler origins and become eager apologists for "high-brow" cultural commodities—opera, orchestra, foreign films, fine wine—while remaining blind to (if not deluded about) the fact that we thereby help legitimate the class divisions such rarefied cultural commodities serve. At the same time, we also tend to denigrate "low-brow" mediums such as rap music, Hollywood movies, or, heaven forfend, comic books. (See Bourdieu, *Distinction: A Social Critique of the Judgement of Taste*, trans. Richard Nice [Cambridge, MA: Harvard University Press, 1984]). Such unreflexive prejudices may be common, but they are unworthy of the *philosopher*, who should indeed *know (themselves)* better. As something of a "high-brow low-brow," a philosopher (or "lover of wisdom") who has long felt love for and drawn wisdom from Hollywood, rap, and—longest of all—comic books, I could hardly refuse when Jeff McLaughlin kindly asked me to contribute a chapter for *Comics as Philosophy*. This title is provocative; *Comics as Philosophy* implies (although McLaughlin himself may not agree) that we should treat comics *as philosophy*, clarifying and discussing the ideas these comics contain, instead of just using comics to illustrate pre-existing philosophical theories. Indeed, demonstrating

the inherent philosophical content of a comic is a more fitting way to give comics their intellectual due than by simply showing that they make for good philosophical examples, which (as in the case of Hollywood films) far fewer would deny.

5. When discussing the maturation of mainstream comic books, Moore is always quick to share the credit (and blame) with Frank Miller. One thinks immediately of *Watchmen* and *The Dark Knight Returns*, but those seminal comics, which changed the genre forever, were made possible by earlier work, including Miller's brilliant work on *Daredevil* and Moore's radical transformation of *The Swamp Thing*. For abundant testimony to Moore's worldwide influence, see Gary Spencer Millidge, ed., *Alan Moore: Portrait of an Extraordinary Gentleman* (Leigh-on-Sea, England: Abiogenesis Press, 2003).

6. This perhaps helps explain why I would choose to go to Berkeley rather than to the more overtly heroic Air Force Academy (one of my own early versions of what Sartre called a "radical choice," a significant parting of the ways on the path of life), and why *Watchmen* would so fascinate me; clearly (in retrospect), I was already in the grip of that ambivalence concerning the hero that *Watchmen* intensified.

7. *Watchmen*'s first and last images are essentially the same, a device which (as in Nietzsche's *Zarathustra*) conveys the circularity of the text and so signals the necessity of rereading it. See Alan Moore and Dave Gibbons (with colorist John Higgins), *Watchmen* (New York: DC Comics, 1986–1987), issue #I, p. 1, panel i and issue #XII, p. 32, panel vii. I will henceforth refer to *Watchmen* by simply listing the issue, pages, and (where relevant) panel numbers, respectively (here: I. 1.i and XII. 32.vii). See also *Watchmen* XI. 23.iii, where the young man who is always reading the comic (within the comic) hints: "I gotta read 'em over."

8. As *Watchmen* XI. 1.iv–v suggests: "this jigsaw-fragment model . . . aligns itself piece by piece. . . . These reference points established, an emergent worldview becomes gradually discernible." Moore explains (in "The Alan Moore Interview") that "with *Watchmen*, what we tried to do was give it a . . . kind of crystalline structure, where it's like this kind of jewel with hundreds and hundreds of facets and almost each of the facets is commenting on all of the other facets and you can kind of look at the jewel through any of the facets and still get a coherent reading." This multidimensional polysemy leads Moore to add (echoing remarks Nietzsche made more ironically about *Zarathustra*) that *Watchmen* is "tailor-made for a university class, because there are so many levels and little background details and clever little connections and references in it that it's one that academics can pick over for years." That is true, but for the most part I leave the monumental task of cataloguing all of the interconnections to others (several web sites undertake this daunting task). I might warn them, however, that if they can exhaustively explain the meaning of an artwork, they have thereby undermined its status *as art*, as I explain in "The Silence of the Limbs: Critiquing Culture from a Heideggerian Understanding of the Work of Art," *Enculturation* 2:1 (1998); see http://enculturation.gmu.edu/2_1/thomson.html.

9. *Watchmen* uses several other devices to multiply meanings, including, most notably, the story within a story (the books, article, journal, magazine, and comic book within the

comic book), which then become (multiple) allegorical frameworks for interpreting the story in which they are placed. Each issue also employs a different recurrent theme and symbol (named in the issue's title and revealed in a quote given fully, and revealingly, only on that issue's last page). My favorite example of this device is issue five, "Fearful Symmetry," in which the entire issue is almost perfectly symmetrical in its panels, colors, figures, etc. (To see this, compare the first and last pages, then work inward to the amazing centerpiece on pp. 14–15, in which the two pages are a "fearfully symmetrical" reflection of one another). Here the point is not merely a display of formal mastery, but to convey the symmetrical relation of life to death—an important and recurring theme throughout the book (cf. V. 15.i with V. 12.xiii).

10. (Cf. Freud, "The 'Uncanny,' " in *Collected Papers*, vol. 4 [New York: Basic Books, 1959], esp. pp. 394–99.) I am thinking of Socrates' notoriously unanswerable elenchtic questioning, his ruthless midwifery in which all his interlocutors' philosophical children either are stillborn or quickly euthanized. The philosophical answers only begin to survive with Plato, whose figure of "the stranger" (in "Parmenides") proposes the patricide, the murder of he without whom one would not be, a murder which is justified as necessary to make room (by clearing the conceptual space) for a better future.

11. (On this revisionary history of comics, see esp. *Watchmen* V. 29–32.) Sridhar Pappu, "We Need Another Hero," *Salon*, 18 October 2000 (http://dir.salon.com/people/feature/2000/10/18/moore/index.html?pn=2).

12. Moore now bemoans this aspect of *Watchmen's* influence, saying: "When I did *Watchmen*, I thought, great, people are going to feel compelled to look at the clever storytelling involved and they'll feel compelled to match me or better me in coming up with ways for telling stories. But instead, it seems what most people saw was the violence, the grimness, the layer of atheist pessimistic politics that was glossed over it. That's what got regurgitated and recycled" (see Moore's "Interview with Jonathan Ross," in *The Idler* (http://www.idler.co.uk/html/interviews/rossmoore.htm). Neil Gaiman's epic *Sandman* saga may be the only mainstream comic that succeeded in meeting *Watchmen's* challenge (of course, one needs to reread the entire *Sandman* series to appreciate this).

13. See *Watchmen* I. 31 ("Under the Hood," 5). It is not uncommon for the fantasy genre to contain a critique of fantasy (as e.g. Anne Rice's vampire novels seek to convince us that we would not really like being immortal), and one can always suspect that such a move is motivated more by "sour grapes" than by an embrace of the human condition as such.

14. Moore lampoons the reactionary, right-wing nature of the superhero, e.g., when he shows the heroes meeting during the Nixon years in order to discuss forming a new team to fight the evils of "promiscuity," "anti-war demonstrations," "campus subversion," "drugs," and "Black unrest" (see *Watchmen* II. 10.ii, II. 11.iv, and VIII. 29–31).

15. See Jean Baudrillard, *The Vital Illusion* (New York: Columbia University Press, 2000), pp. 46–49: "Everywhere we see a paradoxical logic: the idea is destroyed by its own realization, by its own excess. And in this way history itself comes to an end . . . [subsequent] history presents itself as if it were advancing and continuing, when it is actually collapsing."

16. See *Watchmen* XI. 31 (p. 9 of "Nova Express"). Thus Moore describes *Watchmen* (in "The Alan Moore Interview") as "taking these ordinary characters and just taking them a step to the left or right, just twisting them a little bit. . . . *Watchmen* was at the time about as far as I could imagine taking the mainstream superhero comic. It seemed to take it to some place that was so completely off the map."

17. (As Mungo Thomson reminds me, it was this pulp aspect of *Batman* that Frank Miller so influentially revived; Miller's *The Dark Knight Returns* revitalized *Batman* by reconnecting it to its pulp origins.) If one views comics from a sufficient distance, one finds oneself confronting the phenomenon that Joseph Campbell—the great Jungian analyst (whose interpretations of myth demonstrate the appropriateness of applying Jung's notion of the archetype to the idea of the hero)—called *The Hero with a Thousand Faces* (Princeton: Princeton University Press, 1949).

18. See *Watchmen* I. 1.i; on this "true face," cf. VI. 17.iv–vi, VI. 21.ix, and VI. 26.iv. Rorschach's journal also replicates the detective's "voice-over" in classic *film noir*. In Greek drama, the mask amplifies the voice and so focuses, rather than hides, the person within (a point nicely conveyed in Jim Carrey's "The Mask"). Rorschach takes this so far that he disappears into his mask; Night Owl (his former partner) represents a more skeptical ambivalence toward the adoption of the mask of the hero, which (Moore implies) is a kind of "Jesus costume" through which the hero seeks to provide a kind of secular salvation (cf. VII. 8.vi–vii, VII. 24.vii, and VII. 9.viii).

19. (For the connection between Rorschach and the comic within the comic, see V. 22.vi–vii, which speaks of "Raw Shark.") In part to head off the facile response that the idea of comics as projection is merely a projection of Moore himself, the plot of *Watchmen* VI is framed by an ingenious recurring device in which Rorschach himself is subjected to a Rorschach test, a test which he tellingly reverses so that it reveals the unconscious projections of the psychiatrist seeking to administer the test. As a result, the psychiatrist comes to understand his own careerist ambitions as social ideals the internalization of which has alienated him from what he truly cares about, namely, helping people (see *Watchmen* XI. 20.vii), thereby deconstructing these projections, putting them out of play, and so confirming the motto from Nietzsche which bookends the issue: "If you gaze into the abyss, the abyss gazes also into you." See *Watchmen* VI. 28.iv–ix. In the end, the psychiatrist recovers his humanistic ideals, but then dies (in a noble but futile act of ordinary heroism) because of them. This ending is thus more ambivalent about the hero than the conclusion of the comic within the comic itself, which straightforwardly contends that the attempt to become a hero turns one into a monster. This contrast represents an ambivalence about the future of the hero that *Watchmen* itself concludes by posing (see notes 28 and 44 below).

20. See *Watchmen* VI. 28.vii–ix. It is consistent that Rorschach, a character whose very name is synonymous with "projection," should project his understanding of reality as projection onto the world.

21. At least for those who do not simply delude themselves. See *Watchmen* I. 5 ("Under the Hood," 5) and compare *Watchmen* VIII. 27–28 (in which the old, naively

optimistic—indeed, delusional—hero is, in effect, slain by the public). See also VI. 10.iii, in which Rorschach describes his mask (made from the fabric of a space-aged dress ordered by Kitty Genovese—one of *Watchmen*'s many brilliant little details) in symbolically *absolutist* terms: "Black and white. Moving. Changing shape . . . but not mixing. No grey. Very, very beautiful."

22. *Watchmen* IV. 32 ("Dr. Manhattan: Super-Powers and the Super Powers," p. III). The first image after that sentence is of a barely disguised "Jolly Roger" (see V. 1.i), a skull and crossbones which, here, symbolize Rorschach and the projection of meaning onto an empty world. The implication—that Rorschach's nihilism is itself a clear-eyed view of the scientific world—is reinforced at VIII. 18.ix.

23. *Watchmen* I. 21.iii; see also the main debate in IX (through which Moore implies that poetry, not science, will save us). As Night Owl explains (in another of Moore's ironically self-referential passages), "in approaching our subject with the sensibilities of statisticians and dissectionists, we distance ourselves increasingly from the marvelous and spell-binding planet of imagination whose gravity drew us to our studies in the first place." When Night Owl contends that: "A scientific understanding . . . does not impede a poetic appreciation of the same phenomenon. Rather, the two enhance each other," he expresses the hopeful side of Moore's deep ambivalence toward comics (see *Watchmen* VII. 30–31), an optimism which is reinforced by the fact that Night Owl comes out of retirement at the end of *Watchmen* and that *Watchmen*'s signature smiley-face is restored by the recognition that science covers-over the miraculous nature of the everyday (see esp. IX. 27.i–iii).

24. (Remember that the greatest Greek heroes—such as Achilles and Hercules—were *demigods* seeking among mortals to prove themselves worthy of immortality.) When Dr. Manhattan departs for Mars, the juxtaposed text wonders about "the cold distant God" in whose hands fate rested: "Was He really there? Had he been there once, but now departed?" Similarly, Rorschach describes his own defining epiphany in such terms: "Looked at sky through smoke heavy with human fat and God was not there. The cold, suffocating dark goes on forever and we are alone." See *Watchmen* III. 21.vii and VI. 26.ii, (Oblique references to the holocaust abound in *Watchmen*; see e.g. II. 30 ["Under the Hood," 8] and the many appearances of "Krystalnacht").

25. In a baldly self-referential moment, Moore (under the pretext of analyzing the pirate comic contained in *Watchmen*) writes: "In the final scenes, thanks to the skillful interplay of text and pictures, we see that the mariner," i.e., Ozymandias, "is in the end marooned from the rest of humanity in a much more terrible fashion." See *Watchmen* V. 31 ("Treasure Island Treasury of Comics, 61").

26. This helps explain why "The Comedian"—who embraces the nihilism of the world for the licentious freedom it permits him (as if following Dostoyevsky's flawed maxim, "If God is dead, then everything is permitted")—does not seem to be a hero (see *Watchmen* IV. 19.vi).

27. Why approach *Watchmen* from this angle? The very title, *Watchmen*, as a reference to Juvenal's "*Quis custodiet ipsos custodes*" ("Who watches the watchmen?" or, as we might

now say, who polices the police?), is intended primarily as a political question (see *Watchmen* XI. 18.ix, which quotes from the speech J. F. K. was, according to Moore, supposed to read the day he was assassinated: "We in this country, in this generation, are by destiny, rather than choice, the watchmen on the walls of world freedom"), but this reference also implicitly raises the problematic question of the hermeneutic frame (problematic because it seems to generate an infinite regress): From what perspective can one justify one's own interpretive perspective? (On this issue, see Jacques Derrida, *The Truth in Painting* [Chicago: University of Chicago Press, 1987], 37–82). One of the definitive theses of postmodernity is that there can be no privileged interpretive "metanarrative" (whether Marxist, Freudian, existential, or even postmodern) from which to adjudicate between competing interpretive perspectives. (See Jean-François Lyotard, *The Postmodern Condition* [Minneapolis: University of Minnesota Press, 1984]). This postmodern thesis may itself be self-undermining; if it is itself a metanarrative, then it is caught in a paradox of reflexivity (see Reed Way Dasenbrock, "Slouching Toward Berlin: Life is a Postfascist Culture," in *Fascism's Return*, ed. R. J. Golsan [Lincoln: University of Nebraska Press, 1998]). The sentiment dovetails nonetheless with Heidegger's claim that no one interpretive frame can exhaust a true work of art, as well as with Heidegger's warning against the endless task of seeking to situate one's own perspective (to "get back behind one's thrownness"), two points I explain in my aforementioned "The Silence of the Limbs." In this context, it is also interesting to recall the frequently noted fact that in comics, the action always happens outside or between the frames, which are themselves frozen, and that this is especially true of *Watchmen*, which refuses to employ force lines, blurred backgrounds, and any of the other comics shorthand for conveying a sense of motion *within* a single, framed panel. (I owe this latter point to Mungo Thomson).

28. See Isaiah Berlin, *Three Critics of the Enlightenment: Vico, Hamann, Herder* (Princeton: Princeton University Press, 2000); see also Habermas's virulent, neo-enlightenment suspicion of heroes: "It seems to me that whenever 'heroes' are honored, the question arises as to who needs them and why. . . . [O]ne can understand Bertolt Brecht's warning: 'Pity the land that needs heroes.'" (Giovanna Borradori, ed., *Philosophy in a Time of Terror: Dialogues with Jürgen Habermas and Jacques Derrida* [Chicago: University of Chicago Press, 2003], p. 43). Cf. Emmanuel Levinas's depiction of Romanticism's "heroic conception of human destiny," in which "the individual is called upon to loosen the grasp of the foreign reality that chokes it," in *On Escape* [1935] (Stanford: Stanford University Press, 2003), 49–55; Immanuel Kant, "An Answer to the Question: What Is Enlightenment?," *Perpetual Peace and Other Essays*, trans. Ted Humphries (Indianapolis: Hackett, 1983), 41, 44. Ironically, in order to advocate the sober self-guidance which is supposed to lead us beyond such heroizations, Kant himself employs an unmistakably *heroic* rhetoric, proclaiming that "the motto of Enlightenment" is "*Sapere Aude!*" ("Dare to Know!"), and pitting Enlightenment "resolve and courage" against the "laziness and cowardice" of "lifelong immaturity" (41). This is not merely a rhetorical inconsistency, but helps us see that Kant advances his critique of *other*-heroization

(heteronomy) from the perspective of a particular kind of *self*-heroization (autonomy). In other words, rather than a critique of heroization in general, Kant pits one kind of hero (the self) against another (the other). (Of course, the issue of Kant's role in—and the full consequences of—the historical movement of liberal individualism demands a much more careful evaluation than is possible here).

29. Our unconscious solution to the long-anticipated arrival of the millennium was ingenious and revealing; we simply transformed our millennial despair into a technical problem (the quickly forgotten "Y2K Bug") and then channeled our fears into practical attempts to solve this "glitch in the programming." This explains why the dangers of the "Y2K Bug" were so incredibly exaggerated (namely, because it served as a stand-in for our deeper fear of the end of days or apocalypse), and so revealed our (pre-9/11) optimism that we could "de-bug" death from the human genetic "program" (perhaps the ultimate goal of science).

30. See *Watchmen* XI. 32 (p. 10 of "Nova Express"); ironically, here "the world's smartest man" confuses the subconscious with the unconscious. Showing himself to be an extreme disciple of Enlightenment, Ozymandias will later speak of ushering "in an age of illumination so dazzling that humanity will reject the darkness in its heart," and, as he says this, he finds himself confronting a "disappointed" god-figure. See *Watchmen* XII. 17.ii–v.

31. Mungo Thomson informs me that this plot device comes from a 1950's episode of *The Outer Limits* called "The Architects of Fear" (starring Robert Culp, who later figured prominently in the 1980's TV show "The Greatest American Hero," in which the action, drama, and comedy revolve around the Moore-like question, "What happens when you give a 'normal,' gainfully-employed, family-man superpowers?") and points out that Moore cites "The Architects of Fear" at the end of *Watchmen* (it is playing on a TV in the background in XII. 28.ii–iii). When asked, "Who'd believe an alien invasion?," Ozymandias responds by quoting Hitler's dictum, "People swallow lies easily, provided they're big enough" (*Watchmen* XI. 36.iii). *Watchmen*'s climax thus complicates Slavoj Zizek's hypothesis that: "Disaster films might be the only optimistic social genre that remains today, and that's a sad reflection of our desperate state. The only way to imagine a Utopia of social cooperation is to conjure a situation of absolute catastrophe." See Zizek, "Disaster Movies as the Last Remnants of Utopia," interview with Noam Yuran, in *Ha'aretz* (English edition), 15 Jan 2003.

32. Compare *Watchmen* XII. 27.i with XI. 13.vi and XI. 23.i; the obvious parallels between Ozymandias and the would-be savior of his hometown in the pirate comic imply that Ozymandias's "innocent intent" to save the world has destroyed him, undermining not only the "schoolboy heroics" of the traditional superhero but also his own darker and "less obvious heroism" (XII. 17.i). The very name *Ozymandias*, moreover, implicitly connotes the futility of all dreams of empire. (In *Watchmen*, Ozymandias personifies that empire of capitalist imperialism which wears a liberal-democratic mask; Moore was responding to Thatcher's neo-Reaganite policies.) As Moore knows (but does not say in *Watchmen*), the arrogant lines quoted from Shelley (on XI. 28: "My name is

Ozymandias, king of kings:/Look on my works, ye mighty, and despair!") are, in Shelley's poem, found engraved on the base of an ancient monument which now lies shattered in the sand. (This fuller context helps one understand Dr. Manhattan's final answer to Ozymandias: "Nothing ever ends"; see XII. 27.v).

33. By the end of *Watchmen*, Ozymandias changes the fragrance line he sells from "Nostalgia" to "Millennium" (see XII. 31.iv) because he has helped shift the cultural mood from a retrospective pessimism to a forward-looking optimism. Yet, "Millennium," a word with strong thanatological resonances, is an odd name for a product meant to embody the victory of "Enlightenment" over "extinction," and so helps (along with the neo-Nazi aesthetics of the advertising campaign for "Millennium"; one of many ways in which Moore associates Ozymandias with Nazism) to signal the darker undercurrents of *Watchmen*'s conclusion.

34. I hope that my employment of heroic terms ("the three greatest") in a context concerned with questioning such terms will not be seen as begging the question with which we began. I do recognize that it tips my hand a bit, or rather it would, if my epigraph had not done so from the outset by indicating one of the philosophical intuitions guiding me here, *viz.*, that, however problematic, heroes are indispensable for history-making (which, in turn, is needed to transcend the nihilism of the age). I should perhaps also respond to the criticism that I myself am guilty of heroizing Nietzsche, Heidegger, and Moore. On Nietzsche and Heidegger's closely related definitions of the hero (see below), this is true: I not only admire aspects of their thought, but have made those aspects part of my own philosophical identity through a series of creative interpretive appropriations (or philosophical *introjections*). There are, of course, many senses in which I do not want to be anything like them (!); were that not the case, my self-constituting interpretations of their work would not need to be particularly creative. If, as I maintain in my opening paragraph, a hero *functions* as an individual or community's idealized self-projection, a projection which helps focus their guiding sense of self, then certainly these thinkers (among others) play that role for me. This entire chapter, moreover, in that it argues *against* the dispensability of heroes, can be understood as a response to the charge that this heroization constitutes a *criticism* of my work.

35. Although both Kierkegaard and Rorschach keep their identities secret, their masks confer rather than disguise their "true" identities, amplifying and focusing (as in Greek drama) the self, character, or "personality" speaking through the mask. (See note 21 above).

36. See *Watchmen* I. 1.i; XII. 32.vii; and cf. V. 12.vi; *Watchmen* is "closed" only in the sense that a line is closed when it is made into a circle. On the question of the dispensability of the hero, Moore himself now seems deeply ambivalent. In "The Alan Moore Interview," Moore says: "at the time I think I had vain thoughts, thinking 'Oh well, no one's going to be able to follow this, they'll all just have to stop producing superhero comics and do something more rewarding with their lives.'" Yet, the penultimate scene of *Watchmen* is of two aging heroes preparing to return to their "adventuring" (see XII. 30.ii).

37. It is perhaps not too great an over-simplification to point out that a significant strain of the intellectual (or "spiritual," *geistlich*) history of the last few centuries can be sketched as a series of battles in the on-going conflict between Enlightenment and Romanticism: The Enlightenment throws off the "dogmatism" of a religious worldview; Romanticism rejects the triumph of Enlightenment rationality as sober but unsatisfying; the existentialists seek to rehabilitate Romanticism's call for meaning within a broadly Enlightenment framework; Berlin and other liberals reject this Romantic counter-revolution as politically disastrous and call for a return to the Enlightenment; postmodernists rebel against this return to the privileged metanarrative of Reason while nevertheless reviving its suspicion of heroes, master-concepts, and so on.

38. See Nietzsche, *On the Advantage and Disadvantage of History for Life*, p. 10. These "neo-Enlightenment" views may (as with Berlin) or may not (as with postmodernism) share the Enlightenment belief that reason is sufficient for happiness, a view Nietzsche denigrates as "Socratic optimism" in *The Birth of Tragedy* (Cambridge: Cambridge University Press, 1999).

39. If nothing can be an X, then nothing can be made into an X. No liquid, no liquefaction; no heroes, no heroization, and so on. (Someone might object, e.g., that while there are no demons, there are certainly *demonizations*. But a person "demonized" is transformed rhetorically into something that does not actually exist, which helps explain why such rhetorical moves are so objectionable. As I observed in note 35, however, even Kant himself proved incapable of abiding—in his *rhetoric*—by this strict logic of Enlightenment). A would-be "enlightened Kierkegaardian" might try to avoid this problem by insisting that, since Kierkegaard distinguishes the "knight of faith" from the "tragic hero" in *Fear and Trembling*, he does not in fact "heroize" faith. Yet, not only is Kierkegaard's distinction quite *idiosyncratic* (since a *knight* is the very paradigm of the medieval hero), but the distinction turns on Kierkegaard's questionable claim that we can *understand* the tragic hero, but not the knight of faith. (Can one really "understand" Hector, let alone Oedipus? Not, I would argue, without becoming *like* them). As Andrew Cross shows, moreover, Kierkegaard's knight and hero stand in a relation of isomorphic interdependence, each completing the other (each is the other's "better nature"); see Cross, "Faith and the Ethical in *Fear and Trembling*," *Inquiry* 46:1 (2003). If Cross is right, and I think he is, then even *within* Kierkegaard's idiosyncratic conceptual vocabulary, one can say that Kierkegaard gives us a "poetic heroization" (or "heroic poeticization") of faith. (Obviously, however, the concepts of the hero I have analyzed here are significantly broader than Kierkegaard's own). Alternatively, the post-modern Kierkegaardian might try to argue that we cannot say that the Knight of Faith is a heroization of Kierkegaard himself, since Kierkegaard entirely disappears behind (or into) his pseudonymous masks (with even his journals being masks). That, however, only extends the parallel with Rorschach (who also disappears into his masks), while missing the general point that there is almost never a superhero without an unknown "secret identity" (seeming exceptions, like Wolverine, fit the pattern on closer examination), and the fact that this secret identity is not only unknown to the hero's admirers, but is usually popularly

perceived as the very opposite of the hero (think, e.g., of the "nerdy" Peter Parker and Clark Kent, who look cowardly because they are always "running off when trouble starts," and also of the vicious caricatures of Kierkegaard in *The Corsair*) creates a distance which helps *motivate* their continued heroics (potentially into the kind of vicious shame/exhibition cycle Moore analyses in works such as *Miracleman*).

40. See Nietzsche, *Thus Spoke Zarathustra*, p. 124: "*I teach you the superman.* Humanity is something that shall be overcome."

41. On this point, see Moore's *Supreme* and Chabon's *The Amazing Adventures of Kavalier & Clay*, 74–77 and *passim*. The creation of America's famous "Superman" in 1938 was (just like many of the earlier comics) in part an ideologically-motivated response to the Nazi's glorification of Nietzsche's superman (an idea which, in so far as the Nazis conflated it with Nietzsche's "blond beast," they completely misunderstood). Chabon nicely uses his own "Superman" character, "The Escapist," in order to transform the common anti-comics charge of *escapism* into a celebration of comics' "noble" and "necessary" ability to liberate the imagination and so help us escape oppressive regimes and realities (see 575–76, 582, 620). It would be interesting to read Chabon's heroization of escape— escape as resistance to tyrannical "senses of reality" (as Berlin might put it)—in the light of Levinas's earlier idea that "escaping is the quest for the marvelous, the "need to get out of oneself, that is, *to break that most radical and unalterably binding of chains, the fact that the I is oneself*" (*On Escape* [1935], 53, 55).

42. Max Scheler appropriates this Nietzschean idea when he characterizes the "hero" as the exemplary embodiment of "life values." See Manfred Frings, *The Mind of Max Scheler* (Milwaukee: Duquesne University Press, 1997).

43. See *Watchmen* XI. 14.vii. Ozymandias describes his own transformation into a "super-human" (*Watchmen* X. 32), but Moore makes clear that the catch-phrase announcing Dr. Manhattan, "The superman exists, and he's American," was actually a corruption of, "*God* exists and he's American" (cf. IV. 13.i and IV. 31). (Moreover, Dr. Manhattan's human name, Osterman, connotes Easter (*Oster*), and thus divine rebirth, and by the end of *Watchmen* he is no longer this human being; see *Watchmen* XII. 18.ii).

44. For a (Nietzschean) critique of Nietzsche's dangerous conception of the hero, see Alexander Nehamas, "Nietzsche and 'Hitler'" (in J. Golomb and R. S. Wistrich, eds, *Nietzsche, Godfather of Fascism?* [Princeton: Princeton University Press, 2002]). Interestingly, Moore's Ozymandias calls into question Nehamas' rejection of Nietzsche's "evil hero" by providing precisely the kind of example Nehamas himself finds "difficult to imagine" (101).

45. For a sympathetic reconstruction of Heidegger's controversial critique of Nietzsche, see my "Heidegger on Ontological Education, or: How We Become What We Are," *Inquiry* 44:3 (2001), 243–68.

46. See Heidegger, *Being and Time*, trans. J. Macquarrie and E. Robinson (New York: Harper & Row, 1962), 429–39. Jürgen Habermas revealingly (if, once again, reductively) traces back to Kierkegaard Heidegger's understanding of historicality (often misleadingly translated as "historicity"); see Habermas, *The Future of Human Nature* (Cambridge: Polity, 2003), 5–11.

47. This is not to denigrate Marilyn Manson (or Einstein, or Michael Jordan); what really matters, for Heidegger, is that such a "hero" be chosen *authentically* by an individual as his or her hero, with all that entails (see below).

48. "The authentic repetition of a possibility of existence that has been—the possibility that Dasein may choose its hero—is grounded existentially in anticipatory resoluteness; for it is in resoluteness that one first chooses the choice of that which first makes one free for the struggle of loyally following in the footsteps of that which can be repeated" (Heidegger, *Being and Time*, 437). See also Charles B. Guignon, "Authenticity, Moral Values, and Psychotherapy," in Guignon, ed., *The Cambridge Companion to Heidegger* (Cambridge: Cambridge University Press, 1993).

49. None of us are immune from such influences, of course. A few years ago I attended a meeting of the North American Nietzsche Society in which several eminent Nietzsche scholars read papers on the subject of "Nietzsche and Sport"; one after another, they maintained that Nietzsche would have loved the same culturally-banalizing sporting events they themselves seemed to worship—from afar.

50. In *Watchmen* too, the "public" (nicely embodied in the shifting scene surrounding the appropriately Kierkegaardian figure of the newspaper vendor) is distinguished by the refusal of its members to take responsibility for their decisions.

51. See Hubert L. Dreyfus, "Mixing Interpretation, Religion, and Politics: Heidegger's High-Risk Thinking," in Christopher Ocker, ed., *Protocol of the Sixty-first Colloquy of the Center for Hermeneutical Studies*. In the final pages of *Watchmen* (XII. 27.iv–vii), Ozymandias seeks reassurance from Dr. Manhattan (who has become nearly omniscient), asking him, "I did the right thing, didn't I? It all worked out in the end." Dr. Manhattan answers, "Nothing ever ends." Ozymandias's confidence is clearly shaken, and the final image of him (looking away from his own shadow, which is now larger than he is) leaves open the question of whether "the world's smartest man" will be able to live with the uncertainty concerning his own heroics.

52. See Hubert L. Dreyfus, *On the Internet* (London and New York: Routledge, 2001), esp. pp. 73–107. See also Zizek's critical appropriation of Dreyfus's Kierkegaardian critique in "Rhetorics of Power," *Diacritics* 31:1 (2001), 98–103.

53. This work includes Frank Miller's revival of Batman, *The Dark Knight Returns* (which, like so much of Miller's work, embraces the very hero Moore's deconstruction showed to be so problematically right-wing, even while developing Moore's ideas of superman as a dupe of the government and, later, as a kind of god), Neil Gaiman's *Sandman* (a brilliant *Bildungsroman* of the fantasy genre which masterfully reconstructs the hero *Watchmen* deconstructed), Moore's own later work (such as *Miracleman*—an insightful, neo-Nietzschean fable, *Supreme*, *Top Ten*, *Tom Strong*, and *The League of Extraordinary Gentlemen*), as well as—at the very heart of the mainstream—the death and multiple rebirths of *Superman* himself and the very popular *Ultimate* work by Brian Michael Bendis, Mark Millar, and many others.

54. For a discussion of three such recent attempts (comics in which "The Thing" is Jewish, "Rawhide Kid" is gay, and "Captain America" is Black), see Alan Jenkins, "Minority Report," *The Nation*, 12 May 2003, 36–38.

55. I would like to thank Mungo Thomson, Brent Kalar, and Gideon Yafee for generously sharing their brilliant Watchmen insights while I was working on this chapter (I wish I could have incorporated them all), Anne Margaret Baxley, Kelly Becker, Hubert Dreyfus, Kirsten Thomson, and an anonymous reviewer for extremely helpful feedback, the audience of the 25 April 2003 philosophy colloquium at UNM for a stimulating discussion, and Jeff McLaughlin for encouraging me to write this chapter in the first place. (I dedicate it to the philosophers of the future, still happily exiled in the comic book aisles).

Jean-Paul Sartre Meets Enid Coleslaw

Existential Themes in Ghost World

—LAURA CANIS AND PAUL CANIS

Consciousness is a being, the nature of which is to be conscious of the nothingness of its being.

—JEAN-PAUL SARTRE, *Being and Nothingness*

I don't want to go anywhere or do anything. . . . I just want it to be like it was in high school! . . . I guess that's the problem. . . . I feel like I want to become a totally different person. . . . Before I was going to college, my secret plan was to one day not tell anybody and just get on some bus to some random city and just move there and become this totally different person . . . and not come back until I had become this new person. . . . I used to think about that all the time . . .

—ENID COLESLAW, *Ghost World*

In another time, on another continent, there was an underground counter-cultural literature relished and enjoyed by black-clad habitués of smoky coffee shops and other adult rendezvous, who considered themselves defiantly and brutally honest about their world and times, and who turned to this literature as their inspiration and their testimony. The major figures of this counter-cultural movement wrote novels, plays, essays, and manifestos that had a dark, but yet not quite despairing, spirit and worldview. This movement's apparent bleakness was, some said, merely cynical, bitter, or even dangerous. Nonetheless, Existentialism, as this underground liter-ary-philosophical-cultural movement was known, rather quickly came above ground, and became a body of work and way of thinking of keen popular interest and debate in the wake of the certainly unsunny and all-too-grim events of the first half of the twentieth century.

We are speaking here first of all about Europe. The devastations of two incredibly brutal world wars, the shocking rise and rampage of fascist total-itarianism across a number of European nations, the horrors of a method-ically and matter-of-factly implemented genocide against European Jewry and other unwanteds, and then as a *coup de grace*, the dawning of the nuclear age and the mutual drawing by both East and West of an Iron Curtain dividing Europe in two—all of this left the European mind reeling. Happy optimism, faith in the integrity of established social orders and institutions, and even faith in a basic modicum of goodness in the heart of one's neighbor, attitudes such as these were beginning to appear not as merely quaint or sweet, but as in fact possibly outright *delusional*, as bygone and simple-hearted as a belief in Santa Claus. Unlike America, which responded to the end of World War Two by sinking into its collective sofa and dreaming that peculiar American dream of green-planed lawns, nuclear families (albeit huddled, perchance, in a nuclear shelter), cute but rascally youngsters growing up into adoring but comically bumbling spouses, and in general, that entire constellation of optimism and resolve and above all *faith*, that designates what a later American president would hearken back to as that great *morning in America*, for Europe it was not morning. It was twilight. Grey. Shadowy. And not a little foreboding.

Of course, we can add parenthetically that a sense of darkness would not remain limited to Europe. If Europe found it increasingly impossible to feel itself of a sunny disposition as the cruelties and inhumanities of the twentieth century unfolded on its own doorstep, perhaps this is merely an indication of what is required for a people to undergo a critical phase of self-examination. For as we know, while American soldiers and citizens throughout the first half of the twentieth century could return home to placid and unbombed cities and homes, America too was growing its own inward crises that would eventually haunt it the distinctly American crises of ingrained societal racism, a pernicious overtrust in military adventurism, and the ravages of systemic poverty across too many corridors of the American populace.

One can observe, in this context, that America did in fact experience its own existentialist renaissance in the form of the Beat poets and writers, most of whom were themselves avid readers of the existentialist novels and plays that had come over from France and Germany a generation earlier. And indeed, in works such as Jack Kerouac's *On the Road* and Alan Ginsberg's *Howl,* we find America's own version of Existentialism in full-throated native bloom, only this time reacting not to the horrors of Europe, but to the growing sense that America was subtly entering its own twilight time. In fact, it was the American Beats who formed the seedbed of ideas and concerns that would come to fruition in the critical self-examination and counter-culture that developed in the 1960s. One can fairly say that the American version of Existentialism was following on Europe's footsteps, but at a distance of about a quarter century.

But turning to the origins, one of the most important figures at the inception and articulation of European Existentialism was Jean-Paul Sartre (1905–1980), a French philosopher, novelist, playwright, and political activist. We will be focusing specifically on Sartre's idea of and insights into Existentialism as we explore how this body of thought is echoed in the world of some contemporary American comics.

You might be surprised to hear that one can find a robust present-day expression of Existentialism, that serious and sobering philosophy, in, of all places, comic books. Yet, there are myriad examples of Existentialist themes and ideas in numerous of the contemporary underground comix artists. We will be exploring one of the most gifted of these artists, Daniel Clowes, whose carefully drawn and subtly written graphic novels (as aficionados of the genre would rightly insist on calling them) have an intellectual and emotional depth that rivals any serious work of literature.

Existential themes abound in *Ghost World* (Clowes, 1998), the most well known of Clowes's comics. *Ghost World* was made into a pretty decent movie back in 2002, starring Thora Birch and Scarlett Johansson as Enid and Rebecca, and featuring the indie-film heartthrob Steve Buscemi as Seymour, a character based loosely on Bob Skeetes from the comic. But there are some significant differences between the comic and the movie that make reading the actual comic vital to understanding Clowes's ideas and vision, so we highly recommend getting hold of *Ghost World* the comic, whether as the graphic novel (Clowes, 1998) or in the individual episodes serially in issues 11 through 18 of Clowes's *Eightball* comic book (Clowes, 1993–1997).

There are two main reasons why the comic, and not the film, is the real deal for our purposes. First, *Ghost World* the comic is more truly Existential than the movie. In the comic, our heroine Enid confronts her absurd situation for the most part alone, whereas in the movie, she has a romantic interest. Existentialism, however, is about brutally honest self-examination, not love and romance. *Ghost World* the movie is hardly a typical love story, but still, by focusing largely on a romantic story line, the film is nowhere as profound as the comic. One might say, after all, that romantic love is the ultimate and oldest form of escapism, and Existentialism is decisively *not* interested in escapist sentimentality or dreaming. A romance implies two protagonists. In the film version of *Ghost World*, Enid's path of self-examination and discovery occurs as she finds a fellow traveler Buscemi's Seymour in the baffling world she is beginning to see through adult eyes. Seymour is much older and has figured out ways to deal with his alienation in the harsh reality of post-capitalist junk culture. He copes by immersing himself in a more meaningful and authentic time through the great old blues records which he avidly collects and listens to in the quiet monastery of his bachelor's apartment. Enid finds in Seymour a kind of model for becoming authentic for growing up in an alienating world. But in the *Ghost World* comic, Enid has to struggle to mature toward an authentic, non-alienated adulthood without much guidance. Granted, an important part of that struggle involves testing just how big a part her best friend Rebecca will play in this quest. For example, the following conversation.

> Enid: I have to get back and study [for the college entrance exam] pretty soon.
> Rebecca: That's okay, I just wanted to tell you that I might be coming with you.
> Enid: What do you mean? You're driving me to Strathmore?
> Rebecca: Yeah, except I was thinking maybe I'll move there and live with you and get a job around there or something.
> Enid: What are your talking about?
> Rebecca: I knew you didn't want me to come.
> Enid: No, no. . . . It's just weird. . . . I guess I've gotten so used to the idea of being alone, it's like . . . I dunno. . . . (*Ghost World*, 70–71)

Nonetheless, there is no one on the other side to help her across. Enid's father is kind, but mostly he allows his daughter to launch herself into the world on her own unguided course. Enid in the comic is, as the Existentialists knew all too well, ultimately alone in the universe.

The second reason that we recommend the comic has to do with the difference that the drawings make. Far from mere illustrations of the story, Clowes's drawings convey in a really visceral way that unpleasant, skin-crawling, nauseous feeling of pure alienation, a sense of dread or desolation over one's existence, that the Existentialists explored so intently. This has to do not only with Clowes's vision, but also with the nature of graphic images in contrast to fictional writing. Graphics invite participation by the reader in a way that writing cannot. As Jean-Paul Sartre would in fact put it in a discussion of painting, "The writer can guide you and, if he describes a hovel, make it seem the symbol of social injustice and provoke your indignation. The painter is mute. He presents you with *a* hovel, that's all. You are free to see in it what you like. . . . All thoughts and all feelings are there, adhering to the canvas in a state of profound undifferentiation. It is up to you to choose" (Baskin, 306–7). Thus the comic does what all great visual art does: it provides us with the thing itself, it *shows* the world, even as its story line describes it. Each of Clowes's drawings have a directness, a *mute* directness, blunt and to the point that cannot be fully conveyed in the film.

A typical novel has a story and an idea that can be summed up in a few words. Comics also have a story and often an idea, but the addition of the drawings engage the reader's imagination beyond the words and dialogue of the characters. The words in comics play and dart in and around the para-literal imaginative openings that the graphics create. What thus comes out of the interplay between mute drawing, terse writing, and imagination cannot be quickly summed up. It is this level of free and open engagement with *meaning* that makes comics an especially good medium for Existentialist stories and themes.

So what exactly are the Existentialist themes in *Ghost World?*

SARTRE'S EXISTENTIALISM

To begin to explore Existentialist themes in *Ghost World*, we might first take a look at Existentialism, the philosophy of existence, specifically as it was formulated by Jean-Paul Sartre, Existentialism's main proponent. Sartre was a short, pipe-smoking, wall-eyed man with bulbous eyes and lips. As a child, Poulou (as he was called) suffered greatly due to his looks: his abusive childhood chums alternately ignored and taunted him, and in his autobiography *Words*, Sartre even describes himself as a toad.[1] (Coincidentally, Sartre even looks a bit like a Clowes character—compare a photograph of Sartre with Clowes's portrait of Tina from "Like a Velvet Glove Cast in Iron," on the cover of *Eightball* number 10. She's that green thing grasping a tube of lipstick in her pincers.)

But Sartre did not let his off-putting looks, nor his unfortunate experiences with the everyday cruelty of others, stop him from taking on the difficult problem of figuring out the meaning of life, who we are as human beings, and what prospects there are for us to be happy. In fact, Sartre's experiences with social rejection were formative to his philosophy. The proto-Existentialist Friedrich Nietzsche once said that every great philosophy has been the personal confession of its author and a kind of involuntary and unconscious memoir . . ." (Nietzsche, 13). Sartre's philosophy is easily autobiographical. It would not take a large stretch of the imagination to associate Sartre's formulation of, for example, the problem of the encounter with the other" ("Nothingness," 301–556) with his scarring childhood experiences.

At the same time, Sartre was no wimp. He did not hide from confrontation. As a philosopher, he had no patience for philosophizing without action. Sartre's message was one of courage: that each of us alone is responsible for what we make of ourselves. This was more than just an abstract idea; for he thought that any philosopher with a theory of commitment needs to commit to seeing that theory through to action. Words without action are empty, and this is how Sartre lived his life as a philosopher and as a human being. At the outbreak of World War II, when he was a 35-year-old high school philosophy teacher, Sartre voluntarily joined the French army. He was promptly captured by the Germans and lived with 25,000 men in a POW camp for eight months. In the camp, despite hunger, lice, fleas, bedbugs, freezing cold temperatures, and lack of privacy (there were 40 men per shack), Sartre started writing his major philosophical text, *Being and Nothingness*. Then, immediately after being released, he joined the French Resistance movement as a journalist. After the war, Sartre was an anti-colonialist during the French-Algerian war of the mid-1950s through early 1960s. He turned down any honors bestowed upon him by the Establishment. In 1964, he refused the Nobel Prize for Literature because he thought it would interfere with his social and political commitments and his responsibilities to his readers. In 1968, he supported the student protest movement that ripped through France. In the 1970s, he turned down invitations to meet two different French presidents, but then agreed to meet with President Giscard d'Estaing, just so that he could ask for help for the Indochinese boat people. Obviously, for Sartre, to philosophize is always to take a stand.

Along with his activism, Sartre wrote books of philosophy, essays, plays, novels, biographies, and screenplays, all of which explore themes of the meaning of existence. For Sartre, Existentialism was a multimedia philosophy. It was never limited to just good old fashioned, ivory-tower philosophy articles and books. Why? Well, theory is one thing it appeals to the intellect. But art whether painting, fiction, poetry, theater, film, comics, or fully authentic philosophy appeals to the emotions.

Existentialism is not just a theory about the relationship between human beings and their existence; Existentialism expresses a feeling about existence too. Existentialism recognizes that the total human being consists of reason and intellect, but also emotions and instincts. Communicating to our rational part is much different than communicating with our emotional aspect. Authentic philosophy is also art, insofar as it speaks not only to our rational side, but also to our emotions, and to that part of us that is responsible for our taking action. Philosophy as a form of art deals with issues of how we deal with our deep drives and instincts, loves and fears. The philosophy of Existentialism gives a theoretical account of the human condition and appeals to our reason to test whether or not it is accurate. But at the same time Existentialism does not try to convince only with arguments. Existentialism, as an aesthetic philosophy, inclines us in a particular direction, it seduces our feelings and charms us into a point of view, attitude, or perspective without our having to reason it through from the start. The Existentialist movement, with all of its different media, engages us fully because it works on many different aspects of our existence as human beings.

When we turn to Clowes's comics, we see much the same situation. Clowes uses his drawings and stories to *show* rather than intellectually explain the weirdness that is always with us, but that we mostly tune out as we go through our daily lives trying to get stuff done. Clowes's comic world is odd, unsettling, uncanny, unbalanced, and this marks it as a quintessentially Existentialist kind of world. But do this experiment: after reading a Clowes comic, go to the street, the mall, the supermarket, and see what it does to your perceptions and feelings. You just might feel as if you have gained admission to some absurdist circus or freak show, instead of the Safeway or the subway station. This is what art has always been able to do for us: art transports us. Art gives our world a different feel. By heightening our perceptions and sensations, art helps us to see a certain perspective, a buried truth.

But we are not here to give you the art experience. For that, go to Clowes's comics themselves. What we can do in the context of this discussion is to try to enhance your experience of the comics by providing some philosophical tools that you can use to become a little more conscious of the effects that the art is having on you, and so to enjoy it on a deeper level. With that in mind, let's explore some of the details of the philosophy of Existentialism.

One of the questions that philosophers have always tried to answer is, what is a human being? What is the nature, the essence, of the human? What makes us different from other kinds of beings? Existentialist philosophers are particularly interested in this question. An Existentialist, says Sartre, is someone who believes that the *essence* of the human being that which makes us human, that which *defines* us is that we have no essence. Sartre's concise formulation for this idea is that in the case of human nature, our existence comes before essence (EH, 26).

Existentialism takes as its starting point the fact that human beings are literally thrown into the world. We did not ask to be here and we have no control over the circumstances that we are born into—who our parents are, where we live, when we live, or indeed any of our particular circumstances. But Existentialism takes this even further, arguing that we are born without a purpose—no goal, no overarching plan, no predetermined *meaning*. In the beginning, there was . . . nothing. Whatever we make of our lives is our own doing. We live, we make choices, and through those choices we propel ourselves into our own future, we define ourselves, and figure out for ourselves what our purposes are. Man is condemned to be free, says Sartre, because once thrown into the world, he is responsible for everything he does (EH, 34).

In contrast to Sartre's existence precedes essence, earlier philosophies of human nature had said that human beings are born with a purpose, that our essence precedes our existence. For example, God, as our creator, is said to have created us for a purpose, a plan, a meaning. Today one can still find many people, the vast majority of humanity, in fact who still hold and take refuge in this belief. This fact alone that human beings apparently are the only species that seeks after some self-conscious need for a meaning, purpose, and *point* to their existence elevates human beings to a higher level than any other life form on earth.

Taking a radical stance, Sartre proposed that thinking of human beings as created with a purpose or created for a reason in fact does nothing to elevate human beings. On the contrary, it reduces us to the level of mere objects or tools. His reasoning is like this. To have a purpose, an essence, from the start is to have no freedom at all. Artifacts of all kinds—guns, chop sticks, genetically engineered vegetables, you name it—are all created with a purpose. Each one is the fulfillment of a pre-existent plan and meaning. In every case, *the object's essence thus precedes its existence*: each thing is designed and made to do a particular job for us, to fulfill a particular purpose. The objects themselves have no choice in the matter. A gun is made to shoot, period. Even then, the gun has no choice as to if and when it will shoot. Its creators decide that too.

Are we likewise nothing more than products that God or Nature has designed and created? Certainly not, thought Sartre. We are not *creatures*, created with a particular purpose or destiny; we are . . . *freedoms*. There is no determinism, Sartre declares. Man is free, man *is* freedom (EH, 34). We are the being that exists *before* it can be defined. We are the being, among all other beings, with the power to define itself. Our existence precedes our essence.

Does all of this self-defining start at birth? Not really, since as children we are not really free. Parental figures provide us with activities, a sense of purpose, and even an interpretation of the meaning of existence. It is the mature human being that can experience existential freedom. At the same time, the person who does not accept his existential freedom can never be truly mature. One could even claim that the choice to embrace radical freedom marks the beginning of authentic adulthood. In an early entry in his journal, Roquentin, the hero in Sartre's novel *Nausea*, notes, Three o'clock. Three o'clock is always too late or too early for anything you want to do (14). Isn't adolescence a bit like three o'clock? It is too late to depend on the prefabricated world of your parents, yet too early to as yet have your own world. The magic space between the end of high school and the beginning of whatever comes next is the existential moment *par excellence*. It is the brief time when the adolescent limbo comes to a head. Enid in *Ghost World*, is at three o'clock. She exists on the precipice, her fate as either authentically free or self-deceivingly predestined lying in the wait.

But there is more to authentic adult freedom than making the choices that will make my own life more meaningful, more pleasant. Sartre jumps into the cold bath of morality when he argues that when we make a choice for ourselves, we are at the same time choosing for all of humankind. Suddenly, the stakes are a lot higher. My personal choice impacts everybody else, whether I choose to acknowledge it or not. The actions we take are not only a choice of *what* to do. They also make a statement about what we think human life should be like. In Sartre's words, "of all the actions a man may take in order to create himself as he wills to be, there is not one which is not creative, at the same time, of an image of man such as he believes he ought to be. . . . What we choose is always the good; and nothing can be good for us unless it is good for all" (EH, 29). This is why being free is such a burden, and why it feels more like being condemned than bird-like. The responsibility is not only for my own good; it is for the good of all like me, which is, ultimately, everyone.

Let us take an example. Suppose that I decide to play one of eleven bombshell female contestants on a reality dating show on television, even though I am required to sign a contract that makes me promise not to disclose certain facts, such as whether or if the producers of the program have in fact scripted the show's dramatic twists and turns and its winners and losers. My decision to participate is not just a personal choice. You might say that the personal is always universal, for my choice creates a world in which I have thus chosen to live. I have chosen a world, which of course I share with millions of others, where lies are accepted as truth, where lies are in fact systematically called reality itself. In such a world, lying becomes no longer a problem, and such a world contributes to a possible future in which people can be manipulated by anyone in power who wants to, because there are no standards for truth anymore. This would be a world where the idea of telling the truth has devolved into nothing more than a joke.

You might be feeling a bit incredulous at this point. How could all of this be implied in my own private choice to participate in a reality TV show? Yet this is exactly what a truly free person would realize. This level of creative moral imagination is needed in order to act based on the full set of facts, to make informed decisions about what to do. In order to be *truly* free, we must have absolute clarity about the implications and consequences of all of our actions, no matter how seemingly trivial.

There is a further twist, though, to the Existentialist analysis of the human condition. We can always choose, at any moment, *not* to choose. We can choose, paradoxically enough, to *flee* from our responsibility of our freedom. And on top of that, we can choose to pretend that we had no choice in the matter. This utter self-deception about our freedom Sartre calls bad faith. The truth is, to quote the familiar 1970s anthemic Rush ode to existential freedom, "if you choose not to decide, you still have made a choice." To deny that is to act in bad faith, trying to escape the enormous responsibility of being free. We become nothing more than automatons, men in grey flannel suits, Stepford wives.

Another twist in existential freedom is that, since we are always growing and changing, always in process, we can never really be anything. We are constantly becoming. So human beings are not only freedoms; we are also projects. As Sartre puts it, Man is, indeed, a project which possesses a subjective life, instead of being a kind of moss, or a fungus or a cauliflower. Before that projection of the self nothing exists . . . (EH, 28). As projects, we have two distinct areas of freedom: envisioning new possibilities for ourselves in our future, and interpreting the facts of our past in light of new projects and plans. (The term Sartre uses for the facts and givens in our lives is facticity). When we try to establish ourselves as something particular—whether in a social role (waiter, mother, criminal) or as having a certain character (shy, intellectual, cruel)—we are in bad faith. Bad faith is mistakenly considering ourselves as something permanent and settled. This falsely lightens the burden of our freedom. Another form of bad faith is to fool ourselves into thinking that we have infinite possibilities, as if we have all of eternity and all the power and talent in the world to achieve whatever it is that we dream of. In an uncharacteristically judgmental moment, Sartre calls those who are guilty of the first type of bad faith cowards, and those guilty of the second type scum (EH, 52).

Will Enid turn into a coward or scum? Or will she become who she is, authentic, free? One hint: the worst is yet to come! Tune in tomorrow. . . . Same bat time, same bat channel.

EXISTENTIAL ABANDONMENT AND GROWING UP

—This is My Happening, and it Freaks Me Out!

—ENID[2]

Being condemned to be free has some unpleasant emotions associated with it. Sartre offers us the observation that there are three fundamental emotions at the heart of the human condition: anguish, abandonment, and despair. We must fully and deeply experience these profound feelings because these feelings alone are in fact what can prod us into meaningful action in the world. A certain kind of suffering, we can say, is necessary for authentic freedom.

The experience of abandonment is at the heart of our existential suffering, as well as perhaps the most radical of these three emotions, and we will focus here on that particular existential feeling. For Sartre, this feeling is rooted in our recognition of our having been abandoned in some way by God. There are many ways that one can come to this chilling awareness about one's world. For example, one of the common dreads that we can easily call upon is the utter cruelty and depravity of world events in the twentieth century. Two world wars; genocide; purges that would kill millions; more genocide; brutal civil wars around the globe; crushing poverty covering entire continents; more wars; more genocide. Given this world scene, it is impossible to feel that God is in the world. It is impossible to feel that God was superintending at Auschwitz, or nodding in approval as His cosmic plan was being furthered by Pol Pot. The reality of evil finally hit home in the twentieth century: one cannot look at a mass grave and say, God was here. No; that is precisely what one does *not* say, but rather one sees the horror of evil in the world, one sees the crematoriums and sees evidence of the slaughter in the piles of limbs, and one says, *God was not and is not here.*

Even if I feel I have fortunately escaped the ravages of such evil, or if I perhaps feel for some vainglorious reason that the cosmos has purposely decided to protect me in particular among all the many hundreds of millions, what does such an escape or special protection for myself do about the world and the millions of souls in it not so fortunate, or not so specially protected? I can only feel truly fortunate or truly protected insofar as I turn away, ultimately, from the evil itself. When evil becomes so real, vivid, and powerful in the world around me, such as was witnessed by so many in the twentieth century, it is impossible not to feel abandoned and apart from God. But this creates the "problem of evil," as the theologians call it: if it becomes apparent to us that there is all too much that happens to humans in the world that even the most abstruse all-good and all-powerful God could ever actually permit and indulge, then it becomes extremely difficult to believe that God exists—or at least, that our idea of God must have been quite mistaken. God would not have created this kind of a world. God could have nothing to do with this dismal death march called human life. But regardless of whether or not God exists in the form that the Judeo-Christian tradition had long thought, nonetheless the important point for Sartre is that, in any case, we must act as if God has abandoned us; we must take full responsibility. "The real problem," Sartre writes, "is not that of His existence; what man needs is to find himself again and to understand that nothing can save him from himself, not even a valid proof of the existence of God" (EH, 56).

But what of this life then? Humans, not gods, have created it. And in this life, this one life we apparently have, nothing can save us from ourselves except ourselves. This is the attitude of abandonment, and it was and is a disposition familiar in the minds of many of us. What occurs when one is thus bereft of God? Without God, one feels alone, helpless, anxious, and vulnerable, just as we do at the death of someone on whom we thought our very life would depend. But abandonment by God causes not only this grief. When we think through the implications, we see that it causes a tremendous shift in our experience of our place in the universe. Without God, it seems that all of our misery is for nothing. We can no longer say that it was for the best, or it is in God's plan. And without God, there is nothing to guarantee future goodness and rightness. We are faced with the very real possibility of a world that will continue on without an acceptable measure of even the most basic scraps of goodness, truth, and beauty.

Thus, as I experience the emotion of feeling abandoned, I see how fragile and hard-won goodness is. I recognize that there is absolutely no guarantee that evil will not prevail *except through my own actions*. My actions—what I can will to do, what I decide to take on, what I actually perform and see through—are the only events that I can control, so, whatever it is I might discover about the insecurity and rarity of goodness in the world, it is *nevertheless* my responsibility to render *my own* decision about the fate of the world. *Fruitful* awareness of abandonment for Existentialism is exactly this realization on an emotional level that I am left alone, but left alone to figure out what to do. Without a guide or a faith that absolves me of this anguish about my life and this world, I understand myself as the ultimate authority who is ultimately thus *responsible*, the only possible creator I will ever meet in this world. Who creates the world? *I do, everyday*. As Sartre puts it: We are left alone, without excuse. That is what I mean when I say that man is condemned to be free. Condemned, because he did not create himself, yet he is nevertheless at liberty, and from the moment that he is thrown into this world he is responsible for everything he does (EH, 34).

The fact that God is gone is therefore not a completely bad thing. Believing in God, though it feels much more pleasant than experiencing the horrifying despair and anguish of abandonment, nonetheless puts the ultimate restriction on our freedom. We have used the belief in God and His plan for us as a security blanket to pull over our heads to keep us feeling safe, a set of rules to alleviate the Sisyphian labor of every day having to decide anew for oneself, and as a repository for the ultimate meaning of the world. But in a world bereft of God, the consequence is that we humans have the opportunity and the motivation to *evolve ourselves* to the position that the gods have long held. Absent the Divine, *we* become the world's only possible protectors, deciders, and knowers.

This, too, is Enid's task in Clowes's *Ghost World*. The specific central loss that Enid confronts, her specific great absence or abandonment, is the utter absence of what we can term human decency in her world. Where are the decent people in her life and in the world that confronts her each day? Where are things done well among these avenues of stores and people and shuttered houses? Where is the good fight against terrible fate at the diner and on the street corner and in the passing bus? Gone, ever gone, like miners from a ghost town. Hence indeed the title, *Ghost World*.

The specific kind of world that *Ghost World* depicts is an absurd one, which is, from an Existentialist perspective, kind of a best of all possible worlds. An absurd world is one devoid of any thoroughgoing reason or purpose. In an absurd world, the rule is that people are caught up in ludicrous situations, daily lives without meaning or sense, pointless suffering, aimless delusions, and trivial but crucial mistakes, miscues, and miscommunications. Without a faith or hope to salve our worry and buffer us from such a world, we cannot help but become aware that there are in fact no guarantees that we ourselves or anyone, for that matter will ever be happy. In 18-year-old Enid, Clowes has given us a character in the midst of confronting just this quandary of the absurdity of the world. At that moment right after high school, beginning to see the truth of world in glimmers that Clowes shows us all too accurately in the panels of his comic, she is at the beginning of the tightrope that will lead either to authentic adulthood, full of freedom and embracing responsibility, or a kind of inauthentic, perpetual existential immaturity, filled with simmering, subliminal fear and loathing.

Will Enid embrace her responsibility in its fullness, having been prompted by her deeply felt experiences of abandonment, anguish, and despair? Or will she take another route away from abandonment, and hide in the grand self-deception that Someone Else has done the job of determining her life for her? Enid is at the beginning of the tightrope between dependent childhood and free adulthood. *Ghost World* is the story of the tightrope walk, and her creation of herself as an authentic individual along the way.

Before Enid's story even begins to be told, Clowes gives us clues about Enid's character up to the beginning of that summer after her graduation from high school. A drawing of Enid walking alone, head down thoughtfully, passing an apartment window lit by a television's glow and inhabited by a hand holding a fast-food paper cup and straw. On the wall of the building is spray-painted the graffiti GHOST WORLD. Enid is thoughtful and sometimes solitary, while others drown themselves in television and fast food. Scene two, on the dedication page, we get a glimpse of Enid's bookshelf: Little toys like a Japanese plastic egg-laying chicken; a homuncular little angry-faced potato-head-shaped man whom we will later find out is Goofy Gus, a favorite childhood toy. Some weird sunglasses. Comic books, some serious but probably assigned reading (*Oedipus Rex* used), an encyclopedia of unusual sex practices, and some typical teenage-girl items such as CDs and a videotape of Scooby Doo.

What stands out perhaps most of all is a magazine called *Absolutely Normal*—eluding to Enid's most immediate struggle: just how far does she have to go to avoid conformity and a robot-like existence, a life both saved and enslaved by *the norm*? At one point in the story, she and Josh have a significant exchange when they are discussing Enid's new hearse, which Enid thought would make a good vehicle to take to college.

Josh: I'm just surprised. . . . It's not really your style.
Enid: . . . You don't know me, Josh.
J: Apparently not.
E: . . . So what is my style?
J: To defy definition. . . . (GW 68)

The trouble with taking as your style or identity the effort to always defy definition is that, if you truly defy definition, you don't have a core self, an essence, and that must logically involve also never being one who *always* tries to defy definition. This is an *illogical* identity, or to put it into the language of the Existentialists, an *absurd* one. Not to have a core self, not to become defined, is to be committed to having *no self*, an endless flight from ever *deciding* who one is. But, on the other hand, if you are easily defined and experience your self as something stable, a finished product, you risk becoming calcified and constrained as a free person. This dilemma is context for the struggle for authenticity that Sartre describes, and it constitutes the inner tension within every authentic person's life. How much security can I permit myself? How much risk do I need in order to keep my freedom? *When* might I find hope and promise in myself and my world? *When* must I deny it? When must I stay, and when must I go? And where? Whither my self?

In the grotesqueries of the offbeat characters that Enid with her friend, Rebecca, encounter that summer after high school, Enid gradually develops the ability to be able to distinguish the authentic from inauthentic. It might seem at first glance as if nearly everyone in the ghost world lives through some degree of bad faith. All of these people are first of all regarded by Enid and Rebecca as ridiculous freaks of culture, everyone from the pitifully unfunny TV comedian to the homeless panhandler on the street. But what does their regard *say* about Enid and Rebecca? Does it reveal them as cynical, even cruel, teens who spend an otherwise boring summer with their ironic ridicule and scorn? Are they just cop-outs who deal with absurdity through ironic mockery?

Ironic mockery, it might be said, comprises the grim first baby-steps of existentialist enlightenment. It says a great deal about Enid's character, however, that she chooses not to wallow in cynical despair, as a lesser person in her situation might. She will not be depressed, or drown in *ennui*, or fall prey to creeping anxiety. In fact, in and despite the episodes of juvenile mockery and cruelty, her summer with Rebecca is from the start completely satisfying, entertaining, and even edifying, thanks to her talent as a kind of alchemist who can take the detritus of human situations and a messed-up set of characters, and through her eyes make it into a freak show, yes, but this means too: a *carnival, a celebration of the absurd*. Enid, as it turns out, is an *artist*.

The world for Existentialism becomes an arena for self-definition by means of judgement. The self is defined by its judgements and evaluations moral, aesthetic, and spiritual. We become who we are by forming opinions and taking a stand with regard to all kinds of possible models for existing, evaluating people, responding to events, appraising actions, judging ideals and values, and then assessing our own reactions to what our judgments disclose about ourselves and our own values. Enid experiences her self—her free, authentic, adult self—in every response to her situation, as an artist might, always seeking to somehow *transform yet tell the truth* about what she sees.

Nietzsche, who had made an enormous impression on Sartre, once observed that cynicism is the only form in which base souls approach honesty (*Beyond*, 38). It is fascinating to watch Enid's cynicism gradually drop away in this story and become replaced by her artist's eye for the absurd guy on the street. She learns to distinguish between those who truly act in bad faith from those who are struggling to act in good faith, to do things that you would want for everyone—even if, it must be said, these attempts are for the most part utter failures. The episode that best illustrates this transformation within Enid is the one that takes place in Hubba Hubba, The Original '50s Diner. It shouldn't go unnoticed that Enid wears her Holden Caufield-esque people-hunting cap. Enid takes Rebecca on a long bus ride out to the suburbs to check out this diner—Enid: Isn't this the greatest ever!? Rebecca: God, it's pathetic! E: Could they possibly be more clueless? I'm so happy we're here! Once inside, Enid mocks every inaccurate detail of the place, from the waiter with the Rick James mullet-perm— could any hair style be farther from the fifties?—to the music from the wrong decade. She is relentless with the waiter, who despite her poor treat- ment, continues to serve the girls respectfully and in a professional manner. The girls are reading the personals for a laugh. They come across one that sounds especially pathetic, and decide to play a joke on him and pretend they are the redhead he is seeking. Later, they bring Josh out for the joke to be played out. They spot the guy who must be "Bearded Windbreaker," and he is middle-aged, balding, and sad around the eyes. He waits for a half and hour, during which Enid and Rebecca find themselves surprised at their discomfort. They seem to actually feel a little compassion for the guy, and remorse for adding to his lonely unhappiness. Later, as they leave the restaurant, the friendly waiter says goodbye, and Enid, trying to assuage her guilt, runs back and leaves him a huge tip. That wasn't as much fun as the last time, Rebecca comments, as Enid frowns quietly to herself in the back seat on the way home. Thus is human kindness born in Enid.

Enid starts cynical, and finishes authentic. The transformation is complete. She sees the *humanity* even in the failed attempts at authenticity, the freak show, the bizarre melodrama that plays itself out in the streets and behind the closed doors of her hometown. And yet, what you sense in Enid even in her most selfishly cynical moments at the beginning of the summer is her determination to find a place for herself, her own energy for life. She's got chutzpah. She's brave. She is deeply bothered, but not cowed, by the uncertainty of her life. She exercises a boldness in each situation she finds herself in. She is finding that she does not need a shining faith or guide in order to have a sense of self that is worthy of respect.

Her first stab at authenticity had been something she had done since childhood: she experiments with her look, creating a unique assortment of personae from an off-the-rack world. Her transformation as a person, though, comes about as she goes beyond, however, this persona of a mere look, and creates a *purposeful* self in a purposeless world. She becomes, not merely a *poseur*, but one who is without letting go of the truth she sees about the world utterly committed. She refuses to become disoriented by the sleazeballs in the porn shop, but neither does she pretend that such places do not exist. By treating the porn shop as just another Young Miss fashion boutique where she can get herself a cool hat, she claims the place as her own. She orients herself, not hiding from reality, but positioning herself by either saying Yes or No to it, by transforming it into art for herself and those around her, but without sweetening it, without falsifying it. Enid is an artist; but Enid does not *redeem* anything.

Enid is working towards judging each person or situation she encounters according to her own internal standard. She stubbornly insists, indeed demands, that she will be *amused* in a revolting world. It's not simply a dead-end and fruitless sense of irony that causes Rebecca and Enid to, for example, idolize bad comedian Joey McCobb, or to have a semi-religious experience in the run-down and desolate Cavetown, USA. It's a stubbornness that says: I *will* make this my experience. If the comedian's jokes are not funny, I'll find humor in *that*. If Cavetown, U.S.A. or the '50s diner fail to transport, I will be transported by their flagrant deficiencies. I will not succumb to utter boredom and depression. I will not be defeated by the failures in the world, but neither will I take flight from them into a fantasy world where their all-too-vivid sorrow is hidden away *I will be authentic*.

Nietzsche wrote: "When one is young, one venerates and despises without that art of nuances which constitutes the best gain of life . . ." (*Beyond*, 43). Enid's negative but aesthetic responses to the world demonstrates her freedom, her own dawning best gain of life. To say no is a creative reaction to negativity and to exercise it is to express one's ownmost individuality. It is to take a stand and to make one's mark. Likewise, to say yes to an unmistakably bad comedian Joey McCobb, or to say that the poorly conceived and inaccurate '50s diner is good can be the ultimate act of self-creation and self-originality. To learn to say yes to something you may have at one time shunned can be the ultimate act of good faith (for example, Enid's earnest response to a funny-looking old man—"Oh my God, look! That little old man bought those pathetic flowers at the grocery store to take home to his wife! Oh God, it's so cute, I'm dying!" [GW, 55])—a reflective, critical, and conscious decision to evolve and change. The sign of the highest person, the authentic individual, is that they say Yes and No according to their own internal compass. The authentic person is not enslaved by her own past judgments, having developed the capacity to re-evaluate as well as evaluate in the first place. It is a sign of having re-evaluated one's values.

The person of bad faith is half-conscious, self-deceiving, failing to reflect on herself and find a meaningful place or role in the world. Such a person avoids present decisions and hides behind past ones. The most direct example of this is in Enid's friend Rebecca at the end of the story. Rebecca has made the choices that lead to security: a steady job at the bagel place, a relationship with Josh. But is her mood one of deep contentment and energy? Hardly. Her wincing face bespeaks resignation, almost a sense of defeat. Yes, her bagels are waspy. They are phony; they are Mall Bagels. She's being a phony in working there, not living up to her true potential, and she knows it. She is living up to society's expectations and would even be commended as a young adult with her head on straight. But she herself knows, and we know, that she is no longer an individual, she has *stopped creating herself.* The openness and freedom of her self is the high price she has paid for security and good sense.

In contrast to Rebecca, Enid at the end of the story is glowing, virtually bristling with energy and a sense of power in the face of the unknown. But yet Enid is no shining hero. Her energy and her brilliance is an interior quality that does not bleach out the still-absurd and uncertain world and future she faces. She shines in an *existentialist* form of beauty: alone, uncertain, abandoned, but resolved, self-aware, *knowing.*

Enid's comment at the end of the story—"you have grown into a beautiful young woman" (80)—is exceedingly ambiguous. Because of the storyline's preceding panels, it seems to be directed at Rebecca, for one thing, representing Enid's acknowledgment that Rebecca has grown up as best she can, and that she is facing the dilemma of adulthood as best she can; who is she to think she can redeem Rebecca, or to alter the truth of who others are becoming? But Enid says this comment while she is walking down the street alone, walking toward another ride home on the public transit system. Thus she also appears to be saying this comment about herself. It is, in fact, her first self-reflective comment in the whole story. It is the final judgment of her growing up—a judgment finally, about her ownmost self.

People can go about without any completely realized and freed sense of self. If you have an ego (self-identification, a sense of self-interest and demand-for-self, a demand for a me and mine in the world) and a will (an intellectually determined desire, plans and goals in the world), you have enough to make your way in the world—but only to make your way inauthentically. As the joys of that summer come to an end the Satanists break up, Angel's turns into a poser hangout, Enid's college application is rejected—Enid gains a freed self, and she demonstrates this freedom as she walks off into the sunset and gets on Norman's bus, the bus with the unknown destination. She is taking herself down the open road. The message of the story is the open road, being on that road, and not leaving it. Making the self free, then leaving your fate to that self set out on the open road, knowing, transformative, and truthful. As the Existentialists argued, such a stance toward life is perhaps the bravest principle that humans have ever proposed to themselves. The self judging for itself, preserving its own integrity at the same time that it loses itself to the indeterminacy and uncertainty of the world. This too is compassion; it is to stay with the world, to decide not to leave it, to stay with its many stories and sufferings, and to resolve to find freedom nowhere else but *there*. This is what Enid learns at the end of her summer, at the end of her juvenile years, and at the beginning of her becoming an adult.

Looking back on the *Ghost World* story, this flowering of existential compassion in Enid's character is further illuminated by considering Enid's and Rebecca's categorization of human types. In the abandoned ghost world, where decency is optional, there are basically two kinds of people that have survived as the remnants of humanity, like cockroaches surviving a nuclear attack. These are what we might call the creeps and the lameoids. And the pathetic losers. The creeps range from those of weak character to those that are morally vile and genuinely evil. Creeps in the ghost world include the former-priest child pornographer/molesters (and John Ellis, the zine writer who thinks that presenting this guy's work in his zine is a good promotional move), bull dykes who torture high school jocks, and jailed mass-murderers receiving truckloads of fan mail from teenage girls. There are also sell-out creeps like the smug John Crowley, formerly known as Johnny Apeshit, who, when Enid asks what he has been up to, replies, "I've been going to business school. . . . I'm gonna be a *big-ass corporate f#ck!* I'm gonna work for ten years, f#ck things up from the inside as much as I can, and then retire when I'm thirty-five! That's the way to be subversive . . . f#ck this alternative pussy punk rock shit! You gotta get in the f#ckin' *game*, man!" (24). Creeps are at best hypocritical and self-indulgent; at worst, they are fanatical, sociopathic, and dangerous.

The lameoids are those easily-ridiculed weak individuals who have decided that the best way to cope with their station in life is to adapt and conform in predictably ineffectual ways to a schlocky, absurd, and soul-deadening world. The lameoids include the bad comedian; whatever faceless corporate entity came up with the details of the '50s diner; and the lame-brain cashier at the record store. Another lameoid is Enid's childhood chum Mellora, who, though employed by both Greenpeace and a right-wing politician, has almost no cognitive dissonance. Lameoids tend to be lazy, unimaginative, resentful, and captive to their own attempts at coping with the absurdity of the world by denying it.

But there is another group, one that Enid was unable to distinguish from the others at first. These are the victims of fate, and it is this group that, in the end, teaches Enid the truth of human suffering in the world. The victims of fate include the aging prostitute with humongous tits, who Enid conjectures probably became a prostitute precisely because of the size of her breasts ("It's like, if you have giant tits you have no choice *but* to be a slut! . . . I mean, can you imagine being a high school teacher with huge tits? Like what if Mrs. Noyes had *massive, pointy hooters?* There's no way!" [23]). Other victims of fate are high school classmate Carrie Vandenberg, the well-liked, attractive girl whose beauty mark had suddenly grown into a tumorous, veiny, cancerous growth wrapping around the perimeter of her face; and Bearded Windbreaker, the unnamed middle-aged single guy who looks worn and sad but not terrible, and whose pathetic personal ad prompts Enid and Rebecca to prank call him and trick him into showing up at the diner (44–45). Finally, there's Bob Skeetes, whom Enid evaluates first as a grisly, old *con man . . .* Like Don Knotts with a homeless tan . . . [16], but whom she later recognizes as almost a wise soothsayer and a symbol of gutsy survival in the ghost world. There is nothing to indicate that those who are victims of fate *did not* try their best to make authentic decisions, but somehow they could not get out from under certain pressures, whether societal, physical, or even just the pressure of growing older and wear and tear of loneliness.

And then, in a category of his own, there's Josh. Enid and Rebecca are both in love with him. Josh, Enid proclaims, "We love you. You're the only decent person left in the world! Rebecca: Josh, will you marry us?" (49). Josh defies categorization. Josh is a paragon of dignity in a world of misshapen bodies and twisted souls: he's attractive in a simple, understated way; kind and socially concerned; and tolerant of Enid and Rebecca's incessant teasing. But Josh seems also to be perhaps at a loss at what to do with his life. As a regular, decent person, it is difficult for him to find where he fits in— hence, his friendship with weird girls like Enid and Rebecca. There is no trace in his character that he has an idea or even any well-formed wish to rise above that station or to even examine whether or not such a life is the one he wishes to live. Josh, then, just might be what a victim of fate looks like *before* fate has struck: the decent human being who is merely being carried down the road of life by whatever ready option presents itself. The Josh of today could very well be the Bob Skeetes of tomorrow.

In essence, Enid's gradual transformation into an adult awareness of her self and the world around her is provoked by the question: *What am I to do with all of the victims of fate of the world?* With the creeps, it is easy to write them off as simply repulsive, dubious individuals with dubious tales and even more dubious intents. With the lameoids, it is likewise easy to reject them as charlatans, or as intolerably dull. Even in the case of some victims of fate, it is easy to write them off as simply unpleasant reminders of how easily and unpredictably life can backfire. But the appearance of decency in the person of Josh gives pause to Enid's tendency to keep no small distance between herself and the world, and to *merely* artistically transform it into a theater of the absurd. The figure of Josh, not a hero in any sense but also neither an utter waste, teaches Enid compassion in the face of the absurdity of life. And from understanding that *Josh is worthy of compassion*, Enid understands that no loser merits a simple-minded condemnation, and that even the most evil creep is nevertheless a truth of the human condition incarnate. Such compassion such non-judgmental, simple awareness does not redeem any pathetic loser, lameoid, or creep. There can, after all, be no redemption unless the individual person endeavors to undertake it. But yet, *this is the world such as it is*, and as a matter of fact *decency*, in the oddest and most unlikely of places, does sometime flash out at us. In her movement from a cynicism and a one-dimensional ironic mockery of the real, to a willingness to try to discover the deeply threaded humanity that can appear in the midst sometimes of even the most grotesque fabrics of human existence, Enid finds her own tightrope that she knows she must walk. To find compassion for those whom she will nevertheless always leave behind.

NOTES

1. In his autobiography, *Words*, (tr. Bernard Frechtman. New York: George Braziller, 1964), Sartre recalls what happened after his grandfather took him for his first haircut, at age seven: There were shrieks, but no hugging and kissing, and my mother locked herself in her room to cry. Her little girl had been exchanged for a little boy. But that wasn't the worst of it. As long as my lovely ringlets fluttered about my ears, they made it possible to deny my obvious ugliness. Yet my right eye was already entering the twilight. She had to admit the truth to herself. My grandfather himself seemed nonplussed. He had been entrusted with her little wonder and had brought back a toad (p. 104).

2. Enid said this well before Austin Powers, both of whom are possibly consciously quoting Russ Meyer's *Beyond the Valley of the Dolls* (1970), when the Carry Nations meet wealthy rock scenester Z-Man at one of his swank parties, one of which indeed turned into quite the "freak-out."

Making the Abstract *Concrete*

How a Comic Can Bring to Life the Central Problems of
Environmental Philosophy

—KEVIN de LAPLANTE

INTRODUCTION

I first encountered Paul Chadwick's *Concrete* during the summer of 1997, while preparing to teach a course I had twice taught in the past called Introduction to Environmental Philosophy. I was agonizing over the reading selections. The typical student in this class would not be a philosophy major—indeed, for the majority of the students in the class, this would be the only philosophy course they would ever take in their undergraduate careers. The standard environmental philosophy textbooks available at the time were collections of articles that were written, for the most part, by philosophers for philosophers. It was my experience that many students found these articles difficult and/or dry, and they often failed to engage the average student in the central problems of environmental philosophy. Consequently, I was on the lookout for less "academic" teaching resources that would be more effective in presenting these problems in a stimulating and accessible way.

During that summer, I stumbled upon an eight-page black and white comic story written and drawn by Paul Chadwick, titled "Stay Tuned for Pearl Harbor" (Chadwick 1990: 123–30). "Concrete" is the name of both the title and the protagonist of a series of comic stories featuring episodes in the life of Ronald Lithgow, a former speechwriter whose brain has been transplanted by aliens into a twelve hundred pound rock body. Beyond the clichéd origin story, *Concrete* is utterly unlike your standard superhero comic. The *Concrete* stories are thoughtful ruminations on the human condition that use the unusual appearance and abilities of the title character as a device for exploring a range of psychological themes and social issues.

In "Stay Tuned for Pearl Harbor" we accompany Concrete and his two closest friends, Larry and Maureen, as they drive in a pickup truck along a winding highway (Concrete is in the back of the truck; he's too big to sit in the cab). We hear Concrete expressing his anger to Larry over government complicity in promoting industrial pollution, and general public apathy over the looming threats posed by a burgeoning global population. However, Concrete's monologue functions primarily as background and counter-point to the central focus of the story, which is a stunning visual depiction of Maureen's silent, imaginative musings as she stares out the passenger-side window, contemplating her own experiences of nature and the role of perception and the sensory limitations of our bodies in ecological awareness.

I included "Stay Tuned for Pearl Harbor" in the reading package for my fall environmental philosophy course, and the students responded very positively to it. In fact, the comic turned out to be a richer source for discussion topics than I had expected. One student mentioned in passing, at the end of the semester, that the central themes and issues of the whole course were, at some level, "all there" in the *Concrete* story. This is perhaps an overstatement, but the central aim of this essay is to try as far as possible to demonstrate what truth there is in this remark.

The essay is organized as follows. Section 1 gives an overview of the subject matter of environmental philosophy, introducing the important distinction between *environmental ethics* and *radical environmental philosophy*. Section 2 introduces the *Concrete* story. The subsequent sections introduce a variety of conceptual issues that are central to debates in environmental philosophy, and discuss how these issues are expressed, directly or indirectly, through the narrative structure and visual imagery of the story. I focus on the *anthropocentrism/nonanthropocentrism* distinction in section 3, *deep ecology* in section 4, and *ecofeminism* in section 5. I return to the question of how to define environmental philosophy in section 6, and argue for a reconceptualization of the field as a general philosophy of human-environment relations.

1. WHAT IS ENVIRONMENTAL PHILOSOPHY?

For the sake of generality, we can define environmental philosophy as the philosophical study of the relationship between human beings and the broader environmental context in which they live and act. Though the field is traditionally associated with relations to natural environments, it should be noted that environmental philosophy is also concerned with relations to the artifactual environments that are the dominant environmental context of most human beings (cities, cultivated and managed suburban and rural landscapes, etc.). However, environmental philosophy as an academic discipline emerged in the late 1960s and early 1970s in response to growing concerns about human-induced species extinctions, habitat destruction, industrial pollution and human population growth. These concerns have not diminished, and environmental philosophy continues to be motivated and informed by the threat to human and nonhuman welfare posed by human activity and impact on the natural environment. In this essay I'll be dealing exclusively with human relations to nonhuman organisms, populations and ecosystems.

The central themes of environmental philosophy revolve around two related but distinct sets of questions:

(1) Do human beings have moral obligations to protect or preserve the natural environment? If so, what are they, and to whom, or what, are they owed? How are such obligations justified?
(2) What are the root causes of contemporary attitudes and practices with respect to the natural environment, and how can we change them?

These two sets of questions identify two broad, partially overlapping sub-disciplines of environmental philosophy. Answers to the first question effectively define the field of "environmental ethics." Answers to the second question effectively define the field variously known as "political ecology," "radical ecology," or "radical environmental philosophy." Anyone who calls herself an environmental philosopher will have something to say about both sets of questions, but workers in the field tend to focus their attention on one set of questions over the other.[1]

Environmental Ethics

Most people who call themselves "environmental ethicists" are motivated by the belief that the answer to the first question is "yes": human beings do have moral obligations to protect and preserve the natural environment. They also, for the most part, believe that the ethical theories that have dominated Western moral philosophy are, in their traditional forms at least, not well-equipped to justify environmentalist intuitions about the wrongness of environmental pollution, ozone depletion, greenhouse warming, habitat destruction, and accelerated rates of species extinction. Let me elaborate on these points.

Most ethical theories have two components: a theory of *value*, and a theory of *conduct*. A theory of value tells us what sorts of things are intrinsically valuable and worth pursuing for their own sake. A theory of conduct gives us principles for evaluating whether a particular action is morally right or wrong. We can use the ethical theory known as "utilitarianism" to illustrate the distinction, and to motivate the environmentalist critique. The theory of value associated with utilitarianism is a version of what philosophers call "value hedonism," the view that what is intrinsically *good* in the world are experiences of pleasure, happiness, or well-being, and what is intrinsically *bad* are experiences of pain, suffering or unhappiness. The theory of conduct associated with utilitarianism is summarized by the following principle: *the morally right action is the one that will bring about the greatest happiness of the greatest number affected by the action.* The overall aim of utilitarianism, then, is to maximize happiness and minimize suffering.

Utilitarianism was revolutionary in two senses when it was first proposed by Jeremy Bentham and John Stuart Mill in nineteenth century Britain. It was revolutionary in the sense that it made no appeal to God to justify moral beliefs or evaluate moral actions, and it was revolutionary in its egalitarianism: in evaluating the consequences of an action, it was assumed that the happiness of every person must count equally (the happiness of the King could weigh no more heavily than the happiness of the lowliest peasant).

Utilitarianism was regarded, and continues to be regarded by its supporters, as a progressive ideology that can justify a variety of egalitarian social and political reforms. But can it justify environmentalist intuitions concerning the wrongness of pollution, habitat destruction and biodiversity loss? Is it a suitable foundation for a progressive environmental ethic?

Many environmental ethicists would say "no"; utilitarianism, in its traditional form at least, is not a suitable foundation for an environmental ethic. This may seem surprising, since it is clear that unsustainable environmental practices can cause pain and suffering to human beings, and utilitarians are required to take such suffering into account in evaluating an environmental policy or practice. It should not be difficult to come up with good utilitarian arguments for at least some environmentally-friendly policies (pollution control regulations, for example). Furthermore, utilitarians must consider impacts not only on human beings, but on *all sentient creatures*, including mammals, amphibians, birds . . . any creature with a relatively sophisticated nervous and hormonal system that one could argue is capable of experiencing pain. In addition, utilitarianism is the theoretical backbone of the *animal welfare movement* that strongly condemns the suffering inflicted on animals by factory farming practices and animal experimentation in research laboratories. One might think that the animal welfare movement and the environmental movement would have similar political goals and would benefit from a shared ethical framework.

Yet there are instances where the intuitions of environmentalists may come into conflict with those of animal welfarists. An animal welfarist may urge us to save a rare species of *deer*, but an environmentalist may also urge us to save the rare *grasslands* that the deer feed on (what do you do if you can't save both?). Utilitarianism regards the interests of sentient beings as worthy of direct moral consideration, *but this is as far as it goes*. A utilitarian evaluation of a policy regarding, say, the clear-cutting of old growth forests, must consider the happiness and suffering likely to be caused by such a policy on human beings and on the sentient animals that live in such forests, but it does not regard the interests of non-sentient organisms (trees, plants, insects, invertebrates, microorganisms, etc.) as worthy of direct moral consideration, nor does it recognize any intrinsic value in the structure, functioning or existence of "holistic" environmental entities (populations, species, communities, ecosystems, landscapes, etc.). A utilitarian ethic regards sentient beings as having *intrinsic moral value*, but it regards non-sentient beings and entities as having only *instrumental moral value*—i.e. value not for its own sake, but for the sake of something else (in this case, the sake of the welfare of sentient beings). Environmentalists vary in their views on what sorts of entities are suitable bearers of moral value, but many will argue that entities *other* than sentient beings are also worthy of moral consideration. They may believe, for example, that the death of the *last member* of a species is a moral loss distinct from its impact on human welfare, and distinct from the harm suffered by that last individual as it dies (it's not just the end of *this* blue whale, but the end of *all* blue whales, forever). Or they may believe that all living things, sentient and non-sentient, have a good-of-their-own that demands moral respect. In short, many environmentalists want to defend the intrinsic value of non-sentient environmental entities. Classical utilitarianism simply doesn't have the resources to justify such intuitions.

Nor do any other traditional Western ethical theories, for that matter. The *natural law* tradition in ethics (in both its Greek and Judeo-Christian formulations) draws a sharp distinction between the intrinsic moral value of humans and the instrumental value of animals and plants, which are presumed to exist *for the sake of* human beings. *Kantian ethics* and traditional *social contract* theories restrict intrinsic value to beings with at least the potential for rational thought. All of these ethical theories are strongly "anthropocentric" or "human-centered"—i.e. they restrict direct moral consideration to the interests and welfare of human beings. Utilitarianism is the only classical ethical theory that is not strongly anthropocentric, but for many environmentalists it is still too restrictive in scope.

Thus, one of the main goals of environmental ethics is to seek alternative moral foundations, either through the development of new *nonanthropocentric* theories of moral conduct and value, or the *modification* of traditional anthropocentric theories, that would justify environmentalist intuitions. Nonanthropocentric environmental ethics argues for the intrinsic moral value of nonhuman environmental entities, and grounds a theory of conduct on recognition of, and respect for, such value. Modified anthropocentric theories maintain a focus on human values and interests, but allow that the nonhuman environment can have value for humans in a variety of different ways (beyond, say, purely economic value), and argue that the moral intuitions of environmentalists can be justified when the value and importance of the environment is properly understood and appreciated.

Radical Environmental Philosophy

Radical environmental philosophers are also concerned with environmental problems, but their focus is on the historical, cultural and political processes that give rise to attitudes and practices toward the environment. The essential feature of radical environmental philosophy (what makes it "radical") is the view that contemporary environmental attitudes and practices are deeply rooted in historical, cultural, religious and political structures, and that changing these attitudes and practices will require changes in these deep structures (note: "radical" derives from the Latin "radix," meaning "of or pertaining to the root"). Thus, radical environmental philosophers offer specific diagnoses and prescriptions for what is perceived to be humanity's current dysfunctional relationship with the natural environment. There are a number of different schools of radical environmental philosophy, that go by such names as "deep ecology," "social ecology," "socialist ecology," "spiritual ecology," and "feminist ecology" (or as it is more commonly called, "ecofeminism"). Each school differs in its diagnosis of the human-environment condition, and consequently differs in its prescription for ameliorating this condition.

Radical environmental philosophies can differ in many ways. One important way is over how they understand social change. Are the causes of environmental attitudes and practices rooted primarily in the *ideas* that people have about the environment, or in the *economic, technological, and institutional practices* ("material conditions of existence," to use the Marxist phrase) of a culture. Does what we *think* about nature condition what we *do* to it, or does what we *do* to nature condition what we *think* about it? Intuition tells us that the influence probably goes both ways, but many theorists argue for a dominant influence in one direction over the other, and this conviction shows up in their differing strategies for political change. Those who argue that changes in beliefs and values are what drive social change are sometimes called "social idealists"; those who argue otherwise, that changes in the material conditions of existence are the primary determinants of social change, are "social materialists."

Social idealists will focus on changing people's beliefs and values through education, consciousness-raising, criticism, etc. Changes in behaviors and practices, it is hoped, will follow naturally. Among radical environmental philosophers, *deep ecologists* tend towards a social idealist approach to social change. Social materialists will argue that such efforts are wasted unless one also works to change the material conditions (especially, economic organization) that determine how human beings carve out and sustain their social organization through the exploitation of natural resources. *Socialist ecologists* (or *"ecosocialists"*), who target *global capitalism* as a primary cause of environmental problems, support a materialistic conception of social change. Other radical environmental philosophies occupy intermediate positions along the idealist-materialist spectrum.

This brief overview of the field of environmental philosophy is far from complete, but it will suffice as background for what is to follow. In the following sections I take a closer look at Paul Chadwick's "Stay Tuned for Pearl Harbor," and consider how the narrative and imagery in this comic story function to illustrate many of the themes alluded to above.

2. "STAY TUNED FOR PEARL HARBOR"

"Stay Tuned for Pearl Harbor" opens with an overhead shot of a pickup truck with three occupants, Larry, Maureen and Concrete, driving along a winding road through the mountains of the Pacific Northwest. Larry and Maureen are Concrete's two closest friends. Larry is driving, Maureen is in the passenger seat, and Concrete is riding in the back of the truck. We catch Concrete in mid-sentence, complaining of the indifference and lack of accountability of oil companies to the environmental damage caused by drilling and extraction. Larry is listening attentively, but Maureen appears lost in thought; she stares out the passenger window at the passing wilderness landscape:

> "You see so little speeding by. It takes time. And stillness. I remember how aware I became of all the processes, the intricate play of systems, that morning I spent sitting in the woods." (123)

Over the next three pages we enter Maureen's mind as she recalls a recent experience of ecological consciousness. Her narration, and the visual depiction of her experience, is punctuated at points by Concrete's continu-ing dialogue with Larry. We see Maureen sitting cross-legged on the floor of a wooded area. She is actively trying to quiet her thoughts, open her senses, and make an experiential connection with her natural surroundings. Maureen's method is to imagine various extensions and modifications of her perceptual faculties that would allow her to directly experience the mani-fold variety of ecological processes going on around her. Roots extrude from roots her fingertips and wrists, enter the ground, and her circulatory system merges with the root systems of nearby trees. She imagines her extended venous system swelling after a soaking rain, and makes a pointed observation: "Our anatomy determines our picture of the world."

Maureen starts to consider further possibilities for extending our sen-sory experience of the natural world when Concrete's monologue breaks in:

"After all, this administration is hardly hostile to the oil business. And this when we need to be using less oil, for the atmosphere's sake. I swear, Larry. If some people could make a few million bucks, I'm sure they'd gladly do things that would give their grand-children cancer, if only they didn't have to face it too squarely." (126)

This pattern—Maureen's imaginative reverie aimed at promoting greater identification with nature, juxtaposed with Concrete's critical observations and cynicism over human-induced environmental problems—is repeated throughout the story. Chadwick uses Concrete and Maureen to represent two distinct voices within the environmental movement, voices that may be used to illustrate some of the different positions within and between envi-ronmental ethics and radical environmental philosophy.

3. IS CONCRETE AN ANTHROPOCENTRIST OR A NONANTHROPOCENTRIST?

How does Concrete understand the ethical dimensions of environmental degradation? As we saw in section 1, there are two distinct approaches within environmental ethics, anthropocentric and nonanthropocentric. Concrete clearly believes that we have moral obligations to protect and preserve the nat-ural environment, but is he an anthropocentrist or a nonanthropocentrist?

Concrete's primary concern throughout the story appears to be the long-term consequences of unchecked population growth, pollution, and environmental degradation on the welfare of current and future generations of human beings. He believes that there are natural limits to population growth and resource usage that, if surpassed, will likely result in widespread famine, ecological degradation and political desperation among vulnerable Third World countries. This will be our "ecological Pearl Harbor," a wake-up call that will force the First World to radically change its economic and industrial practices in order to avoid ecological catastrophe. He views the root causes of the environmental crisis as arising from a myopic fixation on a narrowly economic conception of growth and material welfare, and a consequent failure to appreciate the negative, long-term impacts of environmental deterioration. Such a position might be described as "enlightened, ecologically-informed anthropocentrism"—it focuses on potential harms to humans, but acknowledges that long-term human welfare is crucially dependent on the sustainable management of natural resources and the continuing existence of diverse, functional ecological communities. Now, Concrete *may also* regard the nonhuman environment as intrinsically morally valuable and worthy of protection and preservation for its own sake, but he isn't explicit about this either way; his criticisms certainly don't rely on any assumptions about the intrinsic moral value of nature. And yet, Concrete clearly identifies with the aims and politics of the environmental movement.

This is a useful point to emphasize. Though environmental ethicists are often critical of traditional Western ethical, political and economic theories for being exclusively concerned with human welfare, it is certainly possible to argue for radical environmental reforms from a purely anthropocentric standpoint. A nonanthropocentric environmental ethic may entail different types of reforms, reflecting particular moral concerns for nonhuman species, communities and ecosystems, than an anthropocentric ethic. But most environmentalists and environmental philosophers will agree that the *differences* between the reforms supportable by a nonanthropocentric ethic and the reforms supportable by an enlightened, ecologically-informed anthropocentric ethic, are *minimal* when contrasted with the enormous distance between the worldview envisioned in either set of reforms, and the current state of environmental awareness and concern exhibited by most government and business organizations.

In fact, it has been argued by pragmatically-oriented environmental philosophers that the anthropocentric/nonanthroprocentric debate has consumed intellectual resources out of proportion to its importance and utility for solving real-world, practical environmental problems. If both approaches are capable of mounting serious objections to the status quo, then the more immediate concern should be on how to implement these objections, how to bring environmental philosophy into more direct and productive contact with environmental education, management, policy, politics, and so forth. This call for practical application over abstract theoretical debate is an emerging voice in environmental philosophy.[2]

4. DEEP ECOLOGY

Concrete's angry monologue is strikingly contrasted with Maureen's silent contemplation. This contrast can help to illustrate some of the differences between environmental ethics and radical environmental philosophy discussed in section 1.

Following on the theme that "our anatomy determines our picture of the world," Maureen imagines herself as a flattened gliding membrane as large as a football field, "skimming the treetops like a hand stroking a cat," bringing into tactile awareness the large-scale textures of the landscape that we normally only ever access perceptually, from great heights. Next, we see her as a giant naked female figure, "a semi-solid ghost, the size of a 747, settling down in the earth, feeling the wary rustlings of burrowing animals, the cool flow of a stream through you." Maureen's appreciation for the natural world is derived from an intimate, experiential identification with nature, rather than from a conception of the environment as an instrument for the satisfaction of human interests, or as an impersonal, abstract object of knowledge and study by ecologists and environmental scientists.

The ethical/philosophical import of Maureen's experiential identification with nature is highlighted on subsequent pages. Larry's truck approaches a small town, and the natural landscape becomes interrupted by power lines, billboards and buildings. Maureen brings her imaginings into the present. Her "membrane-self" glides over the land, heading toward the town.

"Of course, new senses would mean new sources of pain, too. If you were sensitive enough to taste ground-water minerals, you'd be nauseated by the toxins you absorbed." (127) We see Maureen's membrane-self catch and tear on the harsh metal and angular, unyielding edges of billboards and building structures, her head thrown back in a howl of pain. Next, we see bulldozers clearing a large area of land of all visible flora and fauna. Maureen's giant, semi-transparent self is on her back, half immersed in the sand and dirt. Her head is thrown back in pain once again, teeth clenched, fists tight against her chest. Bulldozers run across her body, one very close to the inner thigh of one of her legs. The unmistakable impression is that she is being raped.

From this depiction we are led to understand that Maureen views the harm inflicted by environmental deterioration not as harm to human needs and interests, and not as harm to the objectively described natural world that is the object of traditional scientific knowledge, but rather as harm *to her*. Or rather, harm to an expanded "ecological" conception of her self that does not recognize any firm distinction between "self" and "environment." In identifying closely with nature, Maureen imagines herself as being poisoned by toxins in the soil, torn by the hard metal of the artificial landscape, assaulted by the bulldozers. One could argue that, for Maureen, an environmental ethic is nothing more than an *ethic of self-interest and self-preservation*, but where the "self" in question is not the narrow egoistic self with which we normally identify, but the more expansive "ecological" self that she is attempting to cultivate. To view the self from this perspective is to adopt a conception of self-hood and personal identity that rejects the traditional view that the "me" that is the subject of conscious experience is entirely identical with processes going on within the confines of my skull or even the boundaries of my skin. When imaginatively engaged in identification with the natural world, Maureen's ecological self expands outward into the natural world, making it difficult (perhaps impossible) to say where "she" ends and her "environment" begins.

This depiction of ecological consciousness, and its relation to the justification for environmentalist intuitions concerning the wrongness of environmental destruction, is closely aligned with the worldview of the school of radical environmental philosophy known as "deep ecology," and in particular, the version of deep ecology propounded by Norwegian philosopher Arne Naess. Naess argues that the root cause of humanity's dysfunctional relationship with the natural world is the prevalence of exclusively human-centered (anthropocentric) value systems that deny intrinsic value to the natural world as such. For those environmental ethicists who call themselves nonanthropocentrists, the challenge is to come up with a good argument for attributing intrinsic moral value to the nonhuman natural world, an argument that could function to justify environmental policies that acknowledge and respect this value. Though Naess is a nonanthropocentrist, he views the challenge differently. According to Naess, the challenge posed by the environmental crisis is fundamentally *psychological*—a problem of perception, self-concept, and subjective awareness—rather than an abstract ethical problem. We fail to recognize intrinsic value in nature because, in contemporary (technological, industrial, consumer) society, we are so often denied both the opportunity and the encouragement to engage in meaningful relationships with the natural world, relationships that would promote an experiential awareness of the connectedness and interdependence of organism-environment relations, and an expanded identification of the self with its natural environment. If such identification can be achieved, there is no further need to justify an environmental ethic, for environmentally-friendly attitudes and practices will follow as a natural consequence of self-interested desires and motives. Thus, for the deep ecologist, the challenge is to find ways to promote the kind of psychological reorientation that results in a natural disposition to value and protect the environment.[3]

This discussion of deep ecology helps illustrate the distinction between environmental ethics and radical environmental philosophy introduced in section 1. Deep ecologists are very concerned with promoting nonanthropocentric ethical attitudes toward the natural environment, but they do not focus on developing moral arguments to refute the anthropocentric skeptic. Their main concern is with *social transformation*, and the focus of their philosophical work is on identifying root sources of environmental attitudes, with the aim of restructuring those attitudes in ways that will naturally engender environmentally-friendly practices (this is the "social idealism" implicit in their approach). Deep ecologists view anthropocentric attitudes as a product of a *metaphysical* worldview that, they argue, is presupposed by modern Western industrial society, a worldview that emphasizes the fundamental *separateness* of the human individual from its natural and social environment. Thus, much of their focus is on constructing and promoting alternative metaphysical schemes that emphasize the *holistic interconnectedness* of nature and that view human beings as part of and embedded within nature.

5. ECOFEMINISM

Chadwick's depiction of Maureen's experiential identification with nature has a close affinity to deep ecology, but it is also strongly suggestive of another school, *ecofeminism*. There are many varieties of ecofeminist environmental philosophy, but all them share the core conviction that the *oppression of nature* is historically and conceptually related to the *oppression of women*, and hence, that the environmental crisis cannot be properly understood without simultaneously attending to the role that gender plays in our various conception of nature, and in the root causes and justification for environmental attitudes and practices. Ecofeminists have criticized deep ecologists (and other radical environmental philosophies) for failing to recognize or adequately appreciate the gendered dimension of environmental problems.[4]

Consider, for example, the term "Mother Nature." Nature is identified with the female throughout the Western tradition, and indeed, throughout much of the Eastern and aboriginal traditions of the world. In classical mythology, the male is commonly associated with the heavens above ("Father Sky") and the female with the earth below ("Mother Earth"). Motivations for the association are not hard to understand. Women give birth, and nurse their young from the milk of their bodies (the earth is fertile, it brings for life); women provide for the physical and emotional needs of children, and are traditionally involved more than men in the preparation of food and the maintenance of domestic households (the earth provides sustenance and nurturing for all living creatures); women experience menstrual cycles that involve the shedding of blood and tissue (the earth's fertility is cyclical as well—indeed, the human female menstrual cycle is roughly identical to the lunar month). Women have also been associated with less "motherly" aspects of nature; for example, as a capricious, unpredictable and chaotic force that, on a whim, may bring forth draught and flood, fire and frost, and lay waste the lives and works of human beings.

Chadwick's depiction of Maureen's "ecological self" strongly suggests a conception of nature as female. When I present this story to students, few are consciously aware of the association on a first reading. But then I ask them to consider their impression if the story was described in identical fashion, but with Larry and Maureen's roles reversed. Maureen is driving the pickup truck while Larry looks out the window and imagines himself as Maureen does—say, as a giant bearded man reclining into the earth, feeling the rustling of burrowing animals below ground, and the flow of streams through and around his naked body. Inevitably, many students react strongly to this image—one male student said he found it "unsettling," another said it made Larry look "effeminate." Once their attention is drawn to the image in which Maureen is being "raped" by the bulldozers, there is no longer any doubt that Chadwick's depiction of environmental harm is strongly gendered; I have yet to find a student who does not find this image, in which Larry is replaced with Maureen, as jarring and discordant, if not absurd. Though men can certainly be raped, the convention is to associate sexual violation with harm to women, not to men.

What does any of this have to do with the root causes of environmental problems? A common ecofeminist claim is that the association of nature with the female is very often embedded within a larger conceptual scheme that is both *dualistic* and *hierarchical*. A representative list of such conceptual dualisms would include: mind/body, reason/emotion, fact/value, objective/subjective, active/passive, logic/intuition, culture/nature, and male/female. What makes these pairs dualistic is that they are viewed as mutually exclusive—to be reasonable is to NOT be emotional; to focus on the empirical facts is to NOT make value judgments, etc. What makes the pairs hierarchical is that each of the terms on the left represents something that, in general, is valued more highly than what is represented on the right—the mind is valued *over* the body, reason *over* emotion, fact *over* value, culture *over* nature, and notably, male *over* female. There is, in addition, a broad association between *all* the concepts on the left and *all* the concepts on the right—the male is associated with the mind, reason, logic, objectivity, culture, etc.; the female with the body, emotion, intuition, subjectivity, nature, etc. The association of nature with the female is embedded within a much broader patriarchal conceptual framework that devalues both nature and the female. There is a connection, say ecofeminists, between attitudes and practices that devalue and exploit the natural world, and attitudes and practices that devalue and exploit women. In the *Concrete* story, this connection is made most strongly in the suggested association between environmental degradation and the "rape" of Mother Nature.

Consequently, for ecofeminists, the aims and goals of the environmental movement cannot be separated from the aims and goals of the women's movement, or, indeed, the goals of all oppressed groups that suffer under social systems that express and reinforce dualistic and hierarchical conceptual frameworks. One can see why ecofeminists might be dissatisfied with the deep ecological approach to environmental philosophy. Deep ecologists are keen to break down conceptual dualisms that separate human beings from the natural environments, but ecofeminists argue that they often fail to consider how those dualisms are constructed and maintained in the first place. Ecofeminists are more likely than deep ecologists to focus their critiques on the social, economic and political institutions that serve and are served by patriarchal conceptual frameworks, and place greater emphasis on promoting collective social action as a means for social change, rather than on individual consciousness-raising activities. In this respect they are further away from the idealist end of the idealist/materialist spectrum than deep ecologists. There are, however, many sub-varieties of ecofeminism, and some have closer affinities to deep ecology than others.

6. HUMAN ECOLOGY: THE CORE OF ENVIRONMENTAL PHILOSOPHY?

In section 1 I characterized environmental philosophy as an attempt to answer two sets of questions, one concerning the nature and origins of moral obligations toward the environment, the other concerning the root causes of attitudes and practices with respect to the environment.

The two broad sub-fields of environmental philosophy, "environmental ethics" and "radical environmental philosophy," are respectively associated with these questions. Anyone working in environmental philosophy will be familiar with the main theoretical positions within both sub-fields, but it is not unfair to say that the field is somewhat fragmented, in that workers usually identify with one sub-field or the other, and tend to see the foundational problems of their sub-field as relatively *autonomous*, i.e. not inextricably dependent on the foundational problems of the *other* sub-field. To a certain extent, specialization into sub-fields is to be expected as any discipline matures, but I believe that this view—that the foundational problems of environmental ethics are separable and distinct from the foundational problems of radical environmental philosophy—should be resisted. There is a deeper set of problems that bind these sub-fields together, problems that I believe more accurately characterize the *core* of environmental philosophy.

What is this core? To help think about this, let us consider a different question than the ones we have looked at so far. *What would environmental philosophy look like if there was no environmental crisis, if human beings actually lived in sustainable harmonious relationships with the natural world?* In such a world, would there be any reason to "do" environmental philosophy? If we understand environmental philosophy in terms of the two sets of questions given above, then it would seem the answer is "no." Intellectual support for the environmental movement appears to be the *raison d'être* of environmental philosophy. Why worry about justifying ethical practices toward the environment if our practices are already ethical? Why worry about understanding the root causes of environmental attitudes and practices if there is no felt need to change them?

My own view is that there would be a great deal left for environmental philosophers to do, and it is this that constitutes the core of environmental philosophy. Environmental philosophy is, to quote our initial definition from section 1, "the philosophical study of the relationship between human beings and the broader environmental context in which they live and act." In other words, it is the study of the *ecological dimensions of human nature and human behavior*. We are an evolved species on this planet, unique to be sure, but still fundamentally a product of a complex ecological and evolutionary process that has conditioned not only our biology, but also our psychology and cognitive capacities, and the social dimensions of our existence. Even without the motivating influence of a perceived environmental crisis, there is still much to understand about human-environment relations, questions of a fundamental nature that concern scientists and philosophers alike. My claim is that in attempting to answer the standard questions of environmental ethics and radical environmental philosophy, environmental philosophers invariably run into questions concerning the ecological dimensions of human perception, cognition and activity—what I regard as core questions for environmental philosophy. There isn't room to argue for this in detail here, but our *Concrete* story can help illustrate the point.

Consider Concrete's concern over human population growth. His main worry is that the carrying capacity of the earth is finite, and that exponential growth rates are poised to overshoot this carrying capacity, resulting in mass starvation in Third World countries, a consequence that we all strongly wish to avoid. But what exactly is the carrying capacity of the earth? In population ecology, "carrying capacity" is defined (roughly) as the maximum population that can be sustained within a given environment. For a given population living within a particular ecological niche, the carrying capacity is usually regarded as a fixed constant. But humans can *modify* their environments in ways that no other organism can. And arguably, humans can create *new* resources where none existed before (think of uranium in the ground before and after the development of nuclear technology). Ultimately, Concrete's concerns are based on assumptions about *human ecology* that may reasonably be challenged. Before we can answer the question of how many people *ought* to live on the earth, surely we need to have some understanding of how many *can* live on the earth. This is a problem for human ecology, and hence a problem for environmental philosophy, as I have defined it.

The ecological issues implicit in Maureen's story are even clearer. It is in coming to appreciate the ecological dimensions of her being that Maureen is able to overcome the dualistic thinking that isolates human beings from nature; it is Maureen's experiential identification with her environment and the expansion of her cognitive and sensory capacities that allows her to view the welfare of the environment as a concern for *her*. But Chadwick's depiction of Maureen's imaginative engagement with nature raises deep philosophical questions about the nature of *the self*. We are invited to consider that the self is partly constituted by its relations to the biotic and abiotic environment, but does this imply that there is no self/environment distinction? Or does it simply imply that any conception of self automatically implies a conception of environment that is defined in relation to it? Critics may wonder why anyone would find this depiction philosophically provocative at all, since (they might say) Maureen is just "daydreaming," it's all going on "in her head." The question is a serious one: to what extent do our best theories of perception and cognition support anything like the "ecological" conception of the self that deep ecologists (and to some extent ecofeminists) encourage us to embrace? These too are problems for human ecology, and hence for environmental philosophy. There are many more such problems for a philosophy of human-environment relations.

Contemporary environmental philosophy is what you get when the legitimate fears and concerns of environmentalists are brought to bear on philosophical thinking about human-environment relations. The standard problems of environmental ethics and radical environmental philosophy are a natural outgrowth of these concerns. I suspect, however, that progress on these problems would be better served if the discipline was reconceived as a *general philosophy of human-environment relations*. Such a perspective would focus attention on foundational issues that are too often avoided or glossed over in the environmental literature. At the very least it would encourage productive dialogue between relatively isolated sub-fields of environmental philosophy.

CONCLUSION

I have used "Stay Tuned for Pearl Harbor" in other environmental philosophy classes I have taught, and it never fails to engage student attention and elicit interesting classroom discussion. More importantly, it elicits discussion that is directly relevant to some key issues in environmental philosophy, most notably the anthropocentrism/nonanthropocentrism debate in environmental ethics, and the deep ecology/ecofeminism debate in radical environmental philosophy.

These are important topics, but environmental philosophy is much broader, and encompasses many more topics and issues, than just these. Other commonly discussed topics in environmental philosophy classes include the role of religion in grounding and justifying attitudes toward the environment; the relationship between economics, ethics and ecology; the issue of First World versus Third World responsibility for global poverty and population growth; "ecoterrorism" and the ethics of environmental activism; and many others. The *Concrete* story has been a jumping point for discussions on a number of these issues as well. The success I've had with using comics in these classes has encouraged me to look for other comic stories that might prove useful in teaching other areas of philosophy.[5]

NOTES

1. For a comprehensive overview of issues and debates in environmental philosophy geared to the university classroom see Light and Rolston 2003. For a shorter introduction to environmental philosophy that is perhaps more accessible to a wider audience, see Weston 1999.
2. See Light and Katz 1996 for a collection of essays on "environmental pragmatism."
3. A good source for Arne Naess's environmental philosophy is Naess and Rothenberg 1989.
4. For a good overview of some recent ecofeminist positions, see the readings in Chapter 9 of Armstrong and Botzler 2004.
5. I was embarrassed to discover, at the end of the environmental philosophy course I taught in the fall of 1997, that Paul Chadwick had published a series of six comics featuring Concrete's involvement with the radical environmental activist group known as Earth First!, and that the series had been collected and published by Dark Horse Comics in April 1997. I was using an 8-page black and white comic from 1989, unaware of the existence of a 130-odd page full-color graphic novel on Concrete's involvement with environmental issues published the very year I was teaching my course. I highly recommend Chadwick's 1997 *Concrete: Think Like a Mountain*. The expression "think like a mountain" comes from Aldo Leopold, one of the founding figures of the environmental movement and one of the first to defend a nonanthropocentric environmental ethic (see Leopold 1949). Chadwick, P. (1997) *Concrete: Think Like a Mountain*, Milwaukie, OR: Dark Horse Comics.

The Good Government According to Tintin

Long Live Old Europe?[1]

—PIERRE SKILLING

"A dictionary of philosophy is not the first place you would expect to find Hergé," writes Thierry Groensteen (53), criticizing an attempt to equate Tintin's creator with philosophers such as Kant and Descartes and rejecting all "dogmatic" readings of Hergé's work. Indeed, this multi-faceted work can be approached from many different points of view. *The Adventures of Tintin* have been analyzed from several perspectives, ranging from semiology to psychoanalysis, from sociology to history and art history. But what of philosophy?[2] While he refuses to consider Hergé a philosopher, Groensteen does not dispute the value of a philosophical reading of *Tintin*. Philosopher Michel Serres's brilliant reflections on communication in *The Castafiore Emerald* and *Tintin and the Picaros* bear eloquent testimony to this fact, as do his reflections on fetishism inspired by *The Broken Ear* (Serres). Hergé was himself a self-taught reader of philosophy with, among other things, a special interest in oriental philosophy.

The Adventures of Tintin also lend themselves to a political reading. One of the fundamental questions of political philosophy is that of the best form of government, and Tintin, in the course of his travels around the world, offers his readers some thoughts on this question. His position is simple though not necessarily simplistic. Hergé himself had at best a rudimentary conception of politics and was certainly not a militant, yet through Tintin he introduced hundreds of thousands of children to politics and awakened in them an interest in history and current events.

In my book on the political aspects of *Tintin*, I showed that what makes this series interesting to the children reading it today is not some close link between Hergé's comics and the current political events of the twentieth century but rather the way in which the Belgian creator presents certain political issues in a broader context which far surpasses current and historical events. Of course, it is evident that some of the volumes (especially the early ones), refer to very specific events. For example, *The Blue Lotus* describes in detail events relating to the Sino-Japanese war of the 1930s, starting with the Moukden incident (1931), which corresponds to a railway attack witnessed by Tintin in the story (*Lotus*, 21)[3] and which preceded the occupation of Manchuria.[4] But it is also striking that *The Adventures of Tintin* find many an echo in our own political present, which shows that Hergé, in addition to paying obsessive attention to clarity and detail, knew how to create in many respects a timeless work. The use of imaginary countries as the setting for several of his stories shows an intent to distance the story from the events which inspired the plots: Syldavia and Borduria represent minor Balkan states, San Theodoros, a South American country, Khemed, an oil-producing nation of the Middle East. Tintin's voyages allow him not only to witness history in the making but also to experience a diversity of cultures and societies and, especially, of governments. To cut short, there are basically good and corrupt government leaders. In Hergé's comic books, both exist. Given that children tend to "personify" the government, that is to say that, for a child's point of view, the king—or the president, or the prime minister—"embodies" the government (Easton and Dennis, 139), reading a classic like *The Adventures of Tintin* could still be a good way for the young readers to learn to discriminate between the good and the bad chief.

In political philosophy, the principal legacies of the works of Montesquieu (1689–1755) are, without a doubt his theory of the separation of powers and his theory of forms of government, the latter being a classification of three basic "species" of government, each having its own kind of laws and institutions. According to Montesquieu, whose ideas inspired a number of eighteenth-century revolutionaries, the nature of each form of government (that is a political regime) depends on those who wield sovereign power—as it did for Aristotle by whom Montesquieu was undoubtedly inspired. In

The Spirit of the Laws, Montesquieu uses this notion to identify three kinds of government: republican, monarchical, and despotic:

> Republican government is that in which the people as a body, or only a part of the people, have sovereign power, monarchical government is that in which one alone governs, but by fixed and established laws; whereas, in despotic government, one alone, without law and without rule, draws everything along by his will and his caprices. (II, 1 in Trans. Cohler, Miller, Stone p. 10)[5]

These definitions establish two criteria for recognizing types of government: the number of power holders (one or several) and the extent to which that sovereign power respects fixed and established laws (Aron, 42–43). Yet another categorization of these three basic forms is central in Montesquieu's theory, that is between the moderate government (be it monarchical or republican) and the despotic one. It's only in moderate governments that it is possible to find political liberty, which rests notably in the notion that "it is necessary from the very nature of things that power should be a check to power," to prevent the abuse of power by the sovereign (*Montesquieu* XI, 4). In other words, political liberty prevents the change of a moderate government to despotism (VIII, 8). The idea that "power should be a check to power" leads to the famous theory of the separation of the three powers of the state: legislative, executive, and judiciary. Roughly, to preserve liberty and avoid despotism, each of the powers must keep an eye on the actions of the two others. For Montesquieu, concentration of power in one hand is the ultimate danger.

One of the timeless elements in *The Adventures of Tintin* is undoubtedly Hergé's portrayal of despotic or (now more commonly called) dictatorial regimes. For some (such as Mr. Rumsfeld), the toppling of Saddam Hussein's statue on April 9, 2003, which was shown on CNN and in the world media, may have been reminiscent of the toppling of Lenin's effigies in Eastern Europe at the turn of the 1990s, but for a tintinologist, these statues are also reminiscent of those of Marshal Kûrvi-Tasch in *The Calculus Affair*. In this volume of Tintin, Marshal Kûrvi-Tasch's totalitarian regime is not overturned, but the dictator is visually omnipresent in the capital of Borduria (Szohôd), much like Saddam was visible throughout Bagdad and Iraq even though his actual whereabouts were unknown. In the same way as Saddam made his hold over Iraq felt by representing himself in every possible medium (statues, posters, murals, public place names, etc.), Kûrvi-Tasch and his symbols (the moustache of the Taschist Party[6]) are everywhere in Szohôd: in statues, furniture, public officials' greetings, etc. Moreover, the statue of Kûrvi-Tasch (*Affair*, 47, 12)[7]shows the dictator in a pose similar to that of Saddam, with his right arm raised. Both politicians wear moustaches and are modeled on Stalin (Aburish, 2000).

The basic distinction in modern politics is between liberal democracy and totalitarian regimes—besides which exist different kinds of authoritarian regimes, with diverse degrees of oppression compared with the "total" oppression of totalitarianism (Bénéton, 89–99). Modern politics—that is the conception of politics since the revolutions of the eighteenth century in the Western world—is essentially based on an ideal of liberty and equality for human beings, against the idea of a natural order (e.g. religious explanations of the world). To sum up, liberal democracies consider that these principles have to be realized by legal equality and individual liberty, while totalitarianism promises to shape a better future, to radically change human condition with the means of a revolution which will build a perfect society.

Yet, apparently, Hergé addresses the question of politics in a somehow ancient way. In fact, "for Tintin, the choice is not between democracy and totalitarianism, but between monarchy and dictatorship." Of course, "our young Belgian opts for the former, casting his lot with legitimate sovereigns against the sorry bunch who seek to supplant or even eliminate them" (Vanherpe, 51). In the course of his *Adventures*, Tintin never openly advocates one form of government over another, but when his actions are directed at political leaders, his aim is always to combat the dictators, be they in Latin America or in Eastern Europe. A priori, this does not necessarily, however, make Tintin a democrat in the sense of being an advocate of the rights of citizens to elect their government. Instead, he appears to be on the side on humane monarchs, showed as the only statesmen who can defend the common good.

In the following pages, we will explore the models of power seizure and government which the Belgian hero rejects (dictatorship, sometimes with characteristics of totalitarianism), as well as the legitimate form of government according to Hergé's comics (monarchy). We will ask whether Tintin's political choices are still relevant in our time, which favours democracy, a type of regime whose values seem underrepresented in a classic Franco-Belgian comic strip like *The Adventures of Tintin*.

DICTATORSHIP AND TOTALITARIANISM

Dictatorship as a Political Carnival

In *The Adventures of Tintin*, despotic regimes, especially those of Latin America, are ridiculed. The two stories which take place mainly in San Theodoros (an imaginary country[8]) are *The Broken Ear* (first version in 1937, second in 1943) and *Tintin and the Picaros* (1976), the very last of the series. In these stories, one finds a veritable power struggle corresponding to the type of political legitimacy commonly associated with stereotypical (caricatural) representations of South America. Moreover, in *Tintin and the Picaros* (considered to be one of the least achieved of Hergé's volumes though it is of some interest to us as his "political testament"), Tintin participates in the seizure of power by helping General Alcazar carry out a successful coup d'état.

Over the course of the entire *Adventures of Tintin* series, San Theodoros undergoes a total of five revolutions, or rather coups d'états, bringing to power alternately either General Alcazar or General Tapioca. In these Latin American stories, Hergé seems to offer his readers a caricatural and yet fairly perceptive vision of the political problems of that region, and especially of the role of the military elite. In Latin America, the status of the military elite in the state structure leads them to aspire to central positions of power rather than to limiting themselves to a territorial defence role (Horowitz, 146–89); The number of military coups in San Theodoros corresponds to some degree to reality:

> The frequency, one could almost say the cyclical regularity, of contemporary military intervention suggests that the factors at play here are not only situational but also structural, common to all under-developed countries and Latin America in particular. (Lambert and Gandolfi, 537–38)

Hergé describes the Latin American political situation in straight-forward language. Thus, it seems that Hergé too considers that military coups are part of the very structure of the Latin American system, no matter what the pretext: for Hergé, revolutions are amoral (not immoral). Amoral in the sense that the Latin American dictators do not work for the progress or their nations; they don't believe in any moral duty in their job. They are outside the moral world; they are not tormented by the conflict between good and evil (one cannot expect to see a balloon with an angel and a devil torturing the soul of Tapioca or Alcazar, but it is the kind of torment experimented a few times by Snowy and Captain Haddock). As Tintin witnesses it, revolutions are amoral in their techniques (it's merely a game) as well as in their cause and effect. Actually, their effect is minimal, as shown by two frequently cited scenes in *Tintin and the Picaros*: the departure and return to San Theodoros, which show that obviously, Alcazar's seizure of power has not eliminated misery (*Picaros*, 11 and 62). First, when the plane transporting Captain Haddock and professor Calculus prepares to land in Tapiocapolis (11: 8–9), two frames expose the contrast between the modern city and the extreme poverty of the capital's shantytown. The second frame shows two soldiers patrolling a garbage dump inhabited by the poverty stricken while a nearby billboard proclaims "Viva Tapioca." At the end of the story, the plane leaves with our friends, accompanied by Tintin and Jolyon Wagg's Jolly Follies. The plane flies over a similar scene, the only difference being that the two military personnel inspecting the shantytown are soldiers of Alcazar's government and the billboard now proclaims "Viva Alcazar" (62: 11). Indeed, the effect of the revolution in San Theodoros is neutral. The country does not experiment any good or bad change. But of course, the reader might consider the living conditions of the inhabitants to be immoral....

Whether the revolutions are led by leftist or right-wing groups is immaterial, since for Hergé, the violent changes of government or regime are motivated by personal interest. Hergé's sarcastic vision in this regard was already apparent in *The Broken Ear*: a dictatorship is founded upon fear and governed according to the caprices of the head of power. At the moment at which Tintin is supposed to be shot by Tapioca's troupes, he is drunk and makes an unexpected remark mocking the situation, ridiculing the revolution, summarizing, in a sense Hergé's "political views": "Bing! Bang! Boom!... I'm dead!... Long live General Alcazar and Uncle Tom Cobbleigh and all!" (*Ear*, 21: 14).[9] Moreover, in *Tintin and the Picaros*, the young reporter gets involved in the revolution to help his friend Alcazar regain power not for ideological reasons but to save his friends from Tapioca's clutches, as he explains to the captain (*Picaros*, 46: 1–3). He does not act from political conviction, since the revolution is not based upon any sort of idealism. In Hergé's stories, there is nothing romantic about revolution.

The image of San Theodoros military political leaders presented by Hergé harkens back to that of the *caudillo (Horowitz, 148; Lambert and Gandolfi, 474)*. Although the caudillo's image survives only in folklore, it probably still exerts some influence over the media's representation of the Latin American political figure. However, contrary to popular belief, the caudillo was not necessarily a member of the military, even though he took power through a personal armed guard. "Regardless of his origin, the caudillo was expected to be able to lead his followers in battle and, for that reason, many a landowner, lawyer, or even bandit came to power with a general's rank earned during the revolutions." This explains the confusion—real or imagined, depending on the national context—between political and military powers, for "if civilians could arm their personnel to seize power, it seems logical that military leaders would have been tempted to do the same" (Lambert and Gandolfi, 100–1).

A few of the military governments which have ruled South American countries for decades might have acted as "enlightened despots," promoting implementation of some elements of modernity in their countries. To a certain extent, these governments exhibit local differences and need not be judged as a group. Hergé, however, reduces this phenomenon to a caricature by emphasizing the arbitrary nature of military rule in San Theodoros, arbitrariness forming, in his view, part of the political mores and even being a time-honoured tradition. The coup which brings Alcazar to power in *Tintin and the Picaros* illustrates this well. Tintin opposes these solid Latin American "traditions," to the chagrin even of the deposed leader, General Tapioca. Tintin promises to help Alcazar regain power (by putting an end to alcoholism among his soldiers with the aid of a product invented by Professor Calculus), upon the one condition that no blood be shed, which implies that Tapioca will not be shot. This condition is difficult both for the Picaros leader and Tapioca to accept (*Picaros*, 57). This clash of values is illustrated in the conversation between Alcazar and Tapioca when the latter learns that his life is to be spared:

> *Tapioca*: "For pity's sake don't pardon me! Do you want me completely dishonoured?" [. . .]
> *Alcazar*: "My decision is irrevocable: your life will be spared! An aircraft will be placed at your disposal, to convey you wherever you may wish to go."
> *Tapioca*: "Are you mad?"

Alcazar: "No, I'm not . . . But he is! [pointing to Tintin] . . . This muchacho made me give my word that the coup would be bloodless! . . . I'm desperately sorry!"

[. . .]

Tapioca: "Ah, an idealist, is he? . . . Young chaps nowadays have absolutely no respect for anything. . . . Not even the oldest traditions!"

Alcazar: "We live in sad times." (57: 4–7)

This political violence is provoked by power-hungry individuals. In San Theodoros in particular, power is held by the military and each coup brings the military to power, usually with the help of foreign powers. In *Tintin and the Picaros*, Tapioca heads the government with the support of Borduria, a country which Tintin and Haddock visit in *The Calculus Affair*. Borduria sends Colonel Sponsz to San Theodoros in the capacity of "technical advisor" to Tapioca. Alcazar hopes to overturn Tapioca with the aid of his Picaros. He and his guerillos are apparently backed by a "great power . . . commercial and financial this time: the International Banana Company" (1: 7). Hergé presents a paradox here: the military elite maintains legitimacy at home but depends on foreign aid to establish and maintain that political legitimacy (Horowitz, 146).

Inter-state wars are also "sponsored" by foreign powers, which exploit the vulnerability and instability of these nations led by capricious and infantile leaders. In *The Broken Ear* Alcazar cedes to the pressures of "professional sharks, oil company representatives and arms sellers" (Soumois, 102) and agrees to engage hostilities with the neighbouring country, Nuevo Rico. On the other hand, Tintin, who was hired as a colonel to Alcazar following the hazards of revolution (*Ear*, 22: 2–10), clearly shows his opposition to war.

Hergé's cynicism towards politics and revolution reaches its height in the *Picaros*, while the annual carnival takes place in the capital, Tapiocapolis. In that volume, revolution doesn't look any more serious than a carnival. Politics is so disenchanted that the Picaros—Alcazar's *guerilleros*—become entertainment for tourists: Lampion's bus loses its way, and go through the Picaros' bush—the land of the Arumbaya Indians—to the joy of Jolyon Wagg and his Jolly Follies. The sightseers take pictures, ask a fighter for postcards (*Picaros*, 51: 6), look for a souvenir shop (*Picaros*, 51: 7). . . . General Alcazar is shocked by this masquerade, but Tintin has a plan: the

Picaros, dressed up with costumes of Wagg's troupe, will surprise Tapioca and his guards, and overthrow his government during the first day of the carnival (54–57).

Thus, political instability reigns in South America, generals overturning each other in succession. And once in power, how does Alcazar govern when not engaged in making war? In his own words, "I shall do as I like: I'm in command!" (*Ear*, 22: 7). In other words, he governs arbitrarily, in some accordance with Montesquieu's theory of despotism: a corrupt government by nature, ran according to the prince's personal interest and caprices. In fact, Alcazar is often so busy fulfilling his whims that his office door remains closed even to ministers and ambassadors. One scene shows a work session between the general and Colonel Tintin in which the two men are analyzing "a delicate position:" they are playing chess (23: 13–19 and 31: 4–11), that is, a game whose goal is to capture the king! Thus, every effort is aimed at seizing power. Once this is achieved, the head of state spends his time awaiting the next revolution. . . .

Totalitarianism: The Omnipresence of the Mustache

However, Montesquieu did not foresee all the possible cases of despotism. Inspired largely by a somewhat stereotypical image of "Asiatic despotism" (under which he grouped the empires of Persia, China, India, and Japan), his analysis served as a sort of counter-model to serve as a warning to European monarchies that they must not lose their sense of moderation and must avoid falling into absolutism and arbitrariness (Aron, 36–37). The principle of despotism is *fear* (*Montesquieu*, III, 9): despots govern according to their whims and make their people fear them, and notably their viziers, to extinguish their ambition.

But Montesquieu could not anticipate how far modern nationalism, ideologies and the perfecting of propaganda techniques would bring despotism. According to some authors (such as Hannah Arendt, Carl Friedrich, Raymond Aron, Martin Malia . . .), the twentieth century saw the rise of a new political regime, known as *totalitarianism*. The term is controversial, but according to these political theorists, a totalitarian regime goes even farther than a despotic or dictatorial regime, in that the state encompasses every aspect of public and private life in the nation (political, economic, cultural, etc.) with a religion of power which rules out any possibility of existence outside the boundaries set by the totalitarian state. In a despotic regime according to Montesquieu, religion is "the only limit on the arbitrariness of the ruler" (Aron, 38). In a totalitarian regime, the state and its ideology replaces religion.

In Tintin's universe, there is only one dictator at the head of a political system who could be qualified as totalitarian. This is, of course, Marshal Kûrvi-Tasch. Hannah Arendt, in her classic *The Origins of Totalitarianism*[10] considers Hitler's Germany and Stalin's Russia to be the prototypical totalitarian dictatorships. Hergé, in *The Calculus Affair* (1956), paints a picture of a totalitarian dictatorship which combines elements of Nazi fascism and Stalinist communism. Of course, the *Affair* is not a work of political theory. It is mostly (among other things) an exciting political detective story set against a background of the cold war and the race for scientific progress; it is, nonetheless, a sketch of some of the more visible aspects of totalitarianism (it is, after all, a comic strip!), and the story teems with symbolism and metaphor.

In this story, the Professor is sought after both by Syldavia's and Borduria's secret services, and we witness a breathless chase, in which Tintin and Haddock participate in order to bring their friend back home. Finally, Borduria will lay hands on the famous scientist (*Affair*, 43: 1–3), but Tintin and the Captain will manage to free him (57–60). The purpose of Borduria's secret police is to take possession of an ultrasonic weapon invented by Calculus which can break glass from afar. At the end, back in Marlinspike with his companions, Calculus decides to destroy the microfilms with the plans of the deadly weapon (62: 1–6). Afterwards, he chooses to devote his talent to rather inoffensive research, such as culture of roses in *The Castafiore Emerald*. . . .

In the Borduria of *The Calculus Affair*, we see, essentially, the symbolic face of a totalitarian regime. Hergé presents a sort of Bordurian "façade state."[11] Of course, Arendt goes much farther in analysing the phenomenon, exploring the historical and ideological origins of this political form and analysing its whole internal logic. Nonetheless, some of Arendt's analytical categories seem relevant to the visit to Borduria, an imaginary country created by Hergé (and which had previously tried to annex Syldavia with fascist methods in *King Ottokar's Sceptre*).

Both Hergé and Arendt (with different intentions, of course) see Stalinism and Nazism as prototypes of totalitarian systems, as these two dictatorships were the only known examples of this political form (as defined by Arendt) at the time at which they were writing.[12] In his inimitable style, Hergé tells a story whose political setting and plot in some sense give a brilliant description of the mystical, invasive, omnipresent and indestructible aspects of totalitarianism. Marshal Kûrvi-Tasch is everywhere, but he is never seen in person in Hergé's stories. He appears in portraits and in effigy (*Affair*, 46: 21; 47: 12; 55: 12; 60: 3) sporting the famous whiskers which form the basis of his Taschist Party's whole ideological symbolism. Moustaches are everywhere in the urban landscape of Szohôd, the capital of Borduria. Even the circonflex over the *ô* of *Szohôd* is drawn to resemble a moustache (as are, in fact, all the circonflex accents in the Bordurians' speech in the French original)! It would be futile to attempt to enumerate each one of these countless "Taschist" symbols: they appear on officers' uniforms,[13] on caps, on cars (bumpers, etc.), on public buildings, on furniture and hotel décor, etc. And officials swear "by the whiskers of Kûrvi-Tasch" and greet each other with "Amaïh Kûrvi-Tasch!," an expression whose origin is not hard to guess.[14]

In fact, there is only one mention of a "concrete" sign of his existence as an active political leader, namely in *The Castafiore Emerald*, where a newscaster announces "an exceptionally violent speech" made by Kûrvi-Tasch at the twenty-first Taschist Party Congress in Szohôd (*Emerald*, 49: 1). His presence, which could almost be qualified as virtual, is always through the media or propaganda, although his control over the country is total and unequivocal.

The leader is thus everywhere and nowhere at the same time, thereby effectively demonstrating his absolute power. His symbolic gift for ubiquity translates into a veritable cult of personality (like that of Stalin in the U.S.S.R.) which, in appearance at least, gives him a political aura of indestructibility, like the plexiglass after which he is named in French.[15] What would happen if the Marshal disappeared? Would this put an end to the regime? Perhaps Marshal Kûrvi-Tasch has already disappeared, and his cult lives on despite his absence? In any case, since the regime's strong man is elusive despite his ubiquity Haddock and Tintin can never get at the source of Bordurian power to dislodge him. This is not even their aim, as Tintin, in the *Affair* (the seventeenth book of the series in color), is more preoccupied by personal matters (here, rescuing his friend Calculus) than by saving the world, as he did in some of the first books.[16] But somehow, it would surely be harder to destroy a regime of this kind than make a police investigation on the robbery of a sceptre (see the following section about the monarchy).

Sponsz's Secret Police and the Quest for Domination

In the Borduria of the *Affair*, we find two basic traits of totalitarianism as defined by Arendt: a police force at the centre of power and a foreign policy that openly seeks world domination. The most powerful man that the reader and the hero are allowed to glimpse in *The Calculus Affair* is Colonel Sponsz ("sponge"), head of the secret police or "ZEP" (his name appears for the first time in *Affair*, 49: 11). "And Calculus's fate depends on that man!" (53: 2), says Tintin, who has gone off with the captain in pursuit of his friend who has been kidnapped by agents of Kûrvi-Tasch's regime. He is the most powerful leader the reader sees in person in the story, even though Kûrvi-Tasch is still the supreme head of state.

Despite his considerable power, Sponsz does not pose a threat to Kûrvi-Tasch's government. In a conventional despotic regime, the secret police often pose a potential threat to government authorities because of the information they possess.[17] Even in Western democracies, secret services may eventually disobey the government if they are allowed too much autonomy. In contrast, in a totalitarian regime, the secret police

> [...] is totally subject to the will of the Leader, who alone can decide who the next potential enemy will be and who, as Stalin did, can also single out cadres of the secret police for liquidation [...]. Like the army in a non-totalitarian state, the police in totalitarian countries merely execute political policy and have lost all the prerogatives which they held under despotic bureaucracies. (Arendt, 425)

This dependence is perceptible here through the omnipresence of the ruler's image throughout Borduria and in the rituals of the Kûrvi-Tasch regime officials, which always evoke the name of the leader ("Amaïh Kûrvi-Tasch!") or a symbol referring to him.

Yet Sponsz wields enormous power in Borduria. All true executive and administrative power is in his hands. He is not merely the representative of the law to the Bordurian people; he is in charge of the actual ruling apparatus of the state. It is he who makes the *concrete* political decisions and distributes orders to the supreme head of state:

> Neither dubious nor superfluous is the political function of the secret police, the "best organized and the most efficient" of all government departments, in the power apparatus of the totalitarian regime. It constitutes the true executive branch of the government through which all orders are transmitted. Through the net of secret agents, the totalitarian ruler has created for himself a directly executive transmission belt which, in distinction to the onion-like structure of the ostensible hierarchy, is completely severed and isolated from all other institutions. In this sense, the secret police agents are the only openly ruling class in totalitarian countries and their standards and scale of values permeate the entire texture of totalitarian society. (Arendt, 430)

The fact that Marshal Kûrvi-Tasch has found a confidant in Sponsz illustrates this assertion. No one knows whether it is Sponsz or the Marshal who have taken the initiative, but it is Sponsz's secret police who kidnap Calculus: "[. . .] our secret service have managed to . . . to 'invite' to Borduria a foreign professor, originator of a sensational discovery," says the Colonel to Bianca Castafiore, who plays at Szohôd Opera House where Haddock and Tintin try to hide from the police. "It concerns a secret weapon. Once this has been perfected, it will give us world supremacy" (*Affair*, 55: 4).

If Borduria and its allies are made of plexiglass and the rest of the planet is glass and porcelaine, the world may well quake, as indeed it does in a televised scene presented to the Bordurian État-Major in the *Affair* (51: 8–14) which simulates the destruction of the city of . . . New York! As in Arendt's totalitarian system this "claim to world domination" is openly declared (436): "The day is not far off, gentlemen, when this weapon will make the people of Borduria and their glorious ruler Kûrvi-Tasch, masters of the world" (*Affair*, 51: 9), prophesies the chief of staff. Kûrvi-Tasch's regime succeeds in spreading its ideology as far as South America in *Tintin and the Picaros*.

Colonel Sponsz is assuredly one of the most respected political figures in Szohôd and in Borduria, and also probably one of the most visible. When the Colonel enters a public building with his entourage, the crowd holds its breath and allows him to pass. Everyone recognizes him. Every spectator glances at him, as in the scene at the opera in Szohôd: "Just look, there's Colonel Sponsz" (*Affair*, 53: 1). He wields far-reaching powers, allowing him to threaten summarily with execution those whom he commands: "By all the hairs in the whiskers of Kûrvi-Tasch, if you don't get them back . . . I'll have you shot!" (56: 17). It is noteworthy that General Alcazar, although a friend of Tintin to whom this prerogative is repulsive, allows himself the same power of life and death over his subordinates (*Picaros*, 58: 9 and 12).

The chief of the Bordurian political police never does succeed in getting his claws on the Marlinspike gang. Sponsz may be an elegant, neatly groomed figure of authority, but on the inside, he is rather pathetic. Nonetheless, Tintin magnanimously allows this villain to live, even though Sponsz is out to get him and conquer the world when Tintin foils his plans one last time in *Tintin and the Picaros* (57: 9).

"Pathetic Losers"

Tintin does not recognize the legitimacy of despotic regimes, but in general, he respects the rule of non-intervention in the affairs of a foreign dictatorship with one exception: the rights of citizens of those countries not to be victims to the caprices of their political leader at the price of their lives, a right he accords to even the most dastardly villains. In this, Tintin's political morality is on the side of human rights.[18] Thus, even though Alcazar wins a round against Tapioca thanks, in part, to Tintin's aid, Tintin refuses to allow the enemy to be shot. If he did, the game would continue and the resulting senseless bloodshed is a sacrifice no ideology could justify. Alcazar and Tapioca represent leaders who take power by force of arms, regardless of the messages they defend. In fact, their messages are not even spelled out in any of the Tintin stories, other than in General Alcazar's rather hollow formulaic promise to lead his "[. . .] beloved country forward along the road of economic, social and cultural progress!" (*Picaros*, 56: 11). The ambitions of the leaders of Borduria are just as devoid of content, corresponding to no well-defined ideal. The only use they see for the science of Professor Calculus, whom they have kidnapped, is to satisfy dreams of victory and success.

Conquest and conservation of power and dreams of world dominance are the only ambitions expressed by the despots. They are "pathetic losers" suffering from an incurable lack of morals and with whom it is impossible to reason. They must therefore be watched so that they do not abuse their ambitions. Thus, they can be nothing more than ridiculous or grotesque, even if they seem to be invincible.

THE MONARCHY

Opposed to any tyranny, Tintin seems to favour authority conferred on governments by tradition: he appears to be a royalist, at least if we interpret in this sense his effort to help King Muskar XII to stay on the throne of Syldavia in *King Ottokar's Sceptre*, by rescuing the "supreme sign of the syldav kingship" (*Sceptre*, 21). The sceptre which, traditionally, gives the king the right to reign on this small kingdom, following his ancestors' footsteps. Before taking a look at the Syldavian regime, let's glance at a couple of other sovereigns of the *Tintin* series.

In his work as a defender of justice, Tintin meets several monarchs: a king, a maharaja, an emir, etc. In *Cigars of the Pharaoh*, he meets the Maharaja of Gaipajama (51: 1–4). This Indian sovereign, who invites the reporter to his sumptuous palace, is fighting a powerful drug-smuggling organization (led, unbeknownst to Tintin, by the dastardly Rastapopoulos). By means of Rajaijah juice (the poison of madness) the members of this secret society eliminate those who try to thwart their criminal activities, including hostile politicians and their entourage. The Maharaja and Tintin fight for the same side, a side also championed by Wang Chen-yee and the "Sons of the Dragon" in *The Blue Lotus*. When Tintin succeeds in catching up with the kidnappers of the Indian monarch's son and manages to take him back to his father, this gesture also has political significance, ensuring that the Maharaja once again has an heir to the throne. The state needs successors, which is why monarchs must procreate.

Tintin also meets an Arab sovereign, Mohammed Ben Kalish Ezab, Emir of Khemed (or "Khemedite Arabia"). He is the leader of what might be called a "petroleum monarchy."[19] Unquestionably, the power of Khemed lies in its petroleum resources, which makes this label a fitting one. Moreover, oil is the source of conflict, as the Emir is threatened to be overturned by Bab El Ehr, an adversary who receives support from oil industry magnates.[20] Khemed also has an "old face" and a "modern face," two aspects identified by sociologist Maurice Duverger regarding governments in the

Middle East.[21] However, according to Montesquieu's typology, this regime might more accurately be labelled as despotic since the central distinction between the different types of government listed by Montesquieu is between moderate governments (monarchies, republics) and non-moderate governments (despotism). Despotism is based on fear and the Emir of Khemed uses fear to stay in power. For Montesquieu, monarchies and republics are regimes in which liberty can thrive, but a monarchy gone bad can turn into despotism.

King Muskar's Sceptre: "If You Gather Thistles, Expect Prickles"

However, it is mostly during his adventures in the Balkans that Tintin comes to the defense of royalty. When the young reporter goes to Eastern Europe for the first time, it is to go to the assistance of a figure of legitimate political authority, the king of Syldavia, whose power is threatened by the agents of an annexing power, Borduria. The mysterious and clandestine "Iron Guard," whose Machiavelian plans Tintin discovers at the end of his enquiry, poses a deadly threat to Syldavia.

Syldavia's motto, in the Syldavian language created by Hergé based on a Bruxelles dialect, is "Eih bennek, eih blavek!," which is translated as: "If you gather thistles, expect prickles." The sceptre does, in fact, carry a sting. It is a vital political symbol, the true symbol of authority (Apostolidès, 106). Ottokar's sceptre previously saved an ancient Syldavian king from assassination, namely Ottokar IV, who came to the throne in 1360, after whom the precious artifact is named. According to the tourist brochure that we can read with Tintin (*Sceptre*, 19–21), Ottokar IV is the true founder of the Syldav homeland: "He fostered the advancement of the arts, of letters, commerce and agriculture. He united the whole nation and gave it that security, both at home and abroad, so necessary for the renewal of prosperity" (21). Attacked by Baron Staszrvich, Ottokar saved his own life and his crown by striking the baron's head with the sceptre. Since that time, the sceptre has become more than a symbol: if the king of Syldavia loses it, tradition demands that he lose the right to rule. Moreover, in *King Ottokar's Sceptre*, the king's abdication would entail annexation of the country by Borduria and the transformation of the monarchy into a dictatorship.

Every year, on the national holiday of St. Vladimir's Day, the king of Syldavia makes a great ceremonial tour of the capital, sceptre in hand, while the people "sing the famous anthem":

Syldavians unite!
Praise our king's might:
The Sceptre his right! (*Sceptre*, 21)

The drama which embroils good king Muskar XII is precisely the theft of his sceptre until the eve of the national holiday, which augurs ill for the king and his regime. On the eve of St. Vladimir's, the Prime Minister expresses his concern:

Things are grave, Sire! . . . the people are suspicious: there are rumours that the sceptre is missing. Furthermore . . . Bordurian shops were looted again yesterday. These incidents are of course the work of agitators in the pay of a foreign power, but we are faced with a dangerous situation. And if your Majesty appears before the crowds without the sceptre, I fear . . . (*Sceptre*, 57: 11–12)

The king, a good man who does not want his people to suffer, immediately interrupts him: "Rest assured, Prime Minister, there will be no bloodshed. I will abdicate" (57: 12).

The king of Syldavia is not merely the unifying symbol of the Syldavians. He is not content to reign: he governs. His faithful ministers bow before his authority and do little more than to inform him, as in the scene quoted above. "[They] are anxious old men, incapable of taking the initiative, who come to report to their master in a style deliciously reminiscent of the *Ancien Régime* . . . and then await his orders" (Vanherpe, 45). One example of the king's authority over his ministers is shown when Tintin reveals to Muskar some papers describing a plot by one Müsstler (Mussolini-Hitler), the invisible "mastermind" of the conspiracy, and his accomplices. Two successive frames show Muskar formulating firm decisions to his ministers: "Not a moment to lose! Arrest Müsstler and his associates at once!" (*Sceptre*, 58: 10); "General, the review of the army will not take place tomorrow as arranged. By 8 a.m., crack regiments will occupy defensive positions along the frontier" (58: 11). The two ministers receive the king's orders with a "yes, Sire! . . ." (58: 10).

The plot in question here involves Bordurian agents, lead by Müsstler, the head of the Iron Guard (in reality the Z.Z.R.K.[22]), who have are plotting against King Muskar: they plan to steal the sceptre, that precious artifact which embodies political power and allows its holder to reign over and govern the Syldavian people. It is an "Anschluss" [23] plot, the forced annexation of Syldavia, as proven by the documents found by Tintin (*Sceptre*, 53: 1–4). Tintin, of course, changes the course of history. He saves the king and, by this very fact, the Syldavian people. No blood will be shed. Muskar XII is a good king, worthy of keeping his throne, because he is worthy of the role conferred upon him by his country's monarchical institution. He honours the legacy of Ottokar IV, who unified the country and gave it security and prosperity in the XIVth Century. He proves his merit earlier in the story when he steps out of his royal car unprotected to ensure that the young man (Tintin) who has been hit by the car is alright. "You aren't hurt, I hope?" (40: 3). After Tintin reassured him that he was "not an anarchist" (40: 6), Muskar is disposed to listen to his warning and do the necessary to conserve his nation's liberty. He is a humane king, in some sense a "Tintin" invested with a leader's role.

It is interesting to note that Syldavia is also called, the "Kingdom of the Black Pelican" (Sceptre, 19), a crowned pelican sculpted atop the sceptre. The pelican is a Christian symbol representing abstention and paternal sacrifice.[24] In fact, this Hergé story ends somewhat like the New Testament: the king is ready to abdicate, to sacrifice himself for his people (*Sceptre*, 57: 12), but luckily, the sceptre is found, thereby "restoring" the king to his throne (58: 7–11; 59: 4–5). Muskar is the servant of the Syldavian citizens, hence his responsibility to protect his sceptre, a gage of his authority and the state's political stability. The people's trust is at stake.

The Syldavians are not so much the king's subjects as the king is a sort of guardian of national safety and security, the basis of his legitimacy. The king of Syldavia governs for the good of the country. He wants to protect his citizens from a bloody revolution.[25] Contrary to a dictatorship, in which seizure of power is an end in itself, there is political substance here. Tintin shows himself to be a defender of order and stability, but also of moderation. As the ministry of the Interior—who in the English version also appears to be the Prime Minister of His Majesty—recounts to Tintin, the revolution he has prevented would have provoked the fall of the monarchy and the annexation of Syldavia to Borduria (*Sceptre*, 60: 7), changing a moderate government to a despotic regime, which is "corrupted by nature" (*Montesquieu*, VIII, 10). This monarchy even promotes scientific progress and serves as a beacon for civilization. Thus, it is Syldavia that makes possible the first manned flight to the moon in Hergé's stories (*Destination Moon* and *Explorers on the Moon*), although we never hear again of Muskar XII's rule after the *Sceptre*. Nevertheless, we might wonder what Syldavia has become in the *Affair*, since Syldavian spies, as the Bordurian espionage do, try to capture Professor Calculus and his invention (*Affair*, 28: 10–11 and 29–32; 41: 1–8), but are overtaken by Borduria's agents.

Symbols of Power and Stability

By the fact that the sceptre is an actual object of political power and that power is thus made concrete by Hergé shows that, for him, power can be embodied in a "thing" which can be appropriated, manipulated and exchanged, "For seizure of power is a purely technical problem" (Vanherpe, 49). In short, it seems that political power is not, for Hergé, a force exercised by political leaders on people who obey: this is of secondary importance. The mechanics of power do not interest Hergé. Essentially, power is something which is desired, stolen, taken, or lost. Politics in the world of Tintin looks like of zero-sum game between two persons (or two countries) in competition to take the lead. In other words, there is no sociology of power in *The Adventures of Tintin*, to the extent that in a sociological sense, power can mostly be seen in relational terms: it cannot be reduced to a substance (an energy or a force possessed by someone). In Hergé's work, power *is* a substance. King Muskar's power resides in his authority, which rest on the sceptre; (Apostolidès 110)[26] therefore, power could change of hands simply if the enemy subtilizes the sceptre. In *Tintin and the Picaros*, Tapioca *hands over* "all [his] powers to General Alcazar" (*Picaros*, 56: 11). But where to find a more "sociological" portrayal of power in a children comics? Not easy to find. . . . However, if we stay in the classical Belgian comics tradition, *King Smurf*, a Smurfs story by Peyo (1982 [1965]) is quite interesting in that sense: the reader can see the rise and fall of a tyrant, with his strategies to be obeyed by the inhabitants of the Smurfs' village, and with the tactics of those among the little blue goblins who resist his dictatorship.

Hergé, thus, makes use of a specific technique to simplify the problem of power. Basically, power and the authority attached to it can be embodied in a supreme symbol in Hergé's work, especially in the adventures of Tintin in Syldavia: a sceptre which serves as a measure of the strength and, more importantly, of the legitimacy of the leader's authority over the people. All of this is based purely on a political belief system, but the Syldavian regime rests precisely on such faith. French jurist Georges Burdeau speaks of the political nature of a social fact as resulting "from a colouring of facts" (Burdeau, 1979). Ottokar's sceptre has political clout precisely because the Syldavians perceive it to be an object invested with political virtues. By means of this simplification, Hergé explains to children the extent to which political power can be the object of greed.

In the other *Adventures of Tintin*, not all political leaders have a sceptre or an artefact of symbolic power as extraordinary as Ottokar's sceptre. But in these other stories, power is still reduced to one or two key elements, which would-be usurpers of power can simply steal to threaten the security of the regime and its leaders. For example, in *Cigars of the Pharaoh*, the son of the maharaja is kidnapped, as is Ben Kalish Ezab's son in *Land of Black Gold*. In this fashion, both monarchs lose their succession. Having a son allows the monarch to ensure the longevity of his authority. In the case of the emir of Khemedite Arabia, oil also embodies the strength of the ruling power. If Ben Kalish Ezab loses control of the oil, he is finished as head of the country. The emir's sceptre is oil.

What is the meaning of this praise of monarchy sung in Tintin's world? The Belgian king is a unifying element in the Belgian nation-state who transcends partisan divisions and who, even to this day, maintains credibility in that country. Like the Belgian king, the Syldavian king represents a unifying force, as explained by Delpérée and Dupret in speaking about the Belgian monarch:

> This function is often described as a *symbolic function*. The crown, like the
> sceptre and ermine, are seen as symbols of the kingdom, and, simultaneously,
> as images of the national identity. This formula may be too reductionist as it
> reduces the phenomenon to an emotional and irrational level. However, the
> monarchical institution fulfils a function closely tied to the successful workings
> of political society. (Delpérée and Dupret, 22)

For Hergé, individual safety must be associated with the stability of the political society, and the monarchy is, in his view, one of the best means to achieve such stability. This view conforms to the founding ideals of the Belgian state.[27] Under the Belgian constitution, the king is the guardian of the constitution. A constitution sets the rules for the organisation of power and the rights and liberties of the citizens. Any high-jacking of this constitution, like the theft of Ottokar's sceptre, could result in tyranny or anarchy. The metaphor of the sceptre is, in the end, much less simplistic than it might appear. It is also noteworthy that the Belgian head of state is not called the King *of Belgium*, but King *of the Belgians:* he reigns, not over an abstract nation, but over its citizens.

The Monarch in Fairy Tales

Reading *The Adventures of Tintin* from the perspective of a work aimed at children, the role of monarchical authority takes on yet another dimension. Hergé is not the first children's author to use the magic of kings and queens to introduce children to the universe of power and politics. In fact, the protagonists of many children's stories are kings and queens, starting, of course with many fairy tales. The tales of Perreault or the Brothers Grimm were written at a time when monarchy was the only type of regime existing on the European continent. In many fairy tales, the hero (or heroine), often a prince (or princess), undergoes some hardship, at the end of which he obtains the hand of the king's daughter and a promise that the kingdom will belong to him. According to Bruno Bettelheim's thoughts on the meaning of fairy tales, "Every child at some time wishes that he were a prince or a princess. . . . There are so many kings and queens in fairy tales because their rank signifies absolute power, such as the parent seems to hold over the child. So the fairy-tale royalty represents projections of the child's imagination . . ." (Bettelheim, 205). The "absolute power," is that which the parents exert over the child, and the exercise of this power by parental authority determines, in large part, the child's welfare. A "good" king is the hero's ally: a "bad" king is his enemy. Moreover, the stories never say anything about the exercise of political government by the king or queen in their realm: "There is no purpose to being the king or queen of this kingdom other than being a ruler rather than being ruled" (127). Seizure of power or the preservation of the reigning monarchical order are more important than the actual exercising of authority: "If we are told anything about the rule of these kings and queens, it is that they ruled wisely and peacefully, and that they lived happily. This is what maturity ought to consist of: that one rules oneself wisely, and as a consequence lives happily" (128). From a strictly narrative point of view, it is possible that the attributes of royalty (crown, sceptre, etc.) stimulate the imagination more than does the electoral urn.

What is said about the practices of monarchs in Hergé's stories does not go far beyond what is said about the government of kings in fairy tales. Implicitly, Hergé lets the reader suppose that King Muskar XII of Syldavia, the Maharaja of Gaipajama or the Emir Ben Kalish Ezab of Khemed (all masters of imaginary kingdoms, just like in the fairy tales) are just and benevolent rulers, whose realms are under attack from greedy, scrupulous men seeking to sow mayhem and disorder. While one of these sovereigns, the Emir of Khemed (who might be more accurately considered an "Asian despot" according to Montesquieu's classification), seems to be less reasonable by nature, it remains true that this sovereign of the land of a thousand and one nights undoubtedly lived in peace in his realm before his country became the object of desire of Bab El Ehr and international criminals.

Moreover, Tintin himself aspires to a certain form of nobility, as is clearly seen when he joins Haddock at the château of Marlinspike (we deduce that Tintin moves to the château of the captain's ancestors in *Destination Moon*). Tintin dreams of a sort of "kingdom" which he hopes to win through his exploits, in this way earning the right to establish himself in a unified and happy "family" and to move peacefully into a majestic palace of his own. Even if the château of Marlinspike is not inhabited by a king, it could be plausible that Captain Haddock has Louis XIV in his family tree (Tisseron, 33–72).

AND WHAT OF DEMOCRACY?

Democracy in Marlinspike: A moderate government

But who governs Tintin's country? Who watches over the well-being of the inhabitants of Tintin and Haddock's native country? And what is that country? Is it Belgium? France? Europe? Is Marlinspike a municipality or a state? Hergé never gives a direct response to these questions, though Tintin always identifies himself as European, that is, as a citizen of Europe with no more specific national identity, except that Marlinspike is situated somewhere in western Europe (Skilling, 99–106).

It is clear that Tintin does not live in a dictatorship. But does he live in a democracy? Or in a monarchy? There are no elections in Tintin's world (if we except in his first adventure),[28] nor even any visible government in his country. The only representatives of state authority we meet are police officers, who play a central role in Hergé's narrative universe (Skilling, 39–65). The police are often incompetent (the bungling of the Thompsons enhances Tintin's intelligence), but their work of maintaining order is still shown as indispensable. Moreover, the most respectable police force seems to be the British police (*Island*, 56–62). A reliable police force is one of the guarantors of respect for the law and the rights of the individual within the state. By rejecting dictatorship, Tintin shows that the police and the army must not be involved in politics and must be content to play their role of protectors and defenders of the public.[29]

These then, are values which Tintin's country shares with democracy, even though there do not seem to be any elected politicians in this political community—anyhow, we never encounter any politician of this kind in the series. In fact, we could say that these values are not specifically related to democracy, but more broadly to the idea of a moderate government, somehow in the sense Montesquieu sees it. What the French philosopher opposes to despotic government is a moderate rule, either monarchical or republican.[30] A fundamental quality of a moderate constitution is the separation of powers, namely the executive (governing, such as making peace or war, establishing security, etc.), the legislative (making laws), and the judiciary (punishing crimes and judging disputes between individuals). Police is a component of the third. Accordingly, a moderate government implies an independent and controlled police force, and denies a secret police with an executive power like in a totalitarian regime. If the Borduria of marshall Kûrvi-Tasch is not a democracy but a totalitarian state, it is not basically because there is no election—elections (false ones) exist even in dictatorships, as we can see in *Tintin in the Land of the Soviets* (35–36)—but rather because the secret police is "the true executive branch of the government."

Thus, if a corrupted police is a central element of totalitarianism—and an army pledged to the most recent "caudillo" in a dictatorship, be it a Tapioca or an Alcazar—the fact remains that there can be a reliable police force either in a monarchy or in a democracy. In brief, despotism is always bad, but monarchy can be good at some conditions! In this sense, it is trivial to know if the inhabitants of the château of Marlinspike live in a constitutional monarchy or in a democratic republic; but we can be sure they are governed with moderation!

Are The Adventures of Tintin *Outdated?*

If Tintin is still relevant today, that it is not, according to many, from a political nor sociological point of view. After all, one could say that this series has been created at the turn of the 1930s by a young right-wing catholic Belgian, who gave almost no significant role to any women in his stories (with the exception of the prima donna Bianca Castafiore), and overall proposed a too conventional point of view concerning politics. But as I mentioned at the beginning, Hergé was not a militant, and while he was inspired by history, he distanced his plots from the current events, making his series timeless in many ways. The very first Tintin adventures, though, are the more out of date, because too deliberately politically oriented: *Tintin in the Land of the Soviets* (1929), *Tintin in the Congo* (1930), *Tintin in America* (1931). . . . After that, Hergé became more and more a "graphic novelist," and offered more "food for thought." Let's see if Hergé's depiction of political regimes is still valid.

Reflection on types of government and evaluation of them is one of the oldest questions of philosophy. However, how the question is asked changes according to the time. Some would even say that the question is passé since the fall of the communist regimes of Eastern Europe in 1989–1991, leaving liberal democracy with no rival. Before this major transformation, several political science manuals sorted political regimes in two main models: western liberal democracy vs. the soviet-type political system (which was totalitarian according to its enemies, while its partisans saw it as "socialist democracy"). In fact, liberal democracy has become the dominant political model, and it is the regime of choice of countries emerging from totalitarianism or dictatorship.

Viewed from this perspective, can Tintin still be relevant? Yes and no. Hergé's hero is certainly an enemy of dictatorships, but he remains a royalist, advocating a type of regime which is no longer in vogue, except maybe for readers of tabloids who thrive on the latest gossip about the British royal family. Today, political science and constitutional engineering texts present different electoral systems and the properties of parliamentary and presidential systems, but they do not really place much importance on the advantages and disadvantages of monarchy.

But to what extent is Tintin really a royalist? He rescued a king, but what does it mean to do this task for a European hero? At the beginning of the series, he plays a direct role in political events; but at the end of his adventures, he is almost merely an observer, since his travels are mostly motivated by personal reasons. In the 1930s, Tintin is there to maintain order and stability and fight for justice. During the same period, Alex Raymond's Flash Gordon—inaugurated in 1934—wants to civilize a planet and exports liberal democracy (Berger 133–45). Tintin is less ambitious. From a historical viewpoint, Tintin—born in 1929 and taking part in his last complete journey in 1976—may represent the evolution and decline of the European political power in the twentieth century: this European hero gradually loses his influence on world affairs. In the first stories, he is clearly a defender of a West-European moral superiority over the rest of the world (USSR and communism, Africa needing to be "civilized" by Europe, the United States and capitalism . . .). Afterwards, he resolves international crimes and is directly involved in hostilities in India, China, and South America. When he saves Syldavia's monarchy in the *Sceptre* (composed in 1938–39), he is awarded the Order of the Golden Pelican by King Muskar (60: 1–2), an event which represents the final recognition of his good and faithful service to order, stability, and justice. Next, Tintin becomes less directly concerned by political issues and the world order, yet at a time when Europe is at war: it is at the end of *Red Rackam's Treasure* (1942–44) that Tintin's new friend, Captain Haddock (met in *The Crab with the Golden Claws*), takes on the château of Marlinspike, which will soon become new Tintin's home as well. The teen reporter still travels and do investigations, but mainly, he appears to retire in Marlinspike and work primarily to preserve order in his home and "family" (a metaphor of Europe working on its own construction?). Tintin, Haddock, and Calculus live in a palace which is no longer a royal residence, and which is longing for peace, order, and freedom. How are they governed? Surely by a moderate government.

In their presentation of types of government, Hergé's stories are no doubt somewhat outdated. But even if the Belgian cartoonist presents the issue in a form which seems obsolete to us, he incites us to ask the question "what is good government?" in the most classic manner, therefore, in terms which are still valid today. Aristotle compared the power of governors to that of a ship's captain, as a French sociologist reminds us:

> A captain cannot fulfill his mission unless he takes charge of the ship and all of its passengers. The same is true of politics. A political system which seeks personal gain is corrupt and appears as such to the sane mind. Yet if the system's natural goal is the common good, what is the substance of this common good? Its "core" is fairly undisputed: order, safety, justice. But beyond that, there is much room for debate. (Bénéton, 87)

To tell a story involving democracy (with its deliberations and procedures) in a comic strip aimed primarily at children is maybe not easy (and perhaps not entertaining enough?). Even in some contemporary animated cartoons for children, it is the monarchical symbolism which is preferred: would a "Lion President," or a "Lion Prime Minister," be as pleasant as the "Lion King"?[31] It is much easier to pit the good king, concerned about the well-being of his fellow citizens and striving for the common good, against the tyrant, governing according to his own interests to the detriment of those of his people.[32]

The categorization between the legitimate king and the unlawful tyrant may seem simple and rudimentary, but it is much certainly the oldest one. Subsequent evaluations of governments originate from this classic argument. While Ancient Greece experienced democracy and the early Greek philosophers discussed the merits of democratic government, they contrasted kings and tyrants. Xenophon distinguishes the good and the bad monarchy, the latter—tyranny—being a government of a single leader according to his own will and upon a non-consenting population. Plato does a similar division, adding the government of the few, aristocracy (the riches govern in accordance with the laws) vs. oligarchy (the riches govern unconcerned about the laws), plus a regime in which he sees only a bad version: democracy, the government of the "mob." For his part, Aristotle sees some virtues in democracy, but considers that only a small number of people can really be virtuous enough to hold the power for the common benefit. To him, the bad governments are all sorts of tyrannies (the corrupted versions of monarchy, aristocracy, and republic), while the good ones are conform to the "natural order of politics" (Bénéton, 20). In his taxonomy, monarchy is one of the greatest systems, but is not appropriate for all nations (*Politics*, XII). Aristotle deduces that wisdom leads to a "happy medium" (XIV). Above all, the quality of a government lies in the leader's merits (while for Montesquieu the crucial point is to prevent despotism by arranging a structure when power is strictly controlled). In the Middle Ages, Thomas Aquinas walks on Aristotle's footsteps, as for him a good government is leaded by a righteous chief, but the opposition between royalty (in a wide sense of a devoted sole leader) and tyrannies is even more essential (Bénéton, 21).

Today, the opposition would more likely be between good government and corrupt government, even within liberal democracy. In short, one could simplify by saying that the contrast between monarchy and dictatorship is a way of asking the question of good vs. bad government. Good government ensures order, security and justice. Whereas dictatorships may provide order and security for segments of their population, they can only exercise a caricature of justice, such as in San Theodoros, when the head of State or any army officer can pronounce a sentence on the spot: Tintin is a victim of this expeditious justice without any trial in *The Broken Ear* (18: 6–13), when he is taken to the "Caserna San Juan V," quickly arrested and sentenced to death by the chief officer in the barracks.

Order, security, and justice: Tintin seems to ask no more than this of the heads of governments, but it is, in and of itself, a weighty task. The tasks which a government should or should not undertake for the good of citizens will continue to be the subject of heated debate in the future, but this "nucleus" of a common weal should persevere.

But even in lands living under good governments, some people are victims of prejudices, and citizens more vigilant than others are much desirable. As a model citizen, Tintin defends the rights of those who are too weak to defend themselves. He is, in some ways, more of a police detective than a journalist, but with a mission that goes beyond arresting criminals: he has a political conscience and is a defender of the rule of law and human rights. For instance, he challenges the Thompsons' investigation in *The Castafiore*

Emerald, as the two detectives erroneously suspect gipsies of the theft of Bianca Castafiore's precious jewel. His success in exonerating the bohemians covers a disapproval of a certain police behaviour of those who judge people by their appearance and with preconceptions. One of the two police "brothers" is frustrated by the end result of the story: "Just our luck! The one time we manage to catch the culprits they turn out to be innocent! It's really a bad thing of them!. . ." "You'd think they'd done it on purpose!," adds the other (*Emerald*, 60: 9).

A priori, liberal and republican democracy might seem superior to the constitutional monarchy which seems preferred by Tintin, since it assumes judicial equality of all citizens and denies the right of a man or woman to be head of state on the basis of heredity alone. But even in our day and age, the president tends to surround himself with the pomp and apparatus of the monarchy. Absolute monarchies no longer exist in our time, and even constitutional monarchies are basically democracies. For a comics series aimed mainly at children, and not primarily intended to be a political statement, Tintin probably shows the essential with this manicheism of the "good" leader vs. the "corrupt" politician.

CONCLUSION

So Tintin rejects dictatorship. Big deal! Of course, it's hardly surprising. How could one expect a hero of comics (or of any other art form or media) to promote despotism and oppression? Other French and Belgian comic book heroes—such as *Blake & Mortimer*, created by Edgar Jacobs, a close friend of Hergé, and *Spirou & Fantasio*, conceived notably by André Franquin—are often assigned the same task of halting mad tormentors. In America, among others, Alex Raymond's *Flash Gordon* (beginning in 1934) fought to put an end to the tyranny of Ming, on the Planet Mongo, and classic superheroes such as Superman stand up for liberty and justice.

Obviously, if classic comics heroes combat a form of government abroad, it is to endorse (and even promote) the way things go at home: For Flash Gordon, defeating the despot Ming was to replace the tyranny by a Republic modeled on the United States of America (Berger 143). Tintin also supports a type of government, but he is less ambitious, not working to spread a model of his in foreign countries. Nonetheless, while he opposes dictatorship and totalitarianism, Tintin promotes a quiet and peaceful place to live for everyone. The ideal might be an enlightened and constitutional monarchy, governed by a king who rides himself the royal limousine.

Dictatorship leads to a political carnival. Furthermore, to Hergé as well as for a number of comics artists, seizure of power—that is the only ambition of dictators—is not a serious game. It is a silly one, though with serious consequences for the people. Moreover, the sinister ballet performed by General Alcazar and General Tapioca, stealing power to each other by turns, may echoes in a cynical view of politics in a broader sense: these days, we frequently hear the opinion of disillusioned and sceptical citizens saying that they do not care about who governs, because "politicians are all the same." . . . Maybe it is the reason why Hergé doesn't show us any politician in Marlinspike, a home for retired heroes, far away from the political circus. . . .

Totalitarian regimes are even more terrifying. The totalitarian state has the ambition to ultimately dominate the world. An authoritarian regime like San Theodoros might be motivated to cause trouble by neighbour countries resources, like Alcazar approving a war with Nuevo Rico to lay hands on its oil (*Ear*, 33: 9–10). However, the dictator can be contented with these regional targets. Not the seemingly invulnerable totalitarian leader, whose ideology and propaganda seeks to permeate all his nation's life, and who aspire to extend his domination on all the earth's surface with the help of his secret police, a police vested with executive powers. Marshall Kûrvi-Tasch of Borduria impregnate all his country with his images and symbols (the moustaches), and his plans for world supremacy are unambiguous. In *Tintin and the Picaros*, we notice in fact that Borduria has already captured San Theodoros, saturating that country too with Kûrvi-Tasch propaganda.

Hergé rejects all dictatorships, be they left or right-wing, and favours a monarchical type of authority. In the Tintin stories, non-monarchical regimes arouse scepticism. In short, it seems that only those who are at the head of monarchies, like good King Muskar, are the wisest, have the good of the community at heart, and can assure stability and security. Monarchy appears to be the championed political form in the series: an enlightened monarchy, guaranteeing the well-being of the citizens of the state, who, in turn, venerate their king. While he thought that monarchy has its qualities, Montesquieu was preoccupied by the danger that it could fall into despotism.

To prevent it, his solution was to establish measures to prevent corruption of power and absolute monarchy, that is to assure a moderate government. The key to moderation is that "power should be a check to power": three independent and interrelated powers, that is the executive, the legislative, and the judiciary branches, each supervising the others two. In its imaginary world, Hergé offers another solution to prevent absolute monarchy and despotism: in the kingdom of Syldavia, a strong symbol of authority, King Ottokar's Sceptre, is somewhat a "check to power," or rather an instrument to instil self-discipline into the king. He must protect the sceptre, otherwise he loses his power over his nation. The sceptre is a safeguard against despotism, and a pledge for a good government. There is no need to propagate symbols of power all around Syldavia (like Kûrvi-Tasch in Borduria); the central symbol of the sceptre is sufficient enough. Each year, to deserve what could be compared to a "vote of confidence" from the people, the king has the duty of showing this supreme sign of authority to the crowd, on National Day. For his part, a dictator doesn't maintain his power through trust, but through fear.

However, if compared to crowned heads in fairy tales, monarchy in a children comics like *The Adventures of Tintin* may lose its political significance. In a fairy tale, the king is not a "politician" working for the well-being of the inhabitants of his kingdom, but rather a father protecting his family, a chief from whom we don't know anything about the way he governs. But while *Tintin* is a comics series primarily intended for children—but which of course has readers of all ages—it is not a fairy tale. Even if all the young readers of Tintin don't grasp the political allusions in Hergé's work, there is politics in those stories, though the main political matter is the quest for power.

And what of democracy? Certainly, we don't see elections in Tintin's adventures, and just a couple of panels shows parliamentary work.[33] But democracy is not only about voting and parliamentary debates—crucial aspects of democracy, but it involves more than that. It's also about human rights, and the rule of law. In this sense, it also concerns a reliable police force, independent from the government. In a series like *Tintin*, where the role of detectives and police officers is so considerable, this is not of secondary importance. A sane government is a moderate one. *Tintin* is not a work of political theory, but it shows clearly the "head and tail" of government: the country's leader, and the policeman (or the soldier). If the two are bedfellows, a nation lives under a corrupt government, as in San Theodoros and in Borduria.

Certain philosophers and political thinkers of the past have tried to describe the different forms of government, including democracy, without necessarily championing democracy as the only legitimate political regime, at least not in the same sense as we could see it today. Aristotle and Montesquieu are such examples. A bit in the same way, Hergé will become a classic of his genre, somewhat removed from our reality because the settings and environments will have become outdated, but whose stories will always serve to show us that the world does not change as much as one might believe. Dictatorships may be anachronistic, but they continue to plague too many populations on earth. Furthermore, we may live in democracies, but unfortunately we will possibly see some politicians abusing their power or forgetting their duty to the common good. Fortunately, mechanisms to prevent or punish those conducts may have been established in our countries. Children must learn it. Despite all its qualities, there is no politics in *Harry Potter*. But by chance, there are graphic tales which relate the deeds of the good and the bad kings.

NOTES

1. Some elements of this article are taken from my book *Mort aux tyrans! Tintin, les enfants, la politique*, Quebec: Nota Bene, 2001. [Ed. note: Translated from the French by Annette Dominick.]

2. For their comments, I am grateful to Dr. Jeff McLaughlin, Dr. Mircea Vultur(Institut national de recherche scientifique, Quebec City), Anne Guilbault, and the anonymous reviewer of this paper.

3. Translator's note: All *Tintin* volume page numbers refer to the English *Tintin Three-in-one* series published by Little, Brown & Co.

4. For more on *The Blue Lotus*, see also Peeters (2002, p. 115–26).

5. Translator's note: from the translation by Anne M. Cohler, Basia Carolyn Miller, Harold Samuel Stone (1989). Cambridge University Press, p. 10.

6. Translator's note: In the original French version, the party is called the "Parti Moustachiste." Both the French and English names contain a—*schist* ending reminiscent of the word "fascist."

7. References and quotations from *Tintin* books will be presented in this manner: a key word from the title, followed by page number, and panel(s) number(s) inside the page. Example: *The Calculus Affair*, p. 49, panel 12, is referred to as: (*Affair*, 49: 12). See bibliography for the complete book titles.

8. San Theodoros actually represents Bolivia (Soumois, 103–6), a Bolivia opposed to Paraguay during the so-called "Chaco" war from 1931 to 1936. This conflict was linked to oil and, on a more general level, saw Great Britain and the U.S. at loggerheads. In *The Broken Ear*, Paraguay is called "Nuevo Rico."

9. In the French version of the *Ear*, the quotation even expresses a hint of Belgian "nationalism"(!), Tintin chanting "Vive le général Alcazar et les pommes de terre frites!" ("Long live General Alcazar and French fries!").

10. Translator's note: all quotations from Arendt are taken from the 1966 Harcourt, Brace & World edition. Page numbers refer to this edition.

11. "Totalitarianism in power uses the state as its outward façade, to represent the country in the nontotalitarian world" (Arendt, 420).

12. This assimilation of the two regimes was the object of some criticism levelled against Hergé, for at the time of publication of *The Calculus Affair* (1956), "only the hard-core right would have dared to do what thirty years later would seem self-evident: assimilate the crimes of Stalin to those of Hitler." (Assouline, 291), and many Marxist critics would consider such a position to be proof of allegiance to the hard right. Much as Hergé refused for a long time to acknowledge the Nazi horrors (204), many communist artists and philosophers refused to acknowledge the atrocities of Stalinism. The fact that Hergé placed the two regimes back to back in this way angered several critics of the time.

13. Moreover, the uniforms of the political police of the Taschist Party are styled after those of the Gestapo.

14. The greeting "Amaïh" appears in the French version of *King 'Ottokar's Sceptre*, as a signature on secret documents found by Tintin (53, 1–4). The documents reveal the plot of Müsstler, head of the Iron Guard, to take over Syldavia and annex it to Bordurdia. (Note that Müsstler's name is a contraction of Mussolini and Hitler.)

15. His exact name in French is *maréchal Plekszy-Gladz*, which recalls the toughness of his regime (an evocation that disappears in the English translation, unfortunately to my opinion). Moreover, Calculus makes a comment about glass not being "tough enough" compared to plexiglass (multiplex in the English text) in *Destination Moon* (8, 6).

16. See Apostolidès (164), who explains that Tintin, after *King Ottokar's Sceptre*, is less politically involved and more concerned with his own "family history" (with Haddock, Calculus, etc.).

17. "The secret services have rightly been called a state within the state, and this not only in despotisms but also under constitutional or semiconstitutional governments. The mere possession of secret information has always given this branch a decisive superiority over all other branches of the civil services and constituted an open threat to members of the government" (Arendt, 425).

18. Moreover, Tintin's attitude perhaps comes close to the principle of "right of humanitarian intervention," which appeared in the late 1980s. This principle allows humanitarian assistance to be given in any territory regardless of the state's sovereignty. In other words, human rights are universal, and no state can justify violating the rights of its population on the basis of its sovereignty.

19. Maurice Duverger designates as "petroleum monarchies" those countries "in which highly archaic monarchic and feudal institutions are at work," "which are fabulously wealthy in petroleum resources which give them the highest per capita incomes in the world," and which "use this wealth to accelerate technological modernisation" (Duverger, 415). Among these states he includes Saudi Arabia and the United Arab Emirates.

20. He succeeds in *The Red Sea Sharks*. See also *Tintin in the Land of Black Gold*.

21. The "old face" of these countries relates to the religious nature of political powers and the "very backward" feudal character of the state as described by Duverger, using European regimes as a standard: "The sovereigns care little about political democratization. They are, as a rule, very conservative from the point of view of religion, morality, status of women, private ownership, etc." (Duverger, 415.) Seen from this archaic perspective, the characteristics of the petroleum monarchies enumerated by the Sorbonne political scientist correspond quite closely to the Khemed of Ben Kalish Ezab as drawn by Hergé (who has the same Eurocentric biases as Duverger). The conservatism of this country and its leadership are very visible, and their archaism is most apparent in the area of human rights and justice—see for example *Black Gold* (61, 9), and *Sharks* (30, 9 and 11). According to Duverger, the "modern face" of these regimes is reminiscent of enlightened despotism, an idea of 18th century European philosophers according to which the monarch's absolute power could be used "to modernise his kingdom in the light of new ideas," a way of subscribing to the rational ideals of the Enlightenment in an authoritarian manner.

22. The "Zyldav Zentral Revolutzionär Komitzät," whose goal was to overthrow the monarchy and annex Syldavia to Borduria (*Sceptre*, 60, 7).

23. "Anschluss" was the name given to the forced annexation of Austria by Nazi Germany in March 1938.

24. See Chevalier and Gheerbrant (738). See also Jean-Marie Apostolidès on the Syldavian crisis and its symbolism in the (recently reedited) *Les Métamorphoses de Tintin* (105–15), one of the best books ever written about Tintin.

25. Muskar XII may have been inspired by Albert I, who was King of the Belgians from 1909 to 1934. Albert I was hailed a hero because of the active part he played for the Allies in WWI both on a diplomatic and a military level (Gérard, 355–75). Far from being a passive figure of authority, Hergé's king seems to represent a leader carrying the fate of his fellow citizens upon his shoulders. This is also the image Albert I seems to have had for many Belgians because of his accomplishments during WWI.

26. See Apostolidès (110).

27. Belgium proclaimed its independence in 1830, the national congress voting 174 to 13 in favour of a representative constitutional monarchy as its political system. At the time of the debate, one of the advocates of the monarchy defended his opinion by declaring that this type of system offered "the freedom of a republic, with admittedly a bit less equality in its forms but also with an immense guarantee of order, stability and [. . .] liberty" (Dumont [citing Paul Devaux], 7).

28. The only elections portrayed in all of the *Adventures of Tintin* are the "hijacked" ones in *Tintin in the Land of the Soviets* (35–36).

29. It may have some importance to young readers. As political scientists David Easton and Jack Dennis explained concerning the relationship of children with politics, the police officer has an authority status equivalent with that of the president. According to their studies on political socialization in the United States, the child sees "the head and tail of the political animal with relative sharpness and salience" (Easton and Dennis, 1969: 143).

30. But in fact the best government according to Montesquieu was a mixed one, with a subtle dosage of the features of the two, that is the moderate government established in the English Constitution (*The Spirit of the Laws*, XI, 6).

31. In this logic, a journalist even suggested to me that monarchy was a sort of "infantile stage" of politics (Robitaille, 2003). It's relatively accurate if we consider that in a monarchy in pre-modern times, the struggle for power does not really exists, as the relationship between the people and their sovereign amounts to a celebration of love and devotion for the good king, similar to the love given by a child to his/her father.

32. Yet, since at least the 1960s, there are contemporary comics artists, notably those who create graphic novels for grown-ups, who deal with politics and are concerned with democracy, often with a disenchanted view. For instance, Hermann, a Belgian artist like Hergé, explores various political regimes in his series *Jeremiah* (first volume published in 1979), taking place in a post-nuclear war world grappling with civil war. Some of his stories include democracy and electoral campaigns, but his view is cynical (see Chavanne [1998]). Also, some superheroes stories of the end of the millennium, such as Frank Miller's *Batman: The Dark Knight Returns* (1986), address critics to American democracy (see Blackmore (1991), who associates this work to Alexis de Tocqueville's suspicions, in *Democracy in America*, that democracy could develop into a "tranquil and stable despotism"). Thus, the depiction of democracy in comics seems far from optimistic, at least in this couple of examples.

33. It's in *The Blue Lotus* (60, 2–6), where Hergé portrays a working session of the League of Nations concerning the Japanese occupation in China.

Drawn into 9/11, But Where Have All the Superheroes Gone?

—TERRY KADING

The events of September 11, 2001, so violent and so violently thrust upon us, profoundly altered our own sense of security as the images were replayed multiple times through the media. Within a matter of hours we were compelled to form a new conversation and understanding on a novel and terrifying phenomena. The post-9/11 period has been marked by an attempt to comprehend these events, and re-establish a context of individual and collective security. However, the goal of renewed security eludes us as we are forced to conceive, visualize, and prepare for a whole new set of potential catastrophic eventualities, the likes of which further provoke uncertainty and insecurity. It is this context of high-insecurity and the precarious quest for a renewed sense of safety that will be explored in relation to the medium of *comics*, in particular, the superhero genre. It is suggested that there are several parallels between the events of 9/11, the post-9/11 environment, and the worldview/individual experience within the superhero genre. From several perspectives, then, we may observe how we have been *drawn* into the superhero narrative in such a way that (strangely enough) is the very appeal of superhero genre. The downside of this *comic* source of insight lies in the force for reclaiming our lost security, namely the peculiar powers of the "superhero" (a fact not lost, as we will see, on the comic narrators in response to 9/11). In the first section of the paper the contiguous qualities of the superhero genre and the 9/11 context will be examined, followed by a review of the *comic*/superhero response to 9/11. The final section will address the enigma of these parallels, notably on issues of "good" versus "evil" in understanding the contemporary politics of security and the limits of the superhero narrative in addressing our insecurities.

The superhero genre has always been focused on expanding the bounds of our imagination in ways that offered insights into our immediate reality, while adding a dimension (or twist) that took it just beyond our known experience. Thus, the superhero genre is replete with everyday human characters, activities, and experiences (that prevent it from being classified as "science fiction/fantasy") with a "dash" of the incredible expressed through "beings" with extraordinary powers (talents and technologies). "Heroes" and "villains" are a common theme in many comic narratives, but the superhero genre is distinct from the more classic hero of the Western or the detective series (e.g. the Lone Ranger, Dick Tracy [both expressed through comic form]). Where the heroic figures of the latter were engaged in the defense of "law and order," "righting injustices," and protecting the values of hard work and good character against lawlessness and the predation of "good folk," the scale of the drama played-out was highly localized and the effects limited. In contrast, the superhero narrative offers up everything on a grander scale, where mega-cities, nations, or the globe are vulnerable to the wrath of supervillains. Often placed against the backdrop of a highly developed urban landscape, stark, bleak and anonymous, and defined by towering high-rise buildings, the superhero genre reflects the complexities of urban life in an advanced (post-) industrial setting. This complex environment, while in many ways a recognition of our human ingenuity and advancement, is also a foreboding commentary on the "success" of our science and technology in shaping our lives. All is not "good" and "pure," as crime, poverty, homelessness, urban decay, and questionable characters abound, into which are inserted more powerful and nefarious characters intent on further "shaking up" an already tense and demanding environment. The very benefits, advantages, and continuation of the Enlightenment project (i.e. truth, science, progress, and freedom), are predicated on the intervention of a superhero at various times to ensure that all that has been achieved is not undermined by dark, malevolent, "evil" forces bent on destruction and domination. With such eclectic figures as Superman, Batman, Wonder Woman,

Spider-Man, and Captain America, the superhero genre has established a unique worldview in which the very presence of a superhero prevents the "human experience" from being a permanent dystopia. The prospects for this dystopic human experience stemmed from imagining the potential uses/abuses of unfolding scientific and technological advancements "falling into the wrong hands," or the arrival of forms of "power" we could not yet comprehend or control. With this dilemma emerged new qualities to the binary opposites of "good" and "evil."

In the Western/Detective genres, "evil" was a known quantity, as the desires of the villain were not far removed from our own. They lusted for quick and/or vast wealth, indulged in various forms of instant gratification, and exercised crude but common place forms of "power." The "hero" of the Western/Detective genres was usually then defined by superior marksmanship, a higher level of tactical wisdom, and moral rectitude. In the superhero genre the qualities of "good" and "evil" took on new dimensions, mirroring in many ways our increasing anxieties and concerns over the fact that we had progressed to a point where the scientific and technological "power" under (or not under) our control had significantly expanded. Thus, the villains now possessed the ability to inflict far greater levels of damage and vast numbers of casualties unimaginable in the Western or Detective genres. To right this imbalance the "hero" needed to possess equal (if not greater) levels of powers and abilities, varied and advanced forms of technological superiority, and an acumen for science. Where "good" and "evil" remain as constants in these heroic narratives, with the superhero genre the "evil" has access to a considerable and greater arsenal of evil means. The "good" needs to be more than human, super-human, in order to act as an effective counter to the multiple and diabolical forms that evil acts may be comprised against humanity, and against humanity's greatest defender, the "superhero."

With this combination of forces, it became possible to envision graver and more dramatic scenarios as the imagination became informed by rapid advancements in the scientific fields of astronomy, biology, physics, and chemistry, with the attendant technological and engineering developments. As these areas spawned specialized sub-fields, revealing even more knowledge and our ability to manipulate matter (from elements to human genes), it became possible through the superhero narrative to imagine even greater and horrific possibilities that may be visited upon us. What also emerged were more numerous superheroes, each with peculiar mutations and facilities. While we celebrated and continue to marvel at scientific discoveries and possibilities, the superhero narrative always understood the direct correlation between "knowledge" and "power." With this "knowledge/power" relationship, the nature of "evil" changed from earlier heroic narratives, becoming more abstract in its ends. In the superhero narrative, the villainous figure(s) always possesses a murky political agenda, generally understood as little more than the will to dominate and/or destroy with ease, exercising "power" . . . *Bwah Ha Ha!!!* . . . without discretion, control, or consideration of the innocent. This fits with our understanding of "evil" acts, for as Andrew Linklater observes, "[T]he language of evil carries the obvious implication that there is nothing in the behavior of the victims or the wider society which could be said to explain—or to have contributed to—the acts of violence" (308). With the supervillains, there are no stated ideological or religious precepts invoked offering some superior form or understanding of human organization or emancipation. Differing forms of power are exercised with the simple desire to strike fear, elicit awe, and often directed at the superhero, for by vanquishing the superhero(s) the human species is left defenseless and compelled to be enthralled to a new and more powerful entity. In this respect, the supervillain is narcissistic and vainglorious, and often motivated by a jealous contempt for the near universal adulation of the superhero and their role in human affairs. In the battles that ensue, pitting the powers of the superhero against those of the villain(s), "evil" is clearly evident by villain(s)' willingness to terrify, victimize, and destroy the innocent in pursuit of complete domination. Vile tactics involving the innocent are often used as a form of public declaration, to get the attention of the superhero and draw them out for confrontation, and to use as bargaining devices/hostages in stifling the abilities of the superhero in effectively utilizing their powers. As this life and death battle is played out before our eyes, the fate of the globe hangs in the balance, but the types of power allied against each other are beyond our comprehension, influence, and control. Such a dislocation was best expressed by photojournalist Phil Sheldon, as he grappled with the first arrival of the *Marvels*.

> *Marvels*, I called them . . . and that's what they were. Next to that . . . what were we? Before they came we were so big, so grand. We were Americans . . . young,

strong, vital! We were the ones who got things done. But we'd gotten smaller, I could see it in those same faces . . . faces that had once been confident, so brash. We weren't the players anymore. We were spectators. We were waiting for something . . . without knowing what it was. . . . (Busiek and Ross)

As Phil Sheldon was witness to, we are at the mercy of beings able to command forces in ways that terrify and humble us. Only the virtuous character of the superhero, their willingness to do battle on our behalf, prevents our enslavement to villains capable of wielding incredible powers. In this respect, our natural progression is always vulnerable were it not for the interventions of a superhero character.

The "politics" of the superhero are strictly delineated in relation to human affairs. With the exception of the occasional superhero intervention to prevent a recognizable injustice from occurring (i.e. rape, robbery, or a platitude on contemporary issues; e.g. Spider-Man on drug abuse), the superhero is largely confined to "big-evil." These are not beings or "philosopher-kings" with intentions to pontificate on "human issues" or prescribe a "proper course" of action (i.e. Superman on abortion, Batman on taxation). There are no "policy-experts" in the superhero lineup, no "Policyman!" Shorn of any specific political affiliations or religious convictions, superheroes are above the fray, serving us under very specific circumstances when powerful and malevolent forces overwhelm human abilities to respond in kind. Thus, as the complexities of the human experience persist and progress, larger supervillainous threats that may reverse our course of development are addressed by the very presence of superheroes.

From the overview above, we have a general outline in which the events of 9/11 and our contemporary sense of insecurity may be measured against the superhero genre. We may best understand this collapse of reality and comic representation as two phases of experience, the first involving the traumatic events of September 11, 2001, and the second being the post-9/11 reaction and effort to restore a sense of security. The events of the morning of 9/11 were dramatic, shocking and terrifying for a variety of reasons, several of which have been captured in the narrative of superhero comics. In affect, we have been plunged into a context of personal and collective insecurity that we only before had related to and imagined through the graphic action of the superhero narrative. The morning of September 11 was just another day, unmarked by any commemorative events, until the news reports began to establish an eerie tenor after what initially appeared to be a plane crash/fire involving one of the main towers of the World Trade Center (WTC). But as smoke billowed from the WTC, media speculation was already emerging that something more sinister was afoot. Nothing confirmed this more than with all attention focused on the WTC, a second plane careened into the second main tower of the WTC. As both towers burned, a frantic mood emerged, the likes of which we had no recent memory of, nor reference to, on this scale. As the main towers of the WTC collapsed only hours after being struck, letting loose vast plumes of dust and smoke, a new and frightening atmosphere had been established. Unconfirmed reports spoke of multiple hijackings, unaccounted for aircraft, flights being downed by military fighter jets, attacks on Washington, and potentially tens of thousands dead. Throughout the day the skies over North America remained a constant threat, an unsafe airspace from which an aircraft could appear out of nowhere to inflict massive damage below. Gradually more footage revealed the damage and deaths at the Pentagon and the airplane crash in Pennsylvania, confirming the broad extent of the assault. By this time the trepidation was intense, establishing 9/11 as not a "place" sealed in our memories, but as a shared and deep anxiety separating two distinct contexts of experience. In retrospect, the divide could not have been much greater.

The twelve years separating the end of the Cold War (1989) and 9/11 had been noted for the extent to which security issues did not preoccupy the political agenda. Even the Cold War did not generate the same kind of fears as 9/11, despite the legitimate concerns over the mass annihilation posed by the nuclear standoff between the Soviet Bloc and NATO. Where air raid sirens and "duck and cover" exercises marked the early tensions of the Cold War, in the aftermath of the Cuban Missile Crisis (1961) the Cold War had become a wholly managed affair. The belligerents were highly organized and visible nation-state entities, in which a grudging respect led to numerous agreements (economic, military, diplomatic, cultural). These exchanges allowed citizens in each ideological sphere to go about their daily lives with the Cold War as an accepted backdrop to global life. For fifty years, more fears were expressed over the possibility of accidental missile launches than over outright confrontation, and no one prepared for a "crazed Communist/ Capitalist" intent on razing urban centers. As the Cold War collapsed in a "whimper" through a few public declarations in the East, the political terrain shifted towards a decade where "security" fell from view. In an instant *globalization* became the dominant topic of debate in understanding the fate of national economies, cultural affairs, and political practices (Held and McGrew; Hirst and Thompson). While an accepted definition of *globalization* has not arisen, there was a general agreement that the effects of *globalization* comprised a weakening of the autonomy and powers of individual nation-states. Some speculation even suggested that the "nation-state" was on the verge of extinction, to be replaced by regional and international forms of governance. A concern for some, but for later observers this process opened up the possibilities for new and exciting forms of global governance to address persistent problems in the global system. Taken together, there was an emerging sense that whatever was negative about *globalization*, there was the ability to imagine the possibilities for new multilateral initiatives to address everything from regional conflicts, poverty, AIDS, debt, unemployment to the environment. This was capped off with a call for the formulation and implementation of a global, "cosmopolitan democracy"(Held). Thus, however large the problem, there was a growing consensus that through international cooperation and global action we were on the verge of forging a true "global community." On the home front, the U.S. had experienced an era of prosperity and employment unseen in decades. With no visible threats from abroad, Americans "according to their own opinion polls—had never been feeling more secure. In fact, not since the British burned the White House in 1812 had the U.S. homeland been subject to a direct attack with the threat, in late 2001 at least (though not 1812), of more appalling acts of carnage to follow"(Cox, 154). There is little doubt that the last thing expected or imagined within the academic or the public sphere was an act of terror on an unseen scale. Then came 9/11, a grand and spectacular proclamation in the tradition of the superhero genre, erasing the mood of the time and forcing a broad reconsideration of the aspirations and hopes of the preceding decade for a focus on a singular concern.

As in the superhero genre, we were confronted by a high-tech menace, but not in any anticipated manner. There is something deviously simple about combining "box-cutters" and "fully-fueled passenger jets" into an act of conflagration and self-immolation (taking the ordinary/banal and giving it a novel and potent set of meanings). Behind this, though, lay several years of planning, coordination, (flight) training and (monetary) transactions, to make possible this act, but even collectively these were not the technological advancements that magnified the scope of the act. Rather, what elevated this act "beyond belief" was the fact that a major portion of the event was beamed live, and replayed from numerous angles, in rich technicolor into homes and offices all around the world. The striking images of the second plane altering its trajectory into the WTC, the fiery explosion (caught from both sides and several angles), and the collapse of the towers, were all events that in their affect have best been expressed in the vivid colors of comic representation. The visual effect, due to technological advancements, had brought us into this horrific event like nothing in the past. This was not an act that was "reported," but a gripping event brought to us in real-time, that we would experience over and over again just by changing channels (as if flipping back through the pages of a comic book, focusing on the most graphic images). The dual nature of 9/11, riveting and visually mesmerizing, but horrifying and deeply troubling, parallels earlier observations by Phil Sheldon on the arrival of the first superhero/supervillain conflict.

> To follow the Marvels through their combat, as the Sub-Mariner bolted from landmark to landmark sowing destruction, the Torch a streak of fire on his tail ... it must have seemed like a glorious aerial ballet. Dangerous, beautiful, and thrilling. And maybe it was. But not for us. What we saw was carnage and destruction and confusion ... And frightened people who felt safe a minute or two ago, trying to get out of the way but not sure which way to run. (Busiek and Ross)

From the 9/11 images we could easily place ourselves into the sequences given our familiarity with air travel and the urban landscape, re-imagining them as sites of terrifying horror (as often captured in the facial expressions of individuals in the superhero narrative). Thus, the visual effect, at the time and long after, irrevocably collapsed the distinction between graphic superhero imagery and our own reality, drawing us into the panoramic setting and mood of the superhero narrative, as supervillainous acts altered our daily routines. From this emerged the questions of "who would commit such an act," and "why?" Not surprisingly, this remains the most perplexing of issues, from which the superhero genre lends some insight against questionable explanations that have been put forward.

There have been several disparate explanations put forward in accounting for 9/11. These range from a reaction to *globalization*, a history of U.S.

imperialism, U.S. superpower status, U.S. foreign policy towards the Middle East, to an emerging cultural conflict of "Western secular values versus Islam" (see Booth and Dunne; Halliday). The main limitation of these explanations is the assumption that 9/11 was a "political act" open to logical interpretation as a consequence of some prior sequence of global events and outcomes. From this it is suggested that the events of 9/11 "make sense," rendering the event knowable or comprehendible, albeit reprehensible. But by offering up explanations of questionable veracity we diminish or disregard the unique qualities of the characters and events that comprise 9/11. Of note, the villains or "evil-doers" of 9/11 share qualities of the superhero narrative with respect to the murky political agenda behind what took place, taking their actions to the level of the "bizarre" in defying all political reason or logic in pursuit of a spectacular and destructive end. This may be inferred from what we know of the individuals who commandeered the passenger planes, who by all accounts were of privileged backgrounds, had traveled extensively, studied in Europe, and had university degrees. The "ringleaders" were not particularly religious, nor had they experienced personal life-scarring deprivations due to American foreign policy. We know that 15 of the 19 were from Saudi Arabia (with representatives from Egypt and Yemen), nations that are never listed in the critical literature as having experienced the manipulative effects of U.S. imperialism (unlike, for example, Chile, Nicaragua, Vietnam, Cuba, or Iran). The choice of targets for the attack is just as obscure in meaning and intent. One would be hard-pressed to find any mention of the WTC or the Pentagon in the literature on *globalization* (whereas an attack on the headquarters of the World Bank, International Monetary Fund, or World Trade Organization would have revealed plenty). The World Trade Center as a "symbol of American power" had escaped all academic insights and analysis prior to 9/11, only an after-the-fact addition. Having left no taped messages or written manifestos, we have nothing to confirm 9/11 as a specific economic, religious, cultural, or political grievance, nor anything that implicates the U.S. alone (versus say, Britain, Germany, Brazil). All we have from this group is a second-hand account that "[O]ne of the terrorist pilots is reported to have said that he did not like the United States because it is 'too lax. I can go anywhere I want, and they can't stop me'"(Nye, xi). Where Joseph Nye Jr. interprets this statement as a hatred of certain American values, the sentiment is more bizarre than he realizes. We are quite literally trying to understand someone who is desirous of constant government surveillance, scrutiny, and repression (as if they had read George Orwell's *1984* as a model utopia). This has little to do with any specific "American values" and still leaves no meaningful motivation for 9/11.

It is only the sparse links to Osama bin Laden and Al-Qaeda that provide some context for this violent act, but even here the political logic becomes fuzzy. Prior to 9/11, to the extent that bin Laden's movement was reacting to the presence of foreign military bases in Saudi Arabia, the movement had a recognizable political agenda that was in the tradition of past anticolonial movements. In attacking infrastructure and military targets in and around Saudi Arabia based on nationalistic/religious grievances, the movement could lay claim to legitimate political motives. While we may deplore *acts of terrorism* (by individuals or nation-states) they are by definition recognized as *political acts* when serving an identifiable political agenda. However, the respected scholar on international relations and Middle East affairs, Fred Halliday, has put forward that "The main target of 11 September is not U.S. power or a somewhat carelessly defined 'civilized' or 'democratic' world, but the states of the Middle East themselves"(40). Needless to say, the connection between the attack on the WTC (or the Pentagon) and putting Middle East governments "on notice" seems thin to say the least. Presented with such varied and awkwardly derived explanations, we are still left to ponder the "reasoning/mind-set" that would conceive and orchestrate 9/11. The peculiarity of 9/11, then, is the mystery behind the specific political ends this act was supposed to serve. There were no monetary, territorial, or practical political gains to be derived from such a violent and distant act (in fact quite opposite outcomes in these areas was more easy to deduce well before the attack took place). Furthermore, this was not a long-suffering minority with declining political fortunes, such that some degree of empathy could be attached to the larger community (not that 9/11 would have advanced the claims of any group). Thus, we have a supervillainous act involving the deaths of thousands of innocent individuals, but are left with, at most, the *hubris* of a small cult-like band of stateless actors.

We call this new sort of person a terrorist for lack of any better term, but we do not really have any pigeonholes in which he fits, nor any sense of what institutions and practices will be required to cope with him. Neither armies nor police will do. It turns out that it only takes a few tens of millions of dollars, and a few people prepared to commit suicide, to create an organization able to bring despair to the heart of the West. Such an organization does not need to control a national government or even be allied with one. The catastrophes that rich monomaniacs like bin Laden are now able to cause are more like earthquakes than like attempts by nations at territorial aggrandizement or attempts by criminals to get rich. We are as baffled about how to forestall the next act of mega-terrorism as about how to forestall the next hurricane. (Rorty)

Richard Rorty's observations highlight both the distinctive qualities of 9/11 and the difficulties in preventing another similar attack. Neither the events of 9/11 nor the motives fit neatly into either our legal or political categories of contemporary understanding. This isn't a clearly defined criminally motivated act, as the categories of hijacker, murderer, or vandal come across as too banal to fit the crime. Adding "super-" or "mega-" to these categories of criminality does not do justice to the horrific nature of 9/11. Conversely, as a politically motivated crime, the categories of "foreign invasion," "declaration of war," or genocide convey or conjure up much greater historical precedents which 9/11 (and the cast of characters) does not meet in scale or scope. The term "monomaniacs," in reference to Osama bin Laden (and the actual culprits of 9/11), expresses just that combination of a "singular obsession" and "irrationality" leading to the type of bizarre proclamation that we often attribute to the demeanor of supervillains in relation to their superhero nemesis. In possession of, or having access to material wealth and recognizable talents, they (whether bin Laden and associates or comic supervillains) are willing to squander countless advantages and political options, in lives available to few others, in zealous pursuit of a grandiose but demented act of violence. However peculiar these facets of 9/11, the effect has been extraordinary, forcing us to imagine pessimistic scenarios on a grand scale.

The post-9/11 experience has mirrored the superhero narrative in that we are forced to recognize that supervillains exist, and that we must act accordingly. Just as in the superhero genre, villains are not a "one-act" show. There are more out there, and we feel the need to be prepared. With the establishment of first the Homeland Security Agency (now elevated to permanent status as the Department of Homeland Security) and the creation of a Threat Advisory System, we no longer live without the fear of future attacks. As the

Homeland Security website maintains, "[T]he world has changed since September 11, 2001. We remain a nation at risk to terrorist attacks and will remain at risk for the foreseeable future. At all Threat Conditions, we must remain vigilant" (Department of Homeland Security, "Threats and Protection"). We now continuously fluctuate between a "Low Condition (Green) . . . when there is a low risk of terrorist attacks" to a "Severe Condition (Red)" when there is "a severe risk of terrorist attacks" (Department of Homeland Security, "Threats and Protection"). With each condition/color there are corresponding guidelines and government responses based on the latest intelligence. Beyond this, though, there isn't a clear sense of the criteria that changes the level of risk, or an explanation as to why the Threat Advisory is positioned where it is at a given time. Conversely, no one asks for the details. We just know that we live under constant threat. The other, more disconcerting feature of the post-9/11 environment is that it is defined by our having to push the bounds of our imagination into thinking as a supervillain may in considering potential threats in the future. As the DHS states, "Terrorism forces us to make choices. Don't be afraid . . . Be Ready"(Department of Homeland Security, "Ready.Gov."). To date the list specifies the following concerns: Biological Threat, Chemical Threat, Explosions, Nuclear Blast, and Radiation. However noble the sentiment to "be ready, and not afraid," contemplating the multiple and devastating effects of what has been listed only heightens one's insecurity and vulnerability. As in the superhero narrative, the villains and villainous acts multiply and mutate as our imagination is directed towards considering all possible eventualities. We are to be wary of major public or memorial events, airports, seaports, high-rise office buildings, government buildings, hydroelectric dams, bridges, etc. Everything undergoes an assessment as to the potential threat it may pose as we reexamine our surroundings in light of 9/11. From a new perspective, a dark perspective, we take note of peoples and objects that prior to 9/11 were either anonymous, or synonymous with the conveniences of our modern age. From this unusual atmosphere we are very much living the mood and the tenor of the superhero narrative, but without the benefits of the superhero. We have no reason to direct a Bat symbol at the night sky, or to gaze at the horizon in search of a Fantastic Four alert signal.

With the notable exception of a superhero intervention, there are a number of parallels between the superhero genre and the supervillainy that we have been confronted by, compelling us to accept something novel: a more ominous and insecure environment than we have known. The superhero comic, in response to 9/11, provides a distinct medium from which to reflect on and explore the fears, insecurities, and varied individual reactions generated by the attacks. On the one hand there is the ability to recapture the terrifying and horrific images of 9/11 through vibrant colors and striking detail, a style that has been perfected through decades of expressing the dramatic action between superheroes and supervillains to date. On the other hand there is room to present commentary on thoughts, emotions, and insights as events unfold, thus rendering a novel appreciation of 9/11 and the post-9/11 environment. Through this medium we are first able to view 9/11 from the vantage of a superhero, allowing for an unusual but respectful retrospective on that violent day, and placing the events of 9/11 against the experiences of beings who thought they had seen everything. What stands out in the comic representation/superhero response is the extreme degree of shock and disbelief by the superhero characters, maintaining what was and remains an appropriate reaction to the carnage and death of that morning (Straczynski and Romita Jr.). As Spider-Man arrives to witness from above the collapsing of the main towers of the WTC, the dark black shadows of the surrounding buildings highlight the intense flames, bright smoke, and broad destruction below. His thoughts capture the moment.

Spider-Man:
. . . God . . .
Some Things Are Beyond Words
Beyond Comprehension
Beyond Forgiveness

The following frame is the most abrupt, as Spider-Man swings down to the streets below among the crowd fleeing the collapsing towers and our fictional superhero is confronted by this contemporary reality.

Terrified New York Couple (Amongst Individuals Fleeing Collapsing
 Towers):
Where Were You?!
How Could You Let This Happen?

Caught off guard, Spider-Man can only offer the following observation.

> Spider-Man:
> *I—*
> *How Do You Say We Didn't Know?*
> *We Couldn't Know.*
> *We Couldn't Imagine.*
> *Only Madmen Could Contain The Thought, Execute The Act, Fly The Planes.*
> *The Sane World Will Always Be Vulnerable To Madmen, Because We Cannot Go*
>   *Where They Go To Conceive Of Such Things.*

It is here that one realizes, that with all the madmen/monomaniacs Spider-Man has done battle, they have always aspired to live beyond their destructive deeds to directly confront our superhero. A supervillain with both sociopathic and suicidal inclinations has never been a part of the anticipated Marvel/D.C. story line. As other superheroes arrive to survey the destruction and participate in emergency relief, there is a recognition that this was a unique act of "evil."

> Superheroes (The Hulk, The Avengers, The Fantastic Four) Appear To Help Find
>   Survivors In The Debris:
> *We Could Not See It Coming.*
> *We Could Not Be Here Before It Happened*
>   *But We Are Here Now.*
> *You Cannot See Us For The Dust, But We Are Here.*
> *You Cannot Hear Us For The Cries, But We Are Here.*
> *Even Those We Thought Our Enemies Are Here.*
> *Because Some Things Surpass Rivalries And Borders.*
> *Because The Story Of Humanity Is Written Not In Towers But In Tears.*
> *In The Common Coin Of Blood And Bone.*
> *In The Voice That Speaks Within Even The Worst Of Us, And Says* This Is Not
>   Right.
> *Because Even The Worst Of Us, However Scarred, Are Still Human.*
> *Still Feel.*
> *Still Mourn The Random Death Of Innocents.*

Extolling the courage of "ordinary men and women" for their sacrifices and acts of compassion and bravery, more overt political commentary chastises "the self-serving proclamations of holy warriors of every stripe [images of and reference to both Christian and Muslim fundamentalist leaders] who assume that somehow we had this coming" (Straczynski and Romita Jr.). In response, "We (superheroes and ordinary citizens alike) reject them both, in the knowledge that our tragedy is greater than the sum of our transgressions," observing " . . . that the most harmed are the least deserving." [Image of a young boy awaiting the return of his fireman father, only to see his father's body removed from the 9/11 wreckage as Spider-Man attempts to console the boy]. The retrospective on 9/11 ends with an appeal to "stand tall" through the image of a crowd comprised of peoples of diverse ages, gender, color, and cultural heritage. This is concluded by the image of numerous superheroes intermingled with those personnel (rescue, police, doctors, FBI, military) who responded, and will continue responding, to 9/11 in a variety of ways.

Perhaps noteworthy by their absence, is that there are no declarations affirming faith or trust in political leaders or government institutions, even though our superheroes failed us. Rather, the superheroes admonish contemporary political powers to act as superheroes would. Through "the voice that says all wars have innocents, the voice that says you are a kind and merciful people, the voice that says *do not do as they do, or the war is lost before it is even begun*. Do not let that knowledge be washed away in blood" (Straczynski and Romita Jr., 2002). Overall, the gist of the commentary and images conveys more than just the horrific nature of 9/11, but that superhero qualities are evident in all of us. If we act with restrained determination, never giving in to the urge to respond with senseless or misdirected retaliation, we too can be superheroes. By doing what we can to demonstrate that 9/11 did not undermine our faith in the goodness of humanity, we can recover, rebuild, and continue to uphold the principles that first inspired America [striking visuals of the Statue of Liberty and arriving immigrants]. What emerges from the commentary is that there can be no superhero response as understood and anticipated in the superhero narrative, but only new and unexpected superheroic acts by those around us. No one laid this sentiment out more clearly than Superman (Seagle, Rouleau, and Sown, 14–15).

Superman:
I Can Defy The Laws Of Gravity.
I Can Ignore The Principles Of Physics.
I Can Breathe In The Vacuum Of Space.

I Can Alter The Building Blocks Of Chemistry.
I Can Fly In The Face Of Probability.
I Can Bring Smiles Of Relief To A Thankful Populace.
But Unfortunately . . .
. . . The One Thing I Can Not Do . . .
. . . Is Break Free From The Fictional Pages Where I Live And Breathe . . .
. . . Become Real During Times Of Crisis . . .
. . . And Right The Wrongs Of An Unjust World.
A World Fortunately Protected By Heroes Of Its Own. [Silhouette of a fireman
holding the "Stars and Stripes" in the background]

With this superhero deficit, or vacuum, we witness an act of conversion, as superheroes slide into the background to allow for common, everyday heroes to emerge and be recognized.

From this point, the comic form provides an eclectic and moving account in re-examining numerous facets of the pre-9/11, 9/11, and post-9/11 experience. Most evident is the effort to recognize the real heroes and heroic acts of 9/11. These range from fire personnel, police, emergency services, volunteers to a graphic reenactment/reflection on what may have transpired on Flight 93 before it crashed into a field near Shanksville Pennsylvania, killing all aboard; the passengers deciding to resist their captors, sparing many more lives (Chadwick, 15–18). More poignant are the personal reflections and thoughts of the comic narrators themselves, revealing the varied emotional reactions that they, and those they observed, had experienced as one event and new context gave way to another. There is "hope," but it is not derived from imagining defensive, vindictive, or retaliatory scenarios. Most often this "hope" is directed to the continued recognition of "everyday heroes" and a reevaluation of individual and societal priorities (family and friends before work and status, giving over taking, community members over media appointed idols). Another major theme is the effort to "overcome" the multiple fears and concerns generated by 9/11. These vary from the simple act of boarding a plane, walking in one's neighborhood, to returning to the often mundane tasks of home and work when such routines seem frivolous or "small" against what needs to be done to make the world a safer place to live. For all our efforts to relate to superhero values in response to 9/11, we cannot help but feel as Phil Sheldon did—confused, sometimes angry, and haunted by what we have seen against the specter of more villainous acts to come.

It is perhaps this quandary, where the routines of our lives pale against the violent acts we have seen that marks the significance of 9/11. It presents that day as a solitary and unique event that cannot be easily explained away as part of an ongoing sequence of world events (i.e. a reaction to *globalization*, U.S. foreign policy). This haunting feature of 9/11 is brilliantly captured in an untitled comic piece concerning a young, precocious boy named Sam (Noxon and Huddleston, 89–91). As his mother weeps in despair, having been recently widowed when her husband attempted to help someone in 9/11, Sam blithely plays at her feet with a model airplane, refusing to go to school until "Dad comes home." As his mother attempts again to let Sam know that "Dad can't come home. Not . . . ever," Sam defiantly breaks free of the conversation, and with plane in hand, heads to the backyard. But once there, we see the child with first a look of stern concentration, which gives way to wide-eyed innocence/almost shock, followed by a view from behind the child as he holds his model plane against the silhouette of a passenger jet flying above. We are, in the final frame, looking down at the child from a distance as the boy stares up with his plane limply cradled in one hand by his side. We are left to ponder what the child is thinking. One moment the "plane" is an object of diversion and entertainment, but the next—an object of hope, loss, fear, or despair? Is he still clinging to the hope of his father's imminent return, or are the final frames an awareness that his father is gone, forever to be reminded by every plane passing skyward? Or is Sam's reaction to the passing jet renewed fear and anxiety, as he no longer trusts the intent of the object (and perhaps other high-tech amenities) after what has been done? Or is it uncertainty, that whatever before seemed self-evident, now has become unclear and confusing? Is it innocence lost to a complex reality? The haunted expression on Sam's face says much about the way we feel about the future after 9/11.

Where the comic response to 9/11 lays out a rich intellectual and emotional reflection on 9/11, there is one superhero who cannot fade from view to allow other heroes to emerge. Captain America is not in a position to admit defeat. The symbolic baggage he carries in name and history is too great. Representing the best and the bravest, and singularly identified with the United States, he must act. Drawn too late to prevent or minimize the destructive events of 9/11, Steve Rogers dives into the emergency efforts with an unmatched zeal (Rieber and Cassady, *Captain America*). Unwilling to leave the scene, he balks at the order to be on a plane to "Khandahar" when so much needs to be done at home. Gradually realizing that he has a larger role in the response, he prepares to leave, but not before intervening to save the life of a New York–born citizen named Samir against a father bent on revenge for the 9/11 death of his daughter. As the attacker and the attacked reconcile and shake hands, Captain America finds hope, observing, "We're going to make it through this—We, the people. United by a power that no enemy of freedom could begin to understand. We share—We are— The American Dream" (Rieber and Cassady, *Captain America*). Then, but seven months later, the good people of Centerville, rural USA, are attacked from above by "the monster" Al-Tariq. Showering the region with land mines, Al-Tariq and his men then confine the townspeople to the local church (and during the Easter service!!!), ensnaring them in multiple explosive devices. But this time Captain America has not arrived too late to save the innocent and mete out the appropriate justice (Rieber and Cassady, *Captain America: Fight Terror*). What is intriguing about the Captain America story line is that everything that takes place seems both more than possible in light of 9/11, but also less than what was 9/11. For Captain America, the villains are alive to be confronted and the innocent may be saved. Captain America can maintain an unflinching faith that higher ideals and tactics will prevail when addressing these supervillains. Unfortunately, our reality is much more difficult to address.

The problem of the collapse between the superhero narrative and the reality we now experience is that we are confronted by supervillainous acts, but have no superhero response. We may extol individual acts of heroism in response to 9/11, but we have nothing that approximates the grand and decisive powers of the superhero. We are not capable of mounting a rapid and dramatic act of closure/finality against our supervillains that would permit life to resume as it was. The appeal of the superhero narrative is not just the power of "good" triumphing over "evil" but that the superhero spares us from the plodding, messy, and often unfulfilling dynamics involved in organizing peoples and nation-states in a collective response against further vile acts and continued insecurity. The superhero offers everything: rapid and effective action, a just and proportionate response, and above all, in achieving results no more innocent lives are lost. In the superhero narrative "evil" is not addressed through "evil" (more innocents injured or killed), and we are not brought down to their level and forced to combat villains by vile tactics. There is a clear and persistent separation between "good" and "evil," in that the "good" is able to act and respond with superior means. There are no compromises with questionable characters or nations, calculations concerning the loss of more innocent lives, or limits to freedom/liberty to achieve a safe and secure end. Supervillainous figures are defeated, the sanctity of the innocent preserved, and we quickly return to a secure context knowing that superheroes assure our continued prosperity and progress. In our own more mundane world, though, we are left to our own devices, in affect, to "politics" and "acts of state."

As is often observed, "nation-states" are not moral agents. What is often justified by "nation-states" in the name of expediency, fiscal restraint, national unity, comparative economic advantage, etc. would be frowned upon as unacceptable behavior at the individual level. This is no more evident than in the area of "national security," specifically in times of insecurity, where political decisions often serve the most base of instincts or interests. This involves doing whatever is necessary to ensure the survival or security of the nation, the lead inclination being to retaliate with awesome demonstrations of force and/or abandoning higher ideals of "liberty" and "due process." All of these reversals have been a noticeable reaction to a shocking event that should not have taken place against the most powerful nation in the global system (itself responsible for the security of numerous other nations).

> The terrorist attacks of the World Trade Center and the Pentagon on September 11 involved the worst intelligence failure by the U.S. intelligence community since Pearl Harbor in 1941. It was a failure at all phases of the intelligence cycle, from the setting of priorities and tasks, through the gamut of collection activities, to the analytical, assessment, and dissemination processes which should have provided some warning of the event—and it befell not only the traditional national security and military intelligence agencies but also the myriad law enforcement and specialized agencies involved in counter-terrorist activities. (Ball, 60)

To regain "the edge" requires an arsenal of tactics that the average citizen neither wants to debate nor wants to know of, accepting that the ends will somehow justify the means. Thus, issues of intelligence gathering and early responses to perceived threats involve covert activities on a scale and of a kind seen as discomforting and distasteful, but necessary. From dealing with unscrupulous characters and regimes for information, to bribery, coercion, extortion, torture, assassination to outright forms of armed intervention and military conflict, many ignoble acts have been and will be committed. The closest we come to the panache and accuracy of the superhero response is "precision bombing," and with this there still remains the inescapable "collateral damage." However numerous the parallels of the superhero genre to 9/11, there will be no superhero tactics or superhero ending. We always knew that superhero and supervillains were fictional entities, caught in harmless images from which they could not be released. That we have been confronted by supervillainy is without doubt, but the villains in this real-life narrative are not the powerful and terrifying beings that they once seemed. They were, and are, only humans whose destructive means we may prepare for, mitigate, and perhaps scuttle. Lamentably, without a superhero, the effects of this endeavor have set us back, reversing prior political freedoms and global aspirations for the lone priority of "national security."

Having examined a number of parallels between 9/11 and the superhero genre but finding ourselves experiencing a very non-superhero–like conclusion, or repose to 9/11, we may conclude by observing how the superhero narrative perhaps informs our post-9/11 condition. In the superhero genre, the intervening acts of the superhero provide the relief from the spectacular and traumatic events inspired by nefarious beings committing unexpected acts of carnage. This narrative remains exciting and stirring, as the actions of a few upsets the familiar tedium of our everyday surroundings and daily routines. We are intrigued (even mesmerized) by the diabolical forces arrayed against us, for even though the same storyline is played over and over again, it is always the novel expressions of power (and their attendant forms of destruction) that are so captivating. The insecurity generated by the supervillain(s), though, sets up the expected and much anticipated superhero response, which, initially awkward, poorly timed, and insufficient, has to be adjusted to the novelty of the powers displayed by the supervillain(s). By modifying/refining (tinkering with) their own repertoire of super powers, our superhero(s) adjust to the villainy before them, and after the first "trial and error" set of confrontations, are then able to emerge confident for the final showdown. In the final frames of this storyline, the superhero(s) returns with advanced powers and capabilities, shocking the unprepared supervillain(s) and leaving him incapable of adequately responding . . . the supervillains are vanquished, forced to retreat in humiliation or be annihilated. Thus, however novel the powers of the supervillains, our superheroes are able to adapt and overcome, often issuing grand proclamations in a self-satisfying tone, suggesting that no other outcome was imaginable. Such bravado in victory is captivating and reassuring, completing the sense of finality in ridding the world of a detested villainy. While we are unlikely to ever enjoy this sense of confidence in response to 9/11, perhaps the superhero genre offers enough insight through the narrative of "overcoming." Just as in the superhero genre, we may never fully know the peculiar origins, motivations or anticipated ends of the perpetrators of 9/11 (as with the arrival of the supervillains). It is this mystique that compels us to adjust and become more cognizant of peoples and places that had received little attention prior to 9/11. With 9/11 such an unanticipated, (a literally) "out of the blue" experience marked by obscure "after the fact" explanations (given the lack of villainous testimony), our security is no longer entrusted to the purview of "experts" or political authorities. We have all been forced to consider how to make our world a safer place. As with our superhero(s), this exercise defies any specific political or national allegiances, requiring a collective/international approach to prevent more 9/11s. While bereft of the idealism surrounding "globalization," there nevertheless is recognition for the need for high levels of global collaboration and cooperation to address our collective insecurity. To the extent that 9/11 is not repeated in form or scale, and becomes remembered as but a temporary condition, or an aberration, we may experience a feeling of "success" due to numerous minor and unrecognized heroic acts (i.e. early interventions frustrating the efforts of other 9/11 types). This does not allow for the "triumphalism" of the superhero narrative; however, our real-life villains are not capable of directing novel and awe-inspiring powers against us. They may be capable of novel tactics, but not novel powers of carnage and destruction beyond what we are already familiar from our own history of conflict, or our own imaginations through the superhero genre. They may perpetrate acts of supervillainy, but they are not supervillains, and as such, do not leave us yearning to be rescued by a superhero figure. Superhero(s) may remain, as they always have, trapped in the vivid graphics of the comic medium (and thus, our imaginations), never to be sullied by having to actually intervene in the *real world*.

Bibliography

Abelson, Nathan. "Comics are a Serious Business: Part II of a Study of Comics Magazines." *Advertising and Selling*, Aug. 1946, 80–92.

Aburish, Saïd K. *Saddam Hussein, the Politics of Revenge*. New York: Bloomsbury, 2000.

Anthony Saville. *Leibniz and the Monadology* Routledge, 2000.

Apostolidès, Jean-Marie. *Les Métamorphoses de Tintin*. Paris: Seghers, 1984.

Arendt, Hannah. *Le Système totalitaire*. Paris: Seuil, [1951] 1972.

———. *The Origins of Totalitarianism*. New York & London: Harvest/HBJ, 1973 (1951).

Aristotle, *La politique*. (Texte français présenté et annoté par Marcel Prélot.) Geneva: Gonthier, 1964.

Armstrong, S. J. and Botzler, R. G. eds. *Environmental Ethics: Divergence & Convergence, Third Edition*, New York: McGraw-Hill, 2004.

Aron, Raymond. *Démocratie et totalitarisme*. Paris: Gallimard, 1965. (In English: *Democracy and Totalitarianism: A Theory of Political Systems*. Ann Arbor: University of Michigan Press, [1968] 1990.)

———. *Montesquieu*, in *Les Étapes de la pensée sociologique*, Paris: Gallimard, 1967, 25–76. (In English: *Main Currents in Sociological Thought*. New Brunswick, N. J.: Transaction Publishers, 1998.)

Assouline, Pierre. *Hergé. Biographie*. Paris: Plon, 1996.

Baker, Kyle. *King David*. DC Comics Vertigo Imprint, 2002.

———. *You Are Here*. DC Comics Vertigo Imprint, 1999.

Bakhtin, Mikhail. *The Dialogic Imagination*. Austin, TX: University of Texas Press, 1981.

———. *Rabelais and His World*. Bloomington: Indiana University Press, 1984.

Ball, Desmond. *Desperately Seeking Bin Laden: The Intelligence Dimension of the War against Terrorism*. Ken Booth and Tim Dunne, eds. *Worlds in Collision*. New York: Palgrave Macmillan, 2002.

Barthes, Roland. *The Death of the Author. Image/Text/Music*. London: Fontana Press, 1976.

Becker, Stephen. *Comic Art in America*. New York: Simon and Schuster, 1959.

Bederman, Brenda Gail. *Manliness and Civilization: A Cultural History of Gender and Race in the United States, 1880–1917*. Chicago: University of Chicago Press, 1995.

Bénéton, Philippe, *Les Régimes politiques*. Paris: Presses universitaires de France, 1996.

Benton, Mike. *The Comic Book in America: An Illustrated History*. Dallas: Taylor Publishing, 1989.

Berger, Arthur Asa, *The Comic-Stripped American: What Dick Tracy, Blondie, Daddy Warbucks, and Charlie Brown Tell Us about Ourselves*. Baltimore: Penguin Books, 1974 (1973).

Bettelheim, Bruno, *The Uses of Enchantment: The Meaning and Importance of Fairy Tales*. New York: Vintage Books, 1989 (1975).

Blackmore, Tim, "The Dark Knight of Democracy: Tocqueville and Miller Cast Some Light on the Subject," *Journal of American Culture*, 14, 1. 1991, 37–56.

Bok, Hilary, "Baron de Montesquieu, Charles-Louis de Secondat," *The Stanford Encyclopedia of Philosophy* (Fall 2003 Edition), Edward N. Zalta ed., forthcoming URL http://plato .stanford.edu/archives/fall2003 /entries/montesquieu/.

Booth, Ken, and Tim Dunne, eds. *Worlds In Collision*. New York: Palgrave Macmillan, 2002.

Boyle, James. *Shamans, Software, & Spleens: Law and the Construction of the Information Society*. Cambridge: Harvard University Press, 1996.

———. "A Theory of Law and Information: Copyright, Spleens, Blackmail, and Insider Trading." *Columbia Law Review* 80, 1992.

Burdeau, Georges, *La politique au pays des merveilles*. Paris: Presses universitaires de France, 1979.

Busiek, Kurt, and Alex Ross. *Marvels*. New York: Marvel Entertainment Group, 1994.

Carpenter, Stanford W. "Ethnographic Investigations into the Creation of Black Images in Comic Books." *Journal of Critical Inquiry into Curriculum and Instruction* 2 (3) 2001.

———. "The Tarzan v. Predator Comic Book Mini-Series: an Ethnographic Analysis." *International Journal of Comic Art* v.1 no. 2 (Fall) 1999.

Chadwich, P. *Concrete: Complete Short Stories, 1986–1989*, Milwaukie, OR: Dark Horse Comics, 1990.

Chadwick, Paul. January. "Sacrifice." In *9–11: Artists Respond*. Dark Horse Comics, Inc. Vol. 1, 2002.

Chavanne, Renaud, "Hermann: Jeremiah ou vingt ans de politique," in *Critix*, 7 (1998): 7–26. http://www.imaginet.fr/universbd/albums/critix/critix7.pdf.

Chevalier, Jean, and Alain Gheerbrant. *Dictionnaire des symboles*, Paris: Lafon/Jupiter, 1982.

Clowes, Daniel. *Eightball*, nos. 1–22. Seattle: Fantagraphics, 1989–present.

———. *Ghost World*. Seattle: Fantagraphics, 1997.

———. *Lloyd Llewellyn* (nos. 1–6) and *The All-New Lloyd Llewellyn Special*. Seattle: Fantagraphics, 1986, 1988.

Cox, Michael. "Meanings of Victory: American Power after the Towers." Ken Booth and Tim Dunne, eds. *Worlds in Collision*. New York: Palgrave Macmillan, 2002.

Daniels, Lee. *Marvel: Five Fabulous Decades of the World's Greatest Comics*. New York: Harry N. Abrams, 1991.

Day, Louis Alvin. *Ethics in Media Communication: Cases and Controversies*. 3rd ed. Belmont, Calif.: Wadsworth/Thomson Learning, 2000.

Delpérée, Francis, and Baudoin Dupret. "Le roi des Belges," in *Pouvoirs. Revue française d'études constitutionnelles et politiques*, 54, 1990: 15–24.

Department of Homeland Security. 2003. "Ready.Gov." Retrieved from www.ready.gov.

———. 2003. "Threats and Protection: Advisory System." Retrieved from www.dhs.gov.

Dumont, Georges Henri. *La dynastie belge*. Bruxelles: Elsevier, 1959.

Duverger, Maurice, *Institutions politiques et droit constitutionnel, t. 1: les grands systèmes politiques*. Paris: Presses universitaires de France, 1980.

Easton, David, and Jack Dennis. *Children in the Political System: Origins of Political Legitimacy*. New York: McGraw-Hill, 1969.

E. C. Comics. "The Orphan," *Shock SuspenStories No. 14*, April–May 1954.

Farr, Michael. *Tintin: The Complete Companion*. London: John Murray, 2001.

Friedrich, Carl J., Michael Curtis, and Benjamin R. Barber, *Totalitarianism in Perspective: Three Views*. New York: Praeger, 1969.

Gaines, Jane M. *Contested Culture: The Image, the Voice, and the Law*. Chapel Hill: University of North Carolina Press, 1991.

Gaines, William. Interview by John Tebbel. 4 Aug. 1986.

Gérard, Jo. *Les Grandes heures de la Belgique*, Paris: Perrin, 1990.

Gray, John and G. W. Smith, eds. *J. S. Mill "On Liberty" in Focus*. New York: Routledge, 1991.

Groensteen, Thierry. "Hergé philosophe?," *Les Cahiers de la bande dessinée*, 67 janvier–février 1986, p. 53.

———. "Topffer, the Originator of the Modern Comic Strip" in GA, L1.

Halliday, Fred. *Two Hours That Shook the World*. London: Saqi Books, 2002.

Hanley, Robert W. *Comstockery in America: Patterns of Censorship and Control*. Boston: Beacon Press, 1960.

Held, David and Anthony McGrew. "The Great Globalization Debate: An Introduction." In *The Global Transformations Reader*. David Held and Anthony McGrew, eds. Malden: Balckwell Publishers, 2000.

———. *Models of Democracy*. 2nd ed. Stanford: Stanford University Press, 1996.

Herbert. Johnson. "Why Cartoons—and How," *Saturday Evening Post*, July 14, 1928, 8; and Arthur Prager, *The Mahogany Tree: An Informal History of Punch*, New York, N. Y.: Hawthorne Books, 1979.

Hergé. *The Black Island*. London: Methuen, 1966 (Paris & Tournai: Casterman 1966).

———. *The Blue Lotus*. London: Methuen, 1983 (Paris & Tournai: Casterman 1946).

———. *The Broken Ear*. London: Methuen, 1975 (Paris & Tournai: Casterman 1943).

———. *The Calculus Affair*. London: Methuen, 1960 (Paris & Tournai: Casterman 1956).

———. *The Castafiore Emerald*. London: Methuen, 1963 (Paris & Tournai: Casterman 1961).

———. *Cigars of the Pharaoh*. London: Methuen, 1971 (Paris & Tournai: Casterman 1955).

———. *The Crab with Golden Claws*. London: Methuen, 1958 (Paris & Tournai: Casterman 1943).

———. *Destination Moon*. London: Methuen, 1959 (Paris & Tournai: Casterman 1950).

———. *Explorers on the Moon*. London: Methuen, 1959 (Paris & Tournai: Casterman 1952).

———. *Flight 714*. London: Methuen, 1968 (Paris & Tournai: Casterman 1966).

———. *King Ottokar's Sceptre*. London: Methuen, 1958 (Paris & Tournai: Casterman 1947).

———. *Land of Black Gold*. London: Methuen, 1972 (Paris & Tournai: Casterman 1971).

———. *Prisoners of the Sun*. London: Methuen, 1963 (Paris & Tournai: Casterman 1944).

————. *Red Rackham's Treasure.* London: Methuen, 1959 (Paris & Tournai: Casterman 1943).

————. *The Red Sea Sharks.* London: Methuen, 1960 (Paris & Tournai: Casterman 1958).

————. *The Secret of the Unicorn.* London: Methuen, 1959 (Paris & Tournai: Casterman 1942).

————. *The Seven Crystal Balls.* London: Methuen, 1963 (Paris & Tournai: Casterman 1943).

————. *The Shooting Star.* London: Methuen, 1961 (Paris & Tournai: Casterman 1941).

————. *Tintin and the Picaros.* London: Methuen, 1976 (Paris & Tournai: Casterman 1975).

————. *Tintin in America.* London: Methuen, 1978 (Paris & Tournai: Casterman 1946).

————. *Tintin in the Congo.* London: Sundancer, 1991 (Paris & Tournai: Casterman 1946).

————. *Tintin in the Land of the Soviets.* London: Sundancer, 1989 (Paris & Tournai: Casterman 1929).

————. *Tintin in Tibet.* London: Methuen, 1962 (Paris & Tournai: 1958).

Hirst, Paul and Grahame Thompson. *Globalization in Question.* 2nd ed. Malden: Blackwell Publishers, 1999.

Horowitz, Irving Louis. "The Military Elites," in *Masses in Latin America,* ed. Irving Louis Horowitz. New York: Oxford University Press, 1970: 146–89.

Jacobs, Frank. *The Mad World of William M. Gaines.* Secaucus, N. J.: Lyle Stuart, 1972.

Kiernan, Michael. *Media Ethics: A Philosophical Approach.* Westport, Conn.: Praeger, 1997.

Kihss, Peter. "No Harm in Horror, Comics Issuer Says," *New York Times,* 22 April 1954, 1.

Kimmel, Michael. *Manhood in America: A Cultural History.* New York: The Free Press, 1996.

Kirby, Jack. "Interview Jack Kirby," *Nostalgia Journal.* Ft. Worth, TX: Syndicate Publishers, 1976.

Kirby, Jack, and Simon, Joe. *Captain America: The Classic Years.* New York: Marvel Entertainment Group, 1998.

Kunzle, David. *History of the Comic Strip: Vol. 1, The Early Comic Strip.* Berkeley: University of California Press, 1973.

Lambert, Jacques, and Alain Gandolfi. *Le Système politique de l'Amérique latine.* Paris: Presses universitaires de France, 1987.

Lee, Stan. *Marvel Masterworks: Fantastic Four Nos. 51–60 and Annual No. 4.* New York: Marvel Entertainment Comics, 2000.

Lee, Stan, et al., "Dock Ock Wins!" *Marvel Tales* No. 40, in *Spider-Man vs Dr. Octopus.*

————. "Enter: Doctor Octopus!" *Marvel Tales* No. 38, in *Spider-Man vs Dr. Octopus.*

————. "The Horns of the Rhino!" *Amazing Spider-Man* No. 41, ————.

————. "How Green Was My Goblin!" *Amazing Spider-Man* No. 39, in *Spider-Man Visionaries.*

————. "Spider-Man versus Doctor Octopus." *Amazing Spider-Man* No. 3, in Marvel Characters, Inc., *Spider-Man vs Dr. Octopus* (New York: Marvel Comics, 2000).

————. "Spidey Saves the Day!" *Amazing Spider-Man* No. 40, in Marvel Characters, Inc., *Spider-Man Visionaries: John Romita* New York: Marvel Comics, 2001.

————. "The Tentacles and the Trap!" *Marvel Tales* No. 39, *Spider-Man vs Dr. Octopus.*

————. "Vengeance from Vietnam!" *Amazing Spider-Man* No. 108, in *Spider-Man Visionaries.*

Lefevre, Pascal, and Charles Dierick. "Introduction" in *Forging a New Medium: The Comic Strip in the Nineteenth Century.* Brussels: VUB University Press, 1998.

Leibniz, G. W. *Theodicy*. Ed. Austin Farrer, trans. by E. M. Huggard from C. J. Gerhardt's Edition of the Collected Philosophical Works. La Salle, Ill.: Open Court, 1990.

Leopold, A. *A Sound County Almanac: And Sketches from Here and There*. New York: Oxford University Press, (1949) [1977].

Light, A., and Katz, E., eds. *Environmental Pragmatism*. New York: Routledge, 1996.

Light, A., and Rolston, H., eds. *Environmental Ethics: An Anthology*. Malden, MA: Blackwell Publishing, 2003.

Linklater, Andrew. "Unnecessary Suffering." *Worlds in Collision*. Eds. Ken Booth and Tim Dunne. New York: Palgrave Macmillan, 2002.

Lott, Eric. *Love and Theft: Blackface Minstrelsy and the American Working Class*. New York: Oxford University Press, 1993.

Malia, Martin, *La Tragédie soviétique*. Paris: Seuil, 1999, 1995.

McAllister, Matthew P. "Cultural Argument and Organizational Constraint in the Comic Book Industry." *Journal of Communication* 40 (1990): 55–71.

McBean, George, and McKee, Neil. *The Animated Film in Development Communication. Drawing Insight: Communicating Development Through Animation*. Ed. J. Green and D. Reber. Penang: Phoenix Press, 1996.

McCloud, Scott. *Understanding Comics* Northampton, Mass.: Tundra, 1993.

Montesquieu, Charles-Louis de Secondat, baron de. *De l'esprit des lois, I*. Paris: Gallimard, 1995. (In English: *The Spirit of the laws*. Amherst, N. Y.: Prometheus Books, 2002).

Morales, Robert, and Baker, Kyle. "Hip Hop Wampum." *Vibe Magazine*. June/July 1994, vol. 2, no. 5.

———. "Nirvana Can Wait." *Vibe Magazine*. August 1994, vol. 2, no. 6.

———. "Old School Retirement Home." *Vibe Magazine*. May 1994, vol. 2, no. 4.

———. *Truth: Red, White, and Black*. Part I–VII The Future. Ed. Axel Alonso. New York: Marvel Entertainment Comics, 2003.

Mozgovine, Cyrille. *De Abdallah à Zorrino. Dictionnaire des noms propres de Tintin*. Tournai: Casterman, 1992.

Murdock, Graham. "Back to Work: Cultural Labor in Altered Times." *Cultural Work: Understanding the Culture Industries*. Ed. A. Beck. New York: Routledge, 2003.

Naess, A., and D. Rothenberg. *Ecology, Community, and Lifestyle: Outline of an Ecosophy*. Cambridge: Cambridge University Press, 1989.

Nietzsche, Friedrich. *Beyond Good and Evil*. Trans. Walter Kaufman. New York: Random House, 1989.

Noxon, Marti, and Mike Huddleston. "Untitled." In *9–11: Artists Respond*, January, vol. 1. Milwaukie, Or.: Dark Horse Comics, 2002.

Nyberg, Amy Kiste. "Poisoning Children's Culture: Comics and Their Critics." *Scorned Literature: Essays on the History and Criticism of Popular Mass-Produced Fiction in America*. Ed. Lydia Cushman Shurman and Deidre Johnson. Westport, Conn.: Greenwood Press, 2002.

———. *Seal of Approval: The History of the Comics Code*. Jackson, Miss.: University Press of Mississippi, 1998.

————. *Seal of Approval: The Origins and History of the Comics Code*. PhD diss., University of Wisconsin–Madison, 1994.

Nye, Joseph, Jr. *The Paradox of American Power*. New York: Oxford University Press, 2002 .

O'Brien, Geoffrey "Popcorn Park." *New York Review of Books*, June 2002: 8.

Paul, James C. N., and Murry L. Schwartz. *Federal Censorship: Obscenity in the Mail*. New York: Free Press of Glencoe, 1961.

Peeters, Benoît. *Hergé, fils de Tintin*. Paris: Flammarion, 2002.

————. *Tintin and the World of Hergé: An Illustrated History*. Boston: Little, Brown, 1992.

Peyo. *King Smurf*. New York: Random House, 1982; Marcinelle-Charleroi: Dupuis, 1965.

Plato. *Apology*, trans. Hugh Tredennick. In *Collected Dialogues of Plato*, ed. Huntington Cairns. Princeton, N. J.: Princeton University Press, 1989.

————. *Charmides*, trans. Benjamin Jowett. In *Collected Dialogues of Plato*, ed. Huntington Cairns. Princeton, N. J.: Princeton University Press, 1989.

————. *Euthyphro*, trans. Lane Cooper. In *Collected Dialogues of Plato*, ed. Huntington Cairns. Princeton, N. J.: Princeton University Press, 1989.

————. *Ion*, trans. Lane Cooper. In *Collected Dialogues of Plato*, ed. Huntington Cairns. Princeton, N. J.: Princeton University Press, 1989.

————. *Meno*, trans. W. K. C. Guthrie. In *Collected Dialogues of Plato*, ed. Huntington Cairns. Princeton, N. J.: Princeton University Press, 1989.

————. *Parmenides*. Trans. Mary Louise Gill and Paul Ryan. Indianapolis: Hackett Publishing Company, 1996.

————. *Phaedo*, trans. Hugh Tredennick. In *Plato: The Collected Dialogues*, eds. Edith Hamilton and Huntington Cairns. Princeton, N. J.: Princeton University Press, 1961.

————. *Phaedrus*, trans. R. Hackforth. In *Collected Dialogues of Plato*, ed. Huntington Cairns. Princeton, N. J.: Princeton University Press, 1989.

————. *Protagoras*, trans. W. K. C. Guthrie. In *Collected Dialogues of Plato*, ed. Huntington Cairns. Princeton, N. J.: Princeton University Press, 1989.

————. *Republic*, trans. Paul Shorey. In *Collected Dialogues of Plato*, ed. Huntington Cairns. Princeton, N. J.: Princeton University Press, 1989.

————. *Symposium*, trans. Alexander Nehamas and Paul Woodruff. Indianapolis: Hackett Publishing Company, 1989.

————. *Theaetetus*, trans. M. J. Levett, revised by Myles Burnyeat. Indianapolis: Hackett Publishing Company, 1992.

————. *Timaeus*, trans. Hugh Tredennick. In *Collected Dialogues of Plato*, ed. Huntington Cairns. Princeton, N. J.: Princeton University Press, 1989.

Porges, Irwin. *Edgar Rice Burroughs, The Man Who Created Tarzan*. Porvo, Utah: Brigham Young University Press, 1975.

Reidelbach, Maria. *Completely MAD: A History of the Comic Book and Magazine*. Boston: Little Brown and Co., 1991.

Rieber, John Ney, and John Cassady. *Captain America: Fight Terror*. July 2002, vol. 4, no. 2.

————. *Captain America*. June 2002, vol. 4, no. 1.

Robitaille, Antoine, "Un politologue à la défense de Tintin" (interview with Pierre Skilling), in *Le Devoir* (Montréal), February 2–3, 2003, D7.

Rorty, Richard. "Fighting Terrorism With Democracy." In *The Nation*, 21 October 2002. Retrieved from www.thenation.com/doc.mhtml?I=200021021&s=rorty.

Rotundo, Anthony. *American Manhood: Transformations in Masculinity from the Revolution to the Modern Era.* New York: Basic Books, 1993.

Sadoul, Numa, *Tintin et moi, entretiens avec Hergé.* Tournai: Casterman, 2000. (See a translated excerpt of this seminal book of interviews in *The Comics Journal*, issue #250.)

Sarte, Jean-Paul. *Being and Nothingness: A Phenomenological Essay on Ontology*, tr. by Hazel E. Barnes. New York:Washington Square, 1993.

———. *Essays in Existentialism.* Ed. Wade Baskin. New York:Citadel Press, 1997.

———. *Nausea.* Trans. Lloyd Alexander. New York:New Directions, 1964.

———. *The Words.* Trans. Bernard Frechtman. New York:Vintage Books, 1981.

———. *Existentialism and Human Emotions.* Trans. Lyle Stuart. New York:Carol Publishing, 1984.

———. *No Exit and Three Other Plays.* New York:Vintage Press, 1989.

Seagle, Steven. Duncan Rouleau, and Aaron Sown. "Unreal." In *9–11: The World's Finest Comic Book Writers and Artists Tell Stories to Remember.* DC Comics, vol. 2, 2002.

Serres, Michel. *Hergé mon ami.* Bruxelles: Moulinsart, 2000.

Skilling, Pierre. *Mort aux tyrans! Tintin, les enfants, la politique.* Québec:Nota Bene, 2001.

Soumois, Frédéric. *Dossier Tintin. Sources, versions, thèmes, structures.* Bruxelles:Jacques Antoine, 1987.

Straczynski, J. Michael, and John Romita, Jr. "Amazing Spiderman." In *Mighty Marvel Must Haves*, no. 2. February 2002.

Stuart, Lyle. Letter to James H. Bobo. Records of the Senate Subcommittee on Juvenile Delinquency, National Archives, Washington, D. C. 11 August 1955. TT. TP, 3.

"Tintin and the Intellectuals," in *The Economist*, 29 June 1996, 86–87.

Tisseron, Serge. *Tintin chez le psychanalyste.* Paris: Aubier-Archimbault, 1985.

Toynbee, Jason. "Fingers to the Bone or Spaced Out on Creativity? Labor Process and Ideology in the Production of Pop." *Cultural Work: Understanding the Cultural Industries.* Ed. A. Beck. New York: Routledge, 2003.

U.S. Congress. Juvenile Delinquency (Comic Books: Hearings Before the Senate Subcommittee on Juvenile Delinquency), 83rd Cong., 2d sess., 21–22 April 1954 and June 1954.

U.S. Congress. Motion Pictures: Hearings before the Senate Subcommittee on Juvenile Delinquency. 84th Cong., 1st sess., 15–18 June 1955.

U.S. Congress. Senate Subcommittee to Investigate Juvenile Delinquency. Interim Report: Comic Books and Juvenile Delinquency. 84th Cong., 1st sess., 1955.

Vanherpe, Henry. "Les idées politiques de *Tintin*," in *Revue politique et parlementaire*, 72 (1970): 39–55.

Waugh, Coulton. *The Comics.* New York: Macmillan, 1947.

Wiese, E. "Introduction" in *Enter: The Comics.* Lincoln, Nebr.: University of Nebraska Press, 1965.

Wertham, Fredric. "Is TV Hardening Us to the War in Vietnam?" *Violence and the Mass Media*. Ed. Otto Larson. New York: Harper and Row, 1968. 50–54.

Weston, A., ed. *An Invitation to Environmental Philosophy*. New York: Oxford University Press, 1999.

Williams, J. P. "Why Superheroes Never Bleed: The Effects of Self-Censorship on the Comic Book Industry." *Free Speech Yearbook, Vol. 26* . Ed. Stephen A. Smith. Carbondale: Southern Illinois UP, 1987. 60–69.

Wolfman, Marv. Personal Home Page, www.marvwolfman.com/Q&A.html (visited May 2004).

Wolfman, Marv, and George Pérez. *Crisis on Infinite Earths* (compilation). New York: DC Comics, 2000.

Woodward, Jonathan. *The Annotated Crisis on Infinite Earths*. www.io.com/~woodward /chroma/crisis.html (visited May 2004).

Worcester, Kent. "Kyle Baker Interview." *Comics Journal* (219), 1999.

Contributors

JEREMY BARRIS, Ph.D. (Philosophy), is professor of philosophy at Marshall University, in Huntington, West Virginia. As a philosopher, he is mainly interested in the relations between reality, thinking, style of expression, humour, and justice. He sees comics as allowing us to experience and reflect on many of these relations in uniquely illuminating ways. His most recent book is *Paradox and the Possibility of Knowledge: The Example of Psychoanalysis*, in which he argues that the circularity of knowledge and, with this, its power-effects, are ultimately inescapable, but paradoxically undermine *themselves* to form a foundation for non-circularly established and politically accountable knowledge.

LAURA CANIS received her Ph.D. (Philosophy) from the Pennsylvania State University. She is an associate professor at Baldwin Wallace College near Cleveland, Ohio. Her research interests include phenomenology and existentialism (especially Nietzsche)and cultural rites of passage.

PAUL CANIS received his Ph.D. (Philosophy) from the Pennsylvania State University. He is a part-time instructor at John Carroll University and also part-time graduate faculty at Cleveland State University. He is working on a book tentatively entitled "Logics of the Sublime in Burke, Kant, and Nietzsche." Both he and Laura are valiantly fighting the forces of ignorance, benightedness, and other arch-villains of the mind.

STANFORD W. CARPENTER is a Mellon Postdoctoral in the Department of Anthropology at Johns Hopkins University. The interviews and research for his chapter were supported by a University of Maryland, College Park 2003–2004 David C. Driskell Postdoctoral Fellowship and additional support was rendered by the Friends Research Institute in Baltimore, Maryland. He is currently working on a book that looks at identity in comic books through the eyes of comic book creators for Duke University Press.

ROBERT C. HARVEY, Ph.D. (English literature), is a cartoonist and comics historian whose books run the gamut of the medium. His books include *The Art of the Funnies, The Art of the Comic Book, Accidental Ambassador Gordo: The Comic Strip Art of Gus Arriola*. His most recent book is *Milton Caniff: Conversations*, a collection of two dozen interviews conducted with Caniff over the years of his career. Harvey has contributed numerous cartoonists' biographies to Oxford University Press's American National Biography and has written over 150 short biographies of cartoonists for *A Gallery of Rogues: Cartoonists' Self-Caricatures*. He is a member of the National Cartoonists Society, Comic Arts Professional Society, and an associate member of the Association of American Editorial Cartoonists. He has published cartoons in all the print genre.

TERRY KADING, Ph.D. (Political Science), is an assistant professor in political studies in the Department of Philosophy, History, and Politics at Thompson Rivers University. He teaches courses in Canadian government, American government, Latin American studies, development theory, political theory, and international political economy. His research interests are in the areas of Latin American development and globalization themes, with a focus on the consequences of free trade agreements for the Americas.

KEVIN DE LAPLANTE, Ph.D. (Philosophy), is associate professor of philosophy in the Department of Philosophy and Religious Studies at Iowa State University, where he teaches courses in the philosophy of science and conducts research in the philosophy of ecology and environmental philosophy. In his spare time, de Laplante draws cartoons for a local sustainable farming newsletter. He's a fan of the comic art of Paul Chadwick, Daniel Clowes, Craig Thompson, and Chris Ware.

JEFF McLAUGHLIN, Ph.D. (Philosophy), is assistant professor at Thompson Rivers University in Kamloops, British Columbia. He teaches in a variety of "applied" areas of philosophy including medical ethics and computer ethics. He has published numerous articles on philosophy and information technology. McLaughlin spends a good deal of time in Austria lecturing on information management and educational technology issues. His first paper on comics and philosophy was as first year undergraduate student where he used "The Saga of X-Men's Phoenix" to illustrate the topic of insanity and power. His second paper on comics written some twenty years later, led to the *Comics as Philosophy* project.

AMY KISTE NYBERG, Ph.D. (Mass Communications), is an associate professor of media studies in the Department of Communication at Seton Hall University, South Orange, New Jersey. She holds a doctorate in mass communication from the University of Wisconsin–Madison. Her book *Seal of Approval: The History of the Comics Code*, published by the University Press of Mississippi, is the only full-length historical analysis of comic book censorship.

ALDO REGALADO is a Ph.D. candidate (History) at the University of Miami in Florida. An Americanist, his primary fields include cultural history, urban history, African American history, and comparative slavery. He has presented various papers on the significance of the superhero in American culture, including "Playing in the Dark Knight: Race and Meaning in the Batman Comics" at the 2002 annual meeting of the ASA and "Supermen,

Super-Soldiers, and the Re-Casting of Whiteness" at the 2003 annual meeting of the AHA. He is currently writing his doctoral dissertation, which is a cultural history of the concept of the superhero in America titled *Bending Steel with Bare Hands: Modernity and the American Superhero in the Twentieth-Century*.

PIERRE SKILLING, Ph.D. candidate (Sociology), has a M.A. in political science and is completing graduate studies at Université Laval, Québec City, Canada. Skilling is a specialist of Hergé's *Tintin*, and author of articles on sociopolitical aspects of comics and editorial cartoons; he published a book in 2001 about politics in *Tintin*. Previously the vice-president of ScaBD-Québec (formerly Québec's Comics Artists Association), he has also been editorial assistant for the multidisciplinary journal *L'Image* in Paris. He is a researcher at the Research Department of Quebec's National Assembly with a focus on Democratic institutions.

IAIN THOMSON, Ph.D. (Philosophy), is associate professor of philosophy at the University of New Mexico, where he works mainly on nineteenth and twentieth century continental philosophy, especially Heidegger. His widely reprinted articles have been published by such journals as *Inquiry, Journal of the History of Philosophy, International Journal of Philosophical Studies, Journal of the British Society for Phenomenology, Ancient Philosophy*, and *Philosophy Today*. He is author of *Heidegger on Ontotheology: Technology and the Politics of Education* (Cambridge University Press, 2005). (He has been reading comics since before he could read; indeed, he learned how to read from comics and is still learning.

Index